SOCIAL MEDIA COMMUNICATION

In *Social Media Communication: Concepts, Practices, Data, Law and Ethics*, Jeremy Harris Lipschultz presents a wide-scale, interdisciplinary analysis and guide to social media. Examining platforms such as Twitter, Facebook, LinkedIn, Pinterest, YouTube and Vine, the book explores and analyzes journalism, broadcasting, public relations, advertising and marketing. Lipschultz focuses on key concepts, best practices, data analyses, law and ethics—all promoting the critical thinking professionals and students need to use new networking tools effectively and to navigate social and mobile media spaces. Featuring contemporary case studies, essays from some of the industry's leading social media innovators, and a comprehensive glossary, this practical, multipurpose textbook gives readers the resources they'll need to both evaluate and utilize current and future forms of social media.

Jeremy Harris Lipschultz is Isaacson Professor in the School of Communication, University of Nebraska at Omaha. He is a blogger for *The Huffington Post* and *ChicagoNow* and has authored or co-authored six previous books and dozens of articles. Lipschultz is an international media source and frequently speaks on industry and social trends.

For more information about the book, supplementary updates and teaching materials, follow *Social Media Communication* through Facebook, Twitter and SlideShare.

Facebook:

www.facebook.com/SocialMediaCommunication

Twitter:

@JeremyHL #smc2015

SlideShare:

www.slideshare.net/jeremylipschultz

SOCIAL MEDIA COMMUNICATION
CONCEPTS, PRACTICES, DATA, LAW AND ETHICS

Jeremy Harris Lipschultz

Routledge
Taylor & Francis Group

NEW YORK AND LONDON

First published 2015
by Routledge
711 Third Avenue, New York, NY 10017

and by Routledge
2 Park Square, Milton Park, Abingdon, Oxon OX14 4RN

Routledge is an imprint of the Taylor & Francis Group, an informa business

Library of Congress Cataloging-in-Publication Data

Lipschultz, Jeremy Harris, 1958–
    Social media communication : concepts, practices, data, law and ethics /
Jeremy H. Lipschultz.
      pages cm
    Includes bibliographical references and index.
  1. Social media.   2. Social networks.   3. Online social networks.
4. Social media—Law and legislation.   5. Social media—Moral and ethical
aspects.   I. Title.
    HM741.L563   2015
    302.23'1—dc23   2014007455

ISBN: 978-1-138-77644-9 (hbk)
ISBN: 978-1-138-77645-6 (pbk)
ISBN: 978-1-315-77316-2 (ebk)

Typeset in Garamond Three LT
by Apex CoVantage, LLC

Printed and bound in the United States of America by Edwards Brothers Malloy on sustainably sourced paper.

CONTENTS

4 Social Media in Public Relations   69

5 Social Media in Advertising and Marketing   89

12 Future of Social Media and Information Literacy

TABLES AND BOXES

Tables

Boxes

PREFACE

Facebook, with more than one billion users worldwide, is the largest social network site. However, Princeton University researchers claim it may wither on the vine in the next few years because of the fickle nature of social media use and new applications. The mobile "app" Whisper, for example, has lured some users interested in **posting** "anonymous" memes that suggest more truthful communication, confessions or secrets. Because of the technical nature of the Internet, no message is truly anonymous, yet the idea of anonymous expression has a following. Regardless of which specific platforms grow or wane, social media communication has ushered in a fundamental shift from one-way mass media to interactivity of engagement within media audiences.

This book explores the emerging field of social media communication, as practitioners use new tools to communicate with the public through mass media or directly via social networking. The field of public relations (PR) informs many of the best practices and new rules of social media. At the same time, social media concepts, tools and practices are useful for those studying and working in journalism, advertising and marketing. Social media, collectively, flourish under a broad umbrella for understanding diffusion of social and technological change. In 2012, Barack Obama's @BarackObama Twitter account tweeted a "four more years" photograph of the president and Michelle Obama embracing.

Figure 0.1 This 2012 election night photo was the most popular social media image ever on Twitter and Facebook.

The image was re-tweeted more than 500,000 times and liked by more than 3.5 million people on Facebook on election night, becoming the most popular social media communication ever. It is a complex media world in which online personal branding also may be seen in some contexts (i.e., "selfies") as narcissism. Regardless, social media communication is now big business. Global issues have sprouted, as new media tools are used for political and economic purposes. Journalists, broadcasters, PR practitioners, advertisers, marketers and others in business and non-profit sectors explore effectiveness of developing social network sites, social media and longer-term business plans.

At universities, social media are being studied in the development of communication theory, research methodology and best practices. Academic programs continue to revise curricula. In some cases, new online journalism and digital media courses have been developed and offered. Others have grounded social media use within traditional foundations of media storytelling. While it is possible to incorporate social media skills into journalism, public relations and other writing courses, an interdisciplinary approach to social media is needed. Many concentrations in new media were developed prior to the proliferation of social media, and these tend to be grounded in production techniques. Social media practices, however, extend interpersonal communication skills into mediated, online social spaces. This book is designed to promote critical thinking and media literacy skills needed to effectively use new tools and navigate social media spaces.

It is clear that the media marketplace—from local newspapers to international television channels—is in a state of flux. This book seeks to make a contribution to those academics and professionals exploring curriculum revision, industry convergence and impact on the broad field, which now includes communication studies and media communication.

Social Media Communication is grounded in a wide set of theories and research methods. The author believes readers benefit from the application of traditional media and communication studies concepts, Internet studies, computer-mediated communication (CMC), social networks and other research. Some scholars bristle at the idea that we can move beyond the traditional academic silos of fields, such as journalism, broadcasting and electronic media, public relations, advertising and marketing. However, social media tools such as Twitter promote interaction rather than disciplinary boundaries. Social networks and so-called social media "tribes" form around opinion leaders, influencers and their common interests.

While many newer books describe online media and recent texts focus on social media for journalists, public relations practitioners or marketers, the author seeks to engage all fields in an important dialogue. We will address specific "best practices" but also move toward a larger framework for understanding social media. In this regard, new research exploring virtual teams and collaboration in information technology (IT) offers promising paths. This book will assume that readers have basic experience with tools such as Facebook, Twitter, LinkedIn, YouTube, Pinterest, Instagram, Google+ and FourSquare. Additionally, the text and companion online sites will track newer apps, such as Tumblr, Vine, Yammer, Vimeo, Spreecast, Snapchat, Jelly and Whisper. These sites are often used to spread content on blogs, news sites and other online spaces. Through research findings and case studies, the book will guide the reader toward a greater understanding of what is at stake for social media professionals. As Edelman

Digital Vice President Phil Gomes has observed in talks to students around the country, "the 'source code' of PR is . . . leaking . . . bit by bit, feature by feature." This is similar to the BeTheMedia.com view presented by David Mathison that everyone online essentially has the power to be an online media brand. The re-definition of journalism and public relations toward a social media context requires deeper thinking about the nature of "tweets," "wall posts," "**pins**" and other social media behavior.

The book sees an ever-growing array of social media tools as defining an emerging era of communication, as we move from largely one-way mass communication for large audiences to social networked media communication. While journalists, public relations practitioners, marketers and others will continue to sometimes communicate with large, mass audiences, the perspective of this book is that *influence and trust* are key concepts and will depend, in part, on the strength and character of an individual's or organization's social networks and branding.

Trust is a necessary but not sufficient requirement for communication to be influential through source and message credibility. Pew data have painted a troubling picture: three-fourths of the audience in 2005 said news organizations were more concerned with attracting the largest audience, while less than one-fourth said they cared about informing the public. One of the challenges in the 21st century is to find a balance between individual interests and the greater public interest or good. Trust binds us into social units, and there is a need for trusted information, as well as the individuals and institutions behind narrative storytelling. Trusted stories connect us within social media communication and across social networks. Influencers establish social rules and are leaders when it comes to social media participation.

Social concepts, such as trust, are important in understanding the development of best practices and the use of data within boundaries of law and normative ethics. The audience for new forms of social media needs a media and information literacy framework that critically examines new tools and social norms—whether or not the user engages in social media because of her or his career or for general interest. Taken together with concerns about audience fragmentation and the future of democratic consensus, trust is a key to the future. As an example, consider the 2013 Association for Education in Journalism and Mass Communication (AEJMC) international conference in Washington, D.C. Observation of Twitter users over five days during the convention produced a complex visualization.

Through theory-based concepts, we should be able to measure these data and understand communication patterns. We want to know why people participate in social networks, how they become influential, and what role trust may play in online user engagement. Ultimately, we should see the emergence of reliable predictive analytics.

Of course, these issues are of interest for those in journalism, public relations, advertising and marketing. Every business seeks Return on Investment (ROI) from time and money spent on social media communication. At the same time, fields such as information technology, political science, sociology, criminal justice, education and gerontology also recognize the importance of social media. As social media use continues to rise across the world, this book will be of increasing interest to the general public. The book will clearly define concepts in a way that will be useful to libraries and their readers.

This book, *Social Media Communication: Concepts, Practices, Data, Law and Ethics*, uses the idea of the social network as a heuristic and pedagogical device for understanding social media. It takes the reader beyond a cursory understanding of social media tools toward development of a framework for assessing social media goals, objectives and possible new rules. By applying communication theory, research and understanding, the reader will be prepared to assess each new tool that enters the social media marketplace.

This *Social Media Communication* book could not have happened without the content ideas, insights, editing suggestions and love of my spouse Sandy Shepherd Lipschultz. For more than 30 years, she has been my most important discussion partner on the teaching and research of media. We have been blessed to have two wonderful children, Jeff, age 25, and Elizabeth, 17, who grew up as "digital natives" experimenting with evolving social network sites. We learned a lot from parenting during this time. Daughter-in-law Holly, a blogger and librarian in Chicago, also helped cultivate our understanding about how younger people communicate online.

Aging increases my appreciation for the contributions of those who came before us: my parents, Hank and Maxine; Sandy's parents, Don and Faye; and our grandparents. All of them shared a love for learning and exploring, and in a later time no doubt would have been intrigued by social media communication.

My colleagues at the University of Nebraska at Omaha are knowledgeable, insightful and wonderful. College of Communication, Fine Arts and Media (CFAM) Dean Gail F. Baker, School of Communication Director Hugh Reilly, Associate Vice Chancellor and Graduate Dean Deborah Smith-Howell and the UNO administration have supported my social media communication work, and for this I am extremely thankful. Likewise, AEJMC has been a constant source of enrichment through the Law & Policy and Public Relations divisions, as well as our high quality journals.

My students in Computer-Mediated Communication, Social Media Metrics, Media Regulation and Freedom, and Communication and Technology courses first alerted me to their early adoption of social media communication, and the students continue to challenge our field to offer stronger conceptualization, data and research findings.

At Routledge, Senior Editor Erica Wetter quickly grasped the vision for this project and moved to advance it to publication. Editorial assistant Simon Jacobs provided careful review, editing and processing. My UNO colleague Avery Mazor provided technical help on images.

Finally, from my "tweeps" on Twitter to friends and fans on Facebook, I appreciate our daily social media online activity. Some of my strongest Facebook, Twitter and Google+ connections are found within these pages as thought leaders or sources for important quotation. I hope this book contributes an important piece of our continuing conversation.

Jeremy Harris Lipschultz
February 2014

1 INTRODUCTION TO SOCIAL MEDIA CONCEPTS

> "We live in a time where brands are people and people are brands."
>
> —Brian Solis (@briansolis, 2013)

On a cool mid-April day in 2013, tragedy struck at the finish line of the Boston Marathon. Two bombs were detonated, injuring dozens of runners and spectators. As journalists scrambled to learn what happened and event organizers worked with emergency responders, Twitter instantaneously lit up with a burst of information, images and video. Some of the initial reports by eyewitnesses and media were accurate, but there was also a stream of false information spreading across users' **social networks**. At GolinHarris, their real-time public relations newsroom called The Bridge immediately alerted marketing client Cisco, which pulled content to avoid appearing disconnected from unfolding events (PR News, 2013). It was a correct decision, as the chaotic scene generated massive amounts of information, including numerous factual errors.

Meanwhile, the Twitter **social network site (SNS) hashtag** (#) #BostonMarathon had been used for **live tweeting** photographs and positive news about the annual event, but now it was the online space to track responses to the attack. Unfortunately, even mainstream news media, such as CNN and ESPN, reported inaccurate information in the early hours and days of coverage, as in this tweet: "@SportsCenter: An arrest has been made in the Boston Marathon bombings, CNN reports" (April 17, 2013).

The incorrect tweet was retweeted 13,930 times and made a favorite 2,476 times. As the investigation continued, social media also shared graphic YouTube video of the explosions and aftermath. Six months later, the bombing event continued to attract social media attention—from the Boston Red Sox World Series parade stop at the marathon finish line to the photograph posted online of an inappropriate Halloween costume. A 22-year-old from Michigan dressed as a Boston Marathon victim, and she sparked a large negative reaction from her Instagram photo that was also shared on Twitter.

The online publication *Buzzfeed* reported on the story of Alicia Ann Lynch, who received thousands of negative tweets and even death threats. One called Lynch "an absolutely disgusting human being." Clearly, Lynch's dress was insensitive, but Twitter users went so far as to identify her by sharing a photo of her Michigan driver's license. After deleting social media accounts, Lynch briefly returned on Twitter before having her account suspended. Lynch claimed this later online apology reported by media came from someone else: "@SomeSKANKinMI: Plz stop with the death threats towards my parents. They did nothing wrong. I was the one in the wrong and I am paying for being insensitive" (Nov. 1, 2013). Lynch apologized with a simple "I'm sorry" on Twitter, but the attacks continued. Eventually, some on Twitter accepted the apology and called the continuing online "rage" an example of cyber-bullying and online mob behavior (Zarrell, 2013).

A practitioner of journalism, public relations (PR), advertising or marketing needs to understand how to effectively operate within social media. There is no single way because social media communication can be political and cultural. For example, Shezanne Cassim, 29, spent nearly one year in a Dubai prison for posting a parody YouTube video before the Minnesotan was released in late 2013 (Gumuchian & Sidner, 2013). What might have been considered harmless in the U.S.—poking fun at suburban teens liking hip-hop music culture—was found to be criminal in the United Arab Emirates. However, by developing strategies through planning and creating tactics, it is possible to avoid social media pitfalls and serve many goals within media and other organizations.

📱 BOX 1.1 AIR BERLIN'S FAILED CUSTOMER ONLINE ENGAGEMENT

In a less dramatic example of online engagement, Air Berlin found out the hard way that engaging customers on Twitter might produce unintended results. When the airline lost a business traveler's luggage, the exchange between a social media content manager and customer turned into a very public branding #fail.

@_5foot1: Arrived in Dusseldorf without my bag. @airberlin are useless. No apology, no idea. What happened to German efficiency?
@airberlin—@_5foot1: We're sorry for the inconvenience caused. Did you contact the Lost & Found at Düsseldorf airport?
@_5foot1—@airberlin: of course. Bag left in LDN. No assurance it will be on the next flight. I'm here for business meetings with no clothes.
@airberlin—@_5foot1: We understand how annoying this is and apologise! Unfortunately we can't help you right now, the Lost & Found will contact you

The next day:

@_5foot1—@airberlin: Do you have a number i can call and speak to a human being. The tracking number is giving me no info
@airberlin—@_5foot1: Unfortunately there is no number I can give you, the Lost & Found will get in touch as soon as they found your bag.

While Air Berlin was correct to engage the customer, the conversation probably should have been taken off Twitter and onto a telephone with an eye toward solving the problem through traditional customer service. Perhaps the airline could have offered to buy the customer a set of clothes for his business meeting. The poor experience also could have been converted into positive social media message **engagement**.

Source: Waldman, K. (2013, September 4). I'm Here for Business Meetings with No Clothes. *Slate.* www.slate.com/articles/business/moneybox/2013/09/air_ber lin_lost_luggage_the_german_airline_melts_down_on_social_media.single.html

When Hurricane Sandy hit the East Coast in late October of 2012, it marked what the technology site *Mashable* later called a "Social Storm." The storm, tracked on Twitter as #Sandy, was perhaps the first large-scale natural disaster in which officials coordinated to "disseminate emergency information to residents and provide emergency services in response to residents' posts" (Berkman, 2013, para. 6). On the one hand, citizens were urged to stay indoors and remain safe. On the other hand, the city monitored social media for reports from those venturing outside. One official said, "At no point, did we actively ask the public to collect media."

> "You see an enormous number of people who are using social media and consuming social media, both producing and discovering information, to a much higher extent than you would at any other point," Rachel Haot (@rachelhaot), chief digital officer for New York City, told *Mashable*. (Berkman, 2013, para. 7)

The desire of individuals to engage and participate has its roots in technological developments five decades ago. The origins of this social media revolution can be found in the development of Internet structures, beginning with a 1960s military project called **ARPANET**. Early personal computer users' interest in local bulletin board systems (BBS) in the 1980s was a harbinger of interest in networked communication. The explosive growth of email, which remains the leading online function, and the World Wide Web in the 1990s sparked scholarly interest in the study of **computer-mediated communication (CMC)**. The early site LiveJournal demonstrated that individuals like to share personal information with friends. The popular social sites Friendster, LinkedIn and MySpace launched in 2002–2003. LinkedIn's growth continues today by focusing on professional networks. MySpace remains very active within the music and other select industries. There was a lot of early 21st-century interest in "participatory media, online community newspapers, and citizen journalism" (Mathison, 2009, p. 311). During a subway bombing in London in 2005, the BBC used camera phone video for the first time, along with information from thousands of emails and photographs.

YouTube's first video, "Me at the zoo" had four million views at a time when video streaming was slow and cumbersome. The brief San Diego Zoo video demonstrated that there was audience interest in non-professional video content.

Figure 1.1 The first YouTube video was not very dramatic.

Figure 1.2 "@jkrums: There's a plane in the Hudson. I'm on the ferry going to pick up the people. Crazy."

Source: https://twitter.com/jkrums, posted at: *Los Angeles Times* (2009, January 15). Citizen Photo of Hudson River Plane Crash Shows Web's Reporting Power. http://latimesblogs.latimes.com/technology/2009/01/citizen-photo-o.html#sthash.X2PUIScJ.dpuf

At about the same time, the Craigslist site had grown from an email list developed in the mid-1990s to nearly two billion page views. Wikipedia also was growing in online popularity. Facebook in 2006 evolved from a university student platform to a public site. Twitter was about to burst onto the scene, ushering in communication brevity with its 140-character limitation for each **tweet**. One of the early defining moments of the social media era in the U.S. happened just half a decade ago. A US Airways jet made a crash landing in New York's Hudson River, and entrepreneur Janis Krums (@jkrums) posted a dramatic photograph on Twitter before news media could arrive at the scene.

The news value of the photograph came to symbolize the powerful combination of millions of citizens and their mobile phones. Other top moments in the development of social media include:

- TMZ reported the death of entertainer Michael Jackson in 2009 (http://latimesblogs.latimes.com/technology/2009/12/top-10-social-media-events.html).
- The Library of Congress decided in 2010 to archive all tweets since the Twitter 2006 launch (www.huffingtonpost.com/2010/12/29/social-media-moments-2010_n_802024.html).
- Wyclef Jean's Yele Haiti Foundation raised $1 million through $5 donations on Twitter and mobile following the 2010 earthquake (www.huffingtonpost.com/2010/12/29/social-media-moments-2010_n_802024.html).
- Rebecca Black uploaded a music video to YouTube in 2011, and it went **viral** with more than 160 million views in its first few days (http://mashable.com/2011/12/15/social-media-moments-2011/).
- The **meme** became popular in 2011. After University of California campus police pepper-sprayed student protesters who posted a video, the event was mocked through a series of viral images (http://gawker.com/5861431/uc-davis-pepper-spray-cop-is-now-a-meme/).

Figure 1.3 This University of California Pepper Spray Meme spread as a viral social media image.

- LinkedIn skyrocketed to 90 million registered users by 2011.
- Actor Charlie Sheen joined Twitter in 2011 and had accumulated more than one million followers in just over one day.
- Pinterest, Instagram and Tumblr broadened the social media landscape in 2012 by offering significant competition for user attention (http://mashable.com/2012/12/23/social-media-2012/).
- Vine became the hot app of 2013. By limiting users to six-second looping mobile video, it created Twitter-like communication boundaries (www.youtube.com/watch?v=0wRUDazRh9I).
- Instagram had more than 150 million users by the end of 2013, as Facebook grew to more than 1.5 billion across the globe.

Social media are distinguished from other online uses by a high level of interactivity, the importance of user identity formation and an openness to share content across developing communities. Definitions vary, but the fundamental character of SNS engagement is the linkage of individuals through online technology as a way to communicate using a variety of media forms. Social media also are characterized by the creation of new sites. Many of the newest are focused on **mobile communication**, catering to smartphone and tablet users. This dynamic and evolving nature of technology has helped social media spread in popularity to most of the world.

The global Internet is huge. In China, which blocks sites such as Facebook and Twitter but hosts government-sponsored social media services, there are about 591 million users—nearly as many as all other countries combined (Desilver, 2013). More than 464 million (78.5%) are mobile users, which mirrors international trends (para. 4). While Facebook, YouTube, Google+, Twitter and LinkedIn are the top global sites for social media, Instagram and Pinterest are growing faster, and sites such as Orkut, Badoo, Sina Weibo, Bebo and vkonyakte also have large numbers of international users (Lunden, 2014).

This book focuses on the emergence of social media communication as a primary source of information for people across the world. Drawing from the Edelman PR **media cloverleaf**, social media are among four overlapping environments, which also include traditional media, owned media and hybrid media. Traditional print and broadcast media once were leaders of most public discussion and some public opinion. With the development of the Internet and Web in the 1990s, companies began to develop websites. These owned media, along with application software (**apps**), turned all of those with online identities into media companies. In this century, hybrid media emerged from blogging. *The Huffington Post* was one of the earliest hybrid media to take advantage of the shift by commercializing it and activating a network of citizen bloggers. Finally, social media, through early popular sites, such as Facebook, Twitter and YouTube, empowered individuals to interact as media, promote content and engage new people across social networks.

The rapid **diffusion** of social media over a few short years changed job **roles** for news reporters, **public relations (PR)** people, marketers and others in a wide variety of positions. At the same time, social media are transforming the fields of advertising and marketing. This book examines social media from a communication perspective that focuses on important concepts and practices. For example, some of what we now study as social networking within social media can be examined through Katz and Lazarsfeld's filter hypothesis of personal influence (Katz and Lazarsfeld, 1955, as cited in Schmitt-Beck, 2003). People form social groups, sometimes seek out influencers and gauge social trends: ". . . personal communication mediates the influence of mass communication . . . reinforcing or blocking the impact of media information, depending on the evaluative implications of that information and on the political composition of voters' discussant networks" (p. 233). Influence extends well beyond politics and elections. As Katz (1957) observed about the nature of studying leaders and influencers: "It began to seem desirable to take account of chains of influence longer than those involved in the dyad; and hence to view the adviser-advisee dyad as one component of a more elaborately structured social group" (Katz, 1957, p. 5).

Decades later, Katz (1994) observed that, although we may be able to observe influence, "to activate this knowledge is not as easy . . . (and) tends to be more expensive and more complicated than simply reaching everybody" (p. x). Social media, however, ushered in an era of visualizing human communication, tracking it within large amounts of data—big data—and sometimes placing activation within reach. It is clear that the amount and quality of social media research continues to grow, aligning with the growth in "use of social media for sharing various forms of user-generated content" (Khang, Ki & Ye, 2012, p. 279).

The nature of influence, as well as the contemporary examination of social networks and social media, raises legal and ethical issues. For example, a restaurant review on Yelp, whether or not it is accurate, might cause economic harm to a small business. Despite the challenges of breadth, social media are becoming a force—perhaps the most important communication source—in the 21st century. Despite awareness of potential influence, individual users, including those working for media and corporations, continue to make huge mistakes on social media platforms, such as Twitter. Particularly when it comes to **breaking news** events and **real-time social engagement**, split-second decisions made by professionals frequently miss the mark. In order to better understand the challenges of social networking and social media communication, it is important to develop concepts built upon social research.

Social Media Concepts and Theories

Participants in social media are networked individuals engaging in interpersonal, yet mediated, communication. Through CMC, users create online identities, interact and engage with others, participate in online communities, and may activate groups to respond. Communication behavior may involve politics, power and culture—even when it originates as consumer behavior.

The communication within social media sites, such as Twitter, may trigger **crowdsourcing**, in which audiences piece together bits of information into a larger narrative for **storytelling**. The crowdsourcing question-and-answer program called Jelly, created by Twitter co-founder Biz Stone, is a 2014 mobile media response to user desire to leverage information and rich media images available within personal social network sites.

Effective distribution of stories, images and video requires understanding of specific online **platforms** and context. In marketing, for example, messages must connect with audiences: "With the instant access to social media made possible by mobile devices, there's no such thing as undivided attention anymore" (Vaynerchuk, 2013, p. 4). In this sense, social media content involves human storytelling with a foundation within informational and persuasive communication. SNSs offer different tools to facilitate storytelling: Facebook "walls," Twitter feeds, LinkedIn endorsements. Each new SNS diffuses into the marketplace, but only some are widely adopted by a mass audience. Social media involve the coming together of participants in large SNSs and sharing of information and media content.

((•)) BOX 1.2 THOUGHT LEADER JAMES SPANN

The most important role that social media play in my business is audience engagement during life-threatening weather events. Five years ago, I could not buy a valid storm report from many rural parts of my state; now with one simple tweet, or request via Facebook, Google Plus, or Instagram, I not only have good reports, but pictures as well. Most of these people have not gone through spotter training, but by sending a photo to us, they allow professional meteorologists to evaluate the storm, making the warning process more effective.

In addition, we are able to push critical severe weather information to many who would not consider using television, especially younger people (18–24 year olds). Social media served as a lifeline during our generational tornado out-

Figure 1.4 @Spann.
Courtesy James Spann.

break on April 27, 2011. I think it is interesting that on many days I reach more people via social media than on television. Times are changing.

(continued)

Time management is a big issue for us. We are working social media very hard around the clock, seven days a week, with the same number of people we had five years ago. People expect us to be there via social media to answer their questions and provide weather information on demand. Our job has morphed into a 24/7 kind of thing, which can lead to fatigue and strains on family relationships. You have to maintain a rigid priority table when it comes to managing time.

Another challenge is sorting through bogus weather reports; there are always some people who want to damage the warning process with false information. We have to make decisions "on the fly" concerning the validity of the reports we receive during winter storms and severe weather. Also, for some reason, some people begin circulating old pictures, claiming they are current and related to an ongoing weather event. This is problematic, but we do our best to sort out the bad images and not use them on the air.

For our audience, one of the biggest issues is reliance on Facebook for severe weather information. Facebook is simply a horrible platform for severe weather warning dissemination because only a small percentage of followers/fans actually see the posted warnings on their timeline. Facebook, Twitter, Google Plus, and Instagram are crucial in our communication plan, but with so many on Facebook we have to do a better job of educating them. We prefer people get severe weather warnings via smartphone apps like MyWarn or iMap WeatherRadio, and not rely on social media as their primary source.

We are hoping that video becomes easier to use via social media. For us, it is crucial that we provide live streams of tornadoes. Social science studies have proven that people will take action if they actually see live video of a tornado on TV; if we only provide a radar indication, they will seek confirmation and delay taking action. We have moved our storm spotters over to the Google Hangout platform, and we are very optimistic about its growth and future. We also hope that lower income families have easier access to the Internet and social media clients in coming years; we often struggle to reach that demographic during life threatening weather.

James Spann, CBM, is Chief Meteorologist at ABC 33/40 in Birmingham, Alabama, where he has worked since 1996. He also hosts Weather Brains, reports on two-dozen radio stations, is heard on the Rick and Bubba Network, and is a partner in Big Brains Media and The Weather Factory. He was educated at Mississippi State University. www/alabamawx.com

We know from the **uses and gratifications** communication perspective that media users select content and use it with expectations in mind. Satisfaction and expectation drive future media consumption. At the same time, users will tend to avoid content that does not provide psychological rewards. Over time, then, media user behavior falls into habits built upon stimuli, responses and a set of expectations that may reflect positive, neutral or negative views. These dimensions are particularly important in social media because it is possible to identify user feelings through **sentiment analysis**, which codes media content along a positive–negative continuum.

In a broad sense, social media have the potential to redefine the culture. Voices can be heard through social media that have tended to be ignored by traditional media **gatekeepers**. During most of the 20th century, newspaper and wire service editors, radio news directors and television assignment editors (among others) selected a relatively small number of stories as news, and most events fell through the gatekeeping process. Social media offer new opportunities for sharing events and news, but SNSs may also spread content that is capable of manipulating public opinion and behavior. In this way, traditional media and social media may interact across ideological boundaries, impacting debate and participation (Soo-bum & Youn-gon, 2013).

Advertisers and marketers were some of the first to discover social media as a way to inexpensively reach large numbers of people with their messages. Social media content, like its predecessors, may be fair or not. At first, merely having a Facebook page or Twitter feed was enough to generate some interest. Fairly soon, however, these spaces opened brands to public criticism and required content managers to engage in customer relations. More recently, product and service campaigns have grown to feature strategic plans that include social media **tactics**. Planning creates real-time opportunities to engage in social media during large events, such as the Super Bowl or Academy Awards live television broadcasts. At the same time, brand managers may jump in at any moment when there is an unexpected event. For example, when *Today* show weatherman Al Roker overslept for the first time in nearly four decades of work, Twitter conversation followed.

GolinHarris operates one of the firm's global real-time engagement spaces called The Bridge, which has collaborated with long-time client McDonald's. The Chicago office Bridge Center is the largest of 14 global real-time centers, and is the global headquarters. Since September of 2012, a former Chicago TV journalist has directed the team, which includes experienced real-time engagement analysts. They provide clients with a variety of real-time services—insights, relationship building, hyper-relevant media relations, customer engagement and content creation.

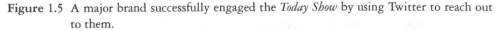

Figure 1.5 A major brand successfully engaged the *Today Show* by using Twitter to reach out to them.

As part of the show making fun of Roker, the tweet was featured during on-air anchor conversation. The **earned media** cost only the time to engage, in contrast to the more expensive cost of advertising within the show, plus it was more valuable coming from show talent. Roker also yawned in a Vine video that poked fun at missing his early broadcast. While the event was brief, it demonstrated how social media conversation may shift and move quickly from one topic to another.

The emergence of a complex social media landscape may seem overwhelming to students and the general public. A social media communication perspective can help. Individuals need to actively develop and use media literacy skills. These can be used to understand how brands make plays within social media. At the same time, open dissemination of information requires all of us to learn how to discern truths from falsehoods.

Social Media in Journalism

Decades ago, journalism was defined by its gatekeeping process, through which editors carefully selected news for distribution. The Associated Press (AP) and United Press International (UPI) maintained a news wire system with local newsroom partners. The wire provided a means to identify, edit and share news to newsrooms. Journalists then shared their selections with audience members. By the early 1980s, journalists were beginning to experiment with portable computers to write and send news reports from a location, such as a courtroom. This Tandy Radio Shack 100 laptop was one of the first mobile devices.

By June of 2009, major news organizations had evolved to begin using Twitter feeds and YouTube videos to report on an Iranian uprising that led to street protests covered by citizen journalists using portable video recording devices.

Journalists today are expected to use social media sites, monitoring content and participating in discussions. For example, the Associated Press (AP), a primary news distribution company, has issued specific social media guidelines for its employees and

Figure 1.6 This TRS-100, an early laptop for journalists, was on display in 2009 at the Newseum in Washington, DC.

journalism practitioners working in "sensitive situations" (AP, 2013). These are based upon news values and journalistic principles:

> The Social Media Guidelines are designed to advance the AP's brand and staffers' personal brands on social networks. They encourage staffers to be active participants in social networks while upholding our fundamental value that staffers should not express personal opinions on controversial issues of the day (AP, 2013).

The AP encourages all journalists to have social media accounts, but this is not universal across journalism. While AP reporters may not post confidential information, they are urged to use a profile photograph and required to identify themselves as AP reporters. They cannot disclose political affiliations or "express political views." The AP (2013) also restricts online opinions, as "AP employees must refrain from declaring their views on contentious public issues in any public forum . . ." Even in the areas of sports and entertainment, the AP (2013) guidelines declare:

- ". . . trash-talking about anyone (including a team, company or celebrity) reflects badly on staffers and the AP"
- ". . . you have a special obligation to be even-handed in your tweets"
- "Posts and tweets aimed at gathering opinions for a story must make clear that we are looking for voices on all sides of an issue"
- "A retweet with no comment of your own can easily be seen as a sign of approval of what you're relaying"

In general, AP (2013) applies its traditional rules of journalism with regard to accuracy and corrections to social media spaces. While journalists are encouraged to promote their stories, they also are warned to be careful online. Journalism, as a profession, is being challenged by the open access and publication nature of the Internet. The WikiLeaks site, for example, challenged the traditional journalistic methods of sourcing and official verification: "Its use of new technologies and the way it puts information into the public domain forces us to reconsider what journalism is and its moral purpose in contemporary global politics" (Beckett, with Ball, 2012, pp. 2–3). Everyone seems to agree that social media has changed journalism. "Regardless of how people get news from the web, this medium has become a dominant channel of communication and has passed newspapers as a primary source of public affairs news and information" (McCombs, Holbert, Kiousis & Wanta, 2011, p. 16).

For these reasons, journalism education has broadened in recent years to emphasize visual storytelling (Green, Lodato, Schwalbe & Silcock, 2012): "News, for many people, now unfolds as a stream of information from various sources—both professional and nonprofessional" (p. 5). Storytelling will continue to evolve because of technological change. For example, **augmented reality (AR)** mobile tools offer the possibility that storytelling "may be transformed into a more interactive, first-person participatory form utilizing the location-based, geographically anchored nature of AR" (Pavlik & Bridges, 2013, p. 41).

Mobile media tool availability appears to predict news consumption among younger users (Chan-Olmsted, Rim & Zerba, 2013). Perceived relative content advantages, utility and ease of use all were predictors of news consumption, suggesting that the younger news user may be driven, in part, by availability of mobile apps. Mobile news users may be some of the first to document news events.

Breaking news reports frequently begin with eyewitness accounts, which may be followed up on as journalists seek facts. Journalism tends to be defined by its key elements: the search for truth, "loyalty" to citizens, verification of information, practitioner independence, and "monitor of power" (Craft & Davis, 2013, p. 41). These are difficult challenges for news organizations seeking business success, which also requires attracting and retaining large audiences through engaging and entertaining content.

Journalists often are urged to develop a personal brand by publishing a **blog**, which tends to be short and frequent posts of information and analysis. Best practices for blogging, according to Briggs (2010, p. 55), include:

- Regularly publish high-quality posts.
- Write effective headlines.
- Participate in the community.

Blogging, however, blurs the lines between news and opinion. While reputable journalists maintain popular blogs, so too do paid bloggers working for corporate clients. At the heart of the emerging conflict between traditional news values practices and online media are the rules of engagement:

> The medium is a way to generate discussion around a particular topic or issue. Great blogs build online communities and encourage user interaction by asking questions and encouraging feedback from readers. Bloggers can share their opinion, but the best blogs also invite readers to share their opinions or comments as well. This open dialog is one of the hallmarks of digital journalism along with interactivity and collaboration. (Luckie, 2011, p. 51)

Internet news is "more horizontal" because its orientation places journalists within large and diverse social networks (Tewksbury & Rittenberg, 2012, p. 5). While traditional journalism informed citizens in order to aid in democratic decision-making through voting, **citizen journalism** has transformed the audience for news, as scholar Jay Rosen observes, through important online discussion. The interaction and **conversation monitoring** itself may be a driver for social change, even as voter apathy has grown. So-called "participatory journalism" features "open gates" that helps explain "fundamental change currently underway" that "transcends national boundaries" (Singer et al., 2011, p. 5).

In such a journalism environment, traditional norms of **objectivity** through balanced opinions and the search for facts has been questioned and studied. Maras (2013) observes that objective journalism is a complex professional ideal in which journalists seek to report "reality," obtain "facts" and avoid "personal opinion" by "[s]eparating facts from opinion," exercising emotional detachment and promoting "fairness and balance" (pp. 7–8). Obviously, these news values directly smash into the openness of the Internet.

While journalism was once defined by elite news organizations competing within a fairly narrow range of media, Internet users no longer are restricted by choices offered within the context of media economics and regulation. "With developments in media technology it is becoming even less clear in which sense it is meaningful to speak of media pluralism, if the media landscape is characterized more by abundance and limit-less choice than by scarcity or lack of options" (Karppinen, in Hesmondhalgh & Toynbee, 2008, p. 40). Journalism, then, is likely to be redefined by emerging SNSs and their business practices. Albarran (2013), for example, observes that social media are defined by a "lack of significant barriers to entry," since almost anyone is free to create social media accounts and user profiles (p. 6). As such, media economists think of social media as a "disruptive communications industry" (p. 14).

Researchers are beginning to study what differentiates the social media landscape. Content dissemination, for example, has been related to news reception, friend behav-ior and partisanship (Weeks & Holbert, 2013): ". . . both reception and friending are highly predictive of dissemination of news within social media" (p. 226). At its core, social media frequently involve distribution of unfiltered news and even rumors. For-mer National Public Radio's (NPR) senior strategist Andy Carvin (@acarvin) describes in his book *Distant Witness* how he has cultivated sources on the ground in Egypt, Syria and other Middle East countries to attempt to verify information circulating on Twitter. Because of the nature of revolutions since the "Arab Spring" uprisings begin-ning in 2009, anonymous sources frequently share videos to YouTube of what appear to be atrocities. Supporters share links on Twitter, but it may be difficult to determine authenticity through crowdsourcing. Still, the technique offers promise for journalists seeking news from dangerous locations. Storyful, a Dublin-based company, works with Yahoo News, Reuters, ABC News and others to verify social media content by monitor-ing for social media "spikes" in traffic and conducting "360 (degree) forensic verifica-tion of video" as an extension of newsrooms:

> And so it explores whether the images are real-time or old. Have they been manipulated? Where did the video come from? What's the history of the account? Was the weather at the time consistent with what the image shows? Is the mosque in the right place? What are the experts saying?
>
> It also gets in touch with the people who shot the video. In Syria, it relies on indirect contacts. But elsewhere, Storyful staffers will talk directly with the people who supplied the material. (Rieder, 2013)

The nature of communication on Twitter is that online communication also gener-ates social networks, which can be observed in real time but also visualized using data analysis tools. For example, a 2011 hockey game played between The Ohio State Uni-versity at the University of Nebraska at Omaha generated a lot of Twitter discussion by home team fans and media. Most users formed a passive audience, but the center of the social network revealed news media, athletic department PR and community boosters—not dissimilar from offline and traditional media interaction.

In a sporting event, it is rare for Twitter users to be faced with trying to confirm facts. However, crowdsourcing usually emerges in the early moments of breaking news stories. Before journalists can do their traditional work of verifying facts, Twitter and other social media sites can be a forum for conflicting eyewitness accounts, as well as attempts by some to spread false and even malicious information.

Social media Twitter users have been called micro-bloggers because tweets are lim-ited to 140 characters of space, including links to images, video or other websites.

Media storytelling, however, can be expanded through the use of blogs and tools, such as Storify, which organizes multiple tweets into a running narrative.

While some have treated the Internet and social media as a sort of Wild West without rules and norms, this approach is not recommended. Similar to their mainstream and traditional media predecessors, social media journalists are constrained by rapidly developing law and regulation (Stewart, 2013). This also applies to those social media users who do not identify themselves as journalists, and those considering themselves PR professionals.

Social Media in PR

Public relations (PR) organizations use social media sites to represent brands and engage with consumers. Coombs and Holladay (2007) suggest that academics and practitioners share frustration that PR "activities are often equated with spin, stonewalling, distortion, manipulation, or lying" (p. 1). In response, modern definitions emphasize "public interest," a "management function," "mutually beneficial relationships," and "relationships with stakeholders" (pp. 22–23). PR discourse may focus on identity and branding. A user:

> . . . packages himself in the language of his relationship to the dominant medium. . . . He can only be better if he frees himself from others' language. The attitude toward choice as digital and self-determined, however, leaves him vulnerable to what is real and what is the complete definition of the self . . . (p. 12)

Global PR efforts face challenges, including being able to communicate and work across cultures. Reid and Spencer-Oatey (2012) identified a "global people competency framework" of knowledge and ideas, communication, relationships and personal qualities:

- Communication management—work partners may have "significantly different norms for communicating in key project contexts, such as in meetings and in emails" (p. 19).
- Shared knowledge and mutual trust—time must be spent "building a common understanding of the meaning of the terminology used in discussions and ensuring that they shared sufficient background/contextual knowledge" (p. 21).

Trust is a relational dimension that may be connected with social interaction and shared values that motivate site usage (Lin & Lu, 2011). Public relations, as a field, has been concerned with the ability of PR practitioners to influence decisions within their organizations. Smith and Place (2013), building upon Grunig's 1992 work, found that integrated structure may have an impact on PR power:

> Through an interconnected structure of blurring functional boundaries that relies upon the skills of each communicator, public relations stands to gain power through the expertise of the individual practitioner *and the use of social media*, which yields tangible evidence for the organization to assess the value of the public relations function. (p. 179, emphasis added)

Smith and Place (2013) relate this to forms of power—expert, legitimate, structural and discursive.

In this book, we use three overarching concepts—**trust, influence** and engagement—to understand the power of social media. Source and message **credibility** may evoke audience trust, which is a driver of influence through strategic engagement. Interactive communication may or may not promote identity and community within social media settings.

PR involves many functions, including:

- Copywriting
- Media relations
- Event planning
- Crisis communication
- Corporate communication
- Reputation management
- Strategic planning

Each of these may incorporate social media tactics for clients, events, messages and branding.

Trust

Trust has been an important concept in media for decades. By the 1960s, for example, journalism researchers began to study what was called source and message credibility. For example, Slater and Rouner (1996) found that message quality may have an effect on the assessment of source credibility. More recently, Eastin's (2006) experiments manipulated source expertise and knowledge about health information online content. Perceptions may be impacted by variation in source and message credibility.

While trust has long been assumed to be important for journalists in their relationship with readers, listeners and viewers, it is only recently becoming central to public relations practitioners. Global PR giant Edleman PR (2012) produces an annual Trust Barometer, which highlights the need for corporate and governmental leaders to "practice radical transparency," establish clear goals for operating, and take note of employee credibility. By doing so, each employee may "spread messages to their networks, which helps build and support trust company-wide" (para. 1).

It is clear that media users value trustworthy information. We want to be able to trust our leaders and the information they share. In a democracy, the availability of accurate information is valued as one way for voters to make decisions. In a world driven by social media content, disclosure of new facts can rapidly change public opinion and policy. By 2009 and 2010, social media contributed to growing **Arab Spring** protests, public awareness and revolution. In Egypt and Libya, longtime leaders were overthrown. In Syria, social media contributed to a spreading civil war. In Iran, public demonstrations were captured on portable video cameras and uploaded to YouTube. In countries ruled by dictators, social media made it more difficult to control **propaganda** and rule by force.

While U.S. reporting by news organizations such as *The New York Times* and NBC News historically has been seen as very trusted, social media are bringing a new global perspective for consumers. For example, when U.S. Special Forces killed Osama Bin Laden, Al Jazeera had early and accurate reporting. Some watched an Internet live stream of the broadcast and shared it to social networks more than an hour before President Barack Obama made an official statement.

Trust also is important for consumer brands. Traditionally, trust was seen as "the critical component in credibility," but new media have redefined these key concepts:

> Trust, we come to find, tends to evolve from audience perceptions of the source's expertise on the topic at hand . . . and is a critical aspect of the advertising persuasion process. Yet, the power of attractive sources cannot be overlooked as an important part of persuasion . . . The Internet itself is not necessarily a reliable source of professionally developed information . . . not only the sender but also, to a great degree, the *medium* are considered as communication sources . . . in the mobile arena, one must look to aspects of credibility other than those impacted by the presentation and actual user interface alone. (Stafford, in Stafford and Faber, 2005, pp. 286–287)

One of the credibility challenges is the nature of online sources (Sundar & Nass, 2011). Cues and context are particularly important in evaluating source and message credibility within a broadening social media sphere.

Influence

Social media sites often are the battleground for influence to determine who we consider to be a **thought leader** or **idea starter**, as described in the Edelman former TweetLevel paradigm, which was designed to measure trust and influence. The PR firm was "assessing new metods" in 2014. The program is one approach among many that attempt to measure trust through influence and other variables.

In May of 2013, President Barack Obama scored an overall 82.8 out of 100 and was categorized as an "amplifier" because of his large number of followers. Obama's account (@BarackObama) had more than 39 million followers on Twitter. This made his account very popular and potentially influential, but this is not based upon much engagement. Instead, the fact that messages sent from the account will likely reach millions of Twitter users, and additionally that some will re-tweet content, helps explain the influence estimate. Obama's TweetLevel scores were: Influence, 82.8; Popularity, 100; Engagement, 59.9; and Trust 66.7. As a diagnostic tool, such measures provide guidance about areas for needed improvement.

Engagement

Engagement is defined as "the collective experiences that readers or viewers have with a media brand" (Mersey, Malthouse & Calder, 2012, p. 698, quoting Mersey, Malthouse & Calder, 2010). Engagement can be understood through consumer beliefs about brands and brand experiences. Engagement has been connected through research to satisfaction and media use, as expectation and evaluation may influence "gratification-seeking behavior" and ultimately includes reading (p. 699).

In social media, reading is an important behavior, but it is not the only behavior. Users process photographs, charts and other visual communication, such as video. These stimuli are consumed and sometimes result in reactions. For example, Facebook "likes" and "shares," Twitter "favorites" and "re-tweets," and Pinterest **board** "pins" follow consumption. At the same time, a user decision to post new content or share content from others may result in additional responses from others.

Social Media in Advertising and Marketing

Early in the development of social media, **marketing** has become an important function. This has impacted the fields of **advertising** and marketing. Online advertising spending has grown across all areas—paid search advertising, display advertising, classified advertising, rich media, referrals of sales leads, sponsorship and email (Tuten, 2008). eMarketer (2013) estimated that retail digital media spending would top $9 billion in 2013, and that 10.5% annual growth was expected through 2017. Indeed, the Interactive Advertising Bureau (IAB) certified a 15.6% growth rate since 2012. Quarterly revenue grew from nothing in 1996 to $2 billion in 2000, to $6 billion in 2007 and to more than $10 billion in 2013.

A 2012 study by Adobe found that a majority of consumers found online advertising annoying (68%) and distracting (51%), and that marketers underestimated these responses. Social media were not seen as places to view advertising compared to magazines and television. More than two-thirds of consumers were using social media, and 57% had liked a brand in social media. Consumers also were asked what they would do if they saw a friend like a product in social media. About 29% responded they would check out the product, but only 2% would buy it. Although the data paint a very rough picture of actual behavior, responses regarding what consumers say they want are valuable. Product reviews, for example, are credible for most—but not all—online users. Likewise, individuals vary in response to different media approaches (Adobe, 2012):

- Advertisements should tell a unique story, not just try to sell (73%)
- A video is worth 1,000 words (67%)
- User product reviews are the best source of truth (67%)
- In-Store experiences trump online experiences (67%)
- Television commercials are more effective than online . . . (67%)

The data support a social media perspective. Tuten (2008) viewed social media as "an umbrella phrase" for understanding SNS, social news, virtual environments and opinion sites:

> Social media refers to online communities that are participatory, conversational, and fluid. These communities enable members to produce, publish, control, critique, rank, and interact with online content. The term can encompass any online community that promotes the individual while also emphasizing an individual's relationship to the community, the rights of the members to collaborate and be heard within a protective space, which welcomes the opinions and contributions of participants. (p. 20)

In this sense, social media have begun to move the discussion of online advertising and marketing beyond the historically favored practice of sponsored search and keyword advertising that has made Google so successful (Jansen, 2011). The online structure allowed advertisers to measure **click-through rates (CTR)** for early banner advertising, but sponsored search allowed advertisers to pay "only when a potential customer clicked on a sponsored result," which allowed for measurement accountability (Jansen, 2011, p. 12). Social media, within this context, empowers potential customers to "share an ad, comment on an ad, and give feedback on an ad" (p. 225). Social media advertising, then, may use a **cost per click (CPC)** pricing structure instead of the traditional audience size estimates.

This helps explain why **word of mouth (WOM)** has become an important marketing phrase for brands wanting to spread word through a growing group of followers and **fans**. So-called "brand ambassadors" may be activated by company and product messages. Through conversation monitoring, brand community managers can assess awareness, spark popularity and even convert followers and fans to loyal customers. They can become part of an earned media strategy that leverages customer passion for a product or service. Social media WOM and "customer evangelism," as some marketing gurus have labeled it, amounts to free advertising by authentic customers who engage with others as trusted spokespeople. Somewhat related are those buyers and purchasers who rate products on sites, such as Amazon.com. These ratings and subsequent conversation may reflect brand loyalty or even competitor attacks.

Community managers are paid to monitor conversation and activity and to engage as needed. For example, if online conversation turns unfairly negative on Twitter, then a company representative may need to engage and participate by providing additional information or offering assistance. Failure to engage when competitors do could be a competitive disadvantage. Some customers may determine product choice based, at least in part, on the quantity and quality of company online engagement. Here, advertising, marketing and PR may converge based upon strategic goals. The cost of online engagement may be considered by a **Return On Investment (ROI)** analysis, although some professionals suggest that this does not make sense for social media. Analogous to ROI for a receptionist, social media may be a cost for doing business in a professional manner. An alternative is the so-called **Cost Of Ignoring (COI)** social media (MacLean, 2013). With more than half of consumers on Facebook and more than one-third on Twitter, the argument is that businesses must be present in order to be listening and engaging in five areas: 1) customer service, 2) reputation management, 3) crowdsourcing to build loyalty; 4) collaboration, and 5) recruitment of job candidates (MacLean, 2013).

The WOM process involves everything from generating conversation through business blogs to hiring paid bloggers (a controversial ethical issue), offering customer relations, triggering viral media content, handling a crisis, managing individual and organizational reputations, and monitoring conversation **buzz**. One of the earliest social media measurement techniques was to track buzz for individual brands and compare it to others. Measurement quickly became more sophisticated.

All online activities are open to measuring **benchmark data**, which establish beginning points for measuring future growth and effects of strategic campaign tactics. Quantitative goals may be set for future growth. Further, qualitative analyses of key conversations may yield clues to marketing and sales successes and failures. Best practices for social media involve development of strategies and tactics for setting specific new media goals.

New Media

Drawing upon the seminal work of Lievrouw and Livingstone (2006), Cheong, Martin and Macfayden (2012) "position new media as information and communication technologies *and* their social contexts" (p. 2). The study of changing technological devices—**hardware** and **software**—is dynamic and driven by continuous change over time. For example, recent development and proliferation of smartphones has driven interest in mobile devices and media. Ling and Campbell (2011) conclude that mobile technologies "rearranged the social scene" by enhancing "some interactions" yet straining others (p. 329).

Consider the apps downloaded and located on a smartphone screen. These represent priorities for the users. However, we live in a multi-screen world in which user attention is split between many screens—sometimes with more than one active in a given moment. Beyond desktop and laptop computers, tablets (the fastest growing device) and smartphones, television screens and place-based screens in public places may each offer engaging content. Social media appear to follow findings of early Internet studies that conclude that user motivations matter. Media may group people into "interpretive communities," which "are neither homogenous nor monolithic" (Mankekar, in Hesmondhalgh & Toynbee, 2008, p. 149). Instead, demographic differences among social media users may produce content that mirrors or departs from existing offline power structures.

One key difference within social media is the rapid spreading of information, even when it is false. When the normally credible @AP Twitter account was hacked with incorrect information in 2013, crowdsourcing was important in users correcting

Figure 1.7 This book author's iPhone 5S "first screen," as viewed in early 2014.

through a variety of other news sources. Eventually, AP had to suspend its account and re-start it. Within one month, AP again had more than two million followers—they re-followed the trusted news source after the brief incident.

The emergence of social media within PR coincides with convergence of traditional practices with advertising and marketing.

((•)) BOX 1.3 THOUGHT LEADER MELANIE JAMES

Using social media to more effectively network and build professional relationships on an international scale has been a "game changer." The ability to join global social media conversations in real time, especially when based in a vastly different time zone from North America and Europe, has delivered insights and opportunities unheard of previously.

The ability to shape personal branding has also contributed to the way my career

Figure 1.8 @melanie_james.
Photograph by George Hyde.

has unfolded in recent years. Social media make it easy to share my own work and that of respected colleagues. This leads to more exposure and more opportunities. Closer to home, social media has also fundamentally changed the way communication takes place with my colleagues, clients and students. Negotiating the personal and the professional, which previously had been very distinct, has been at the center of these changes.

Defining what appropriate return on investment in social media looks like for organizations remains challenging, as this can vary widely depending on the nature of the entity's mission. Integrating social media into traditional public relations activities, many of which have not diminished as a result of social media's rise, is placing strain on PR departments. Power plays and turf wars are becoming evident within organizations as people fight for control of digital communication. This also has negative impacts for women—research has shown that men are more likely to want to have control over what are seen as technical areas, and if technology is involved, such roles are likely to pay higher.

The way success is viewed in public relations will change. Whereas once organizations looked at measures such as attitudinal or behavioral change as the primary desired outcome for PR, this instead will only be the beginning. Success won't have been achieved until target publics have both changed their attitude or behavior *and* propagated the idea that others do the same through social media networks. People will increasingly "wise up" to the way their social sharing benefits business and will want to be rewarded for this "work." The use of network analysis in PR will further rise as organizations seek to map how and through whom such propagation takes place. PR practitioners will need to "up-skill" to be able to not just provide this information but to use it to inform decision-making on future campaign investments.

There are opportunities in research applying social network and actor network theories to examine the role and influence of the social media technologies themselves. There will be a need to better understand how they constrain and enable PR practice, but also how they constrain and enable desired responses from target audiences. With organizations under more public scrutiny than ever before via social media, PR practitioners will be empowered to argue for more ethical approaches to practice as the issue of establishing and maintaining a social license to operate becomes increasingly prominent.

Melanie James, Ph.D., is Senior Lecturer in Communication and Public Relations and researcher in the Centre for Social Research in Energy and Resources, University of Newcastle, Sydney area, Australia. Her research on new media, PR and blogging as an educational assessment tool has been widely cited. James joined the university in 2006 after working in senior management roles in PR—strategic, government and marketing communication. She was an early adopter of social media in PR practice and education and is a strategic communication consultant. James sits on the National Education Advisory Committee of the Public Relations Institute of Australia.

Engaging consumers—within the context of PR, advertising or marketing—appears to be "more about conversations, connections, and shared control and less about passive consumption of packaged content" (Tuten, 2008, p. 3). It is a fundamental shift that will continue to have an effect on PR and other professionals for years to come.

Ahead

In the next chapter, computer-mediated communication will be used to explore the importance of **identity**, **interaction** and **community** within social media spaces. As new ideas and technologies spread, online communication may influence cultural change in powerful ways. A large number of social media tools are now in use within journalism and public relations. These occupations now borrow **branding** techniques from advertising and marketing, as **convergence** continues to take hold across many media industries.

Entrepreneurs creating new businesses, investing in **start-ups**, and constantly creating new media industries are driving some of the change. The **innovation** culture often ignores old media organizations and practices in favor of fundamental change.

The new media landscape is not without challenges. As we will learn in this book, "big data" collection and analysis raise concerns about personal **privacy**. There are legal and ethical issues surrounding social media technologies, and there are calls for global regulation. Perhaps the best we can hope for right now is the development of **best practices** by journalists, PR practitioners and others. We can learn from case studies that expose social media successes and failures. More can be learned through use of social media **metrics** and **analytics**. For example, **search engine optimization (SEO)** rules affect the words we should use in effectively spreading online content. At the same time, popular measurement tools—Google Analytics, Hootsuite, SproutSocial, Topsy and others—offer new intelligence about communication behavior. As we will see in this book, SEO may be positively or negatively impacted by social media conversation, from online engagement to product and service sales. The quality of those sites linking to a story, conversation or site may raise or lower the prominence of content at any given moment. This can be important for story placement on search engines, such as Google, but it also has implications within social media conversation over time. Likewise, Facebook insights data help community brand managers select and promote social media storytelling. Knowing which stories are liked, shared and commented upon offers important explanations about why content is moving through social networks.

Some are turning to **media literacy** as a way to explore best practices of journalists and PR people. In order to effectively engage within a social network, strategies and tactics must constantly return to concerns about online trust and influence.

■ DISCUSSION QUESTIONS: STRATEGIES AND TACTICS

1. The Boston Marathon explosions provided challenges for journalists, PR practitioners, advertisers and marketers: How does each respond to a breaking news story? What are the challenges? What legal and ethical concerns exist? How should social media users judge source and message credibility of information during a crisis?

2. What are the similarities and differences in roles and functions for journalists, PR practitioners, advertisers and marketers? How do social media blur the lines between these fields? What are the challenges for practitioners moving from journalism to PR? What about moving from PR to journalism? What is an example you recall of social media engagement that did not seem to be authentic?

3. How do you determine whether or not to trust a social media voice? How do social media change the nature of influencing others compared to traditional word-of-mouth sharing? How do you influence others within social media spaces? How will your influence evolve as a social media professional?

References

Adobe (2012, October). *Click Here: The State of Online Advertising*. www.adobe.com/aboutadobe/pressroom/pdfs/Adobe_State_of_Online_Advertising_Study.pdf

Albarran, A. B. (Ed.) (2013). *The Social Media Industries*. New York, NY: Routledge.

AP (2013, May). *Social Media Guidelines for AP Employees*. www.ap.org/Images/Social-Media-Guidelines_tcm28–9832.pdf

Beckett, C., with Ball, J. (2012). *Wikileaks, News in the Networked Era*. Cambridge, UK: Polity Press.

Berkman, F. (2013, October 29). Sandy Was Our Social Storm. But at What Cost? *Mashable*. http://mashable.com/2013/10/29/sandy-social-media-storm-safety/

Briggs, M. (2010). *Journalism Next*. Washington, DC: CQ Press.

Chan-Olmsted, S., Rim, H., & Zerba, A. (2013). Mobile News Adoption Among Young Adults: Examining the Roles of Perceptions, News Consumption, and Media Usage. *Journalism & Mass Communication Quarterly 90*(1), 126–147.

Cheong, P. H., Martin, J. N., & Macfadyen, L. P. (Eds.) (2012). *New Media and Intercultural Communication, Identity, Community and Politics*. New York, NY: Peter Lang.

Coombs, W. T., & Holladay, S. J. (2007). *It's Not Just PR, Public Relations in Society*. Malden, MA: Blackwell.

Craft, S., & Davis, C. N. (2013). *Principles of American Journalism, An Introduction*. New York, NY: Routledge.

Desilver, D. (2013, December 2). China Has More Internet Users Than Any Other Country. *Pew Research Center*. www.pewresearch.org/fact-tank/2013/12/02/china-has-more-internet-users-than-any-other-country/

Eastin, M. S. (2006). Credibility Assessments of Online Health Information: The Effects of Source Expertise and Knowledge of Content. *Journal of Computer-Mediated Communication 6*(4). http://onlinelibrary.wiley.com/doi/10.1111/j.1083-6101.2001.tb00126.x/full

Edelman PR (2012). *2012 Edelman Trust Barometer*. www.edelman.com/insights/intellectual-property/2012-edelman-trust-barometer/

Edelman PR (2014). *TweetLevel*. http://tweetlevel.edelman.com/

eMarketer (2013, June 11). *When Will Desktop Ad Spending Peak?* www.emarketer.com/Articles/Print.aspx?R=1009959

Green, S. C., Lodato, M. J., Schwalbe, C. B., & Silcock, B. W. (2012). *News Now, Visual Storytelling in the Digital Age*. Boston, MA: Pearson.

Gumuchian, M.-L., & Sidner, S. (2013, December 23). American Gets 1-Year Prison Sentence for Parody Video. *CNN*. www.cnn.com/2013/12/23/world/meast/uae-american-sentence/index.html

Hesmondhalgh, D., and Toynbee, J. (Eds.) (2008). *The Media and Social Theory*. London, UK: Routledge.

Jansen, J. (2011). *Understanding Sponsored Search, Core Elements of Keyword Advertising*. New York, NY: Cambridge University Press.

Katz, E. (1994). Forward. In G. Weimann (Ed.), *The Influentials, People Who Influence People*, pp. ix–xi. Albany, NY: State University of New York Press.

Katz, E. (1957). The Two-Step Flow of Communication: An Up-To-Date Report on an Hypothesis. Departmental Papers (ASC). Annenberg School for Communication. http://repository.upenn.edu/cgi/viewcontent.cgi?article=1279&context=asc_papers

Khang, H., Ki, E.-J., & Ye, L. (2012). Social Media Research in Advertising, Communication, Marketing, and Public Relations. *Journalism & Mass Communication Quarterly 89*(2), 279–298.

Lievrouw, L. A., & Livingstone, S. (Eds.) (2006). *Handbook of New Media* (Updated Student Edition). London: Sage.

Lin, K.-Y., & Lu, H.-P. (2011). Intention to Continue Using Facebook Fan Pages from the Perspective of Social Capital Theory. *Cyberpsychology, Behavior, and Social Networking 14*(10), 565–570.

Ling, R., and Campbell, S. W. (Eds.) (2011). *Mobile Communication, Bringing Us Together and Tearing Us Apart*. New Brunswick, NJ: Transaction.

Luckie, M. S. (2011). *The Digital Journalist's Handbook*. Lexington, KY: Mark S. Luckie.

Lunden, I. (2014, January 21). Instagram is the Fastest-Growing Social Site Globally, Mobile Devices Rule over PCs for Access. *Tech Crunch*. http://techcrunch.com/2014/01/21/instagram-is-the-fastest-growing-social-site-globally-mobile-devices-rule-over-pcs-for-social-access/

MacLean, H. (2013, May 28). The Cost of Ignoring Social Media. Sales Force Marketing Cloud. www.salesforcemarketingcloud.com/blog/2013/05/cost-of-ignoring-social-media/?d=70130 000000tH3O

Maras, S. (2013). *Objectivity in Journalism*. Malden, MA: Polity Press.

Mathison, D. (2009). *Be The Media*. New York, NY: natural E creative.

McCombs, M., Holbert, R. L., Kiousis, S., & Wanta, W. (2011). *The News and Public Opinion, Media Effects on Civic Life*. Malden, MA: Polity Press.

Mersey, R. D., Malthouse, E. C., & Calder, B. J. (2012). Focusing on the Reader: Engagement Trumps Satisfaction. *Journalism & Mass Communication Quarterly 89*(4), 695–709.

Pavlik, J. V., & Bridges, F. (2013, Spring). The Emergence of Augmented Reality (AR) as a Storytelling Medium in Journalism. *Journalism & Communication Monographs 15*(1), 1–59.

PR News (2013, October 21). PR Teams Build Internal Newsrooms as Communications Strategies Shift. www.prnewsonline.com/topics/media-relations/2013/10/21/pr-teams-build-internal-newsrooms-as-communications-strategies-shift

Reid, S., & Spencer-Oatey, H. (2012). Beyond Stereotypes: Utilising a Generic Competency Approach to Develop Intercultural Effectiveness. In V. Carayol & A. Frame (Eds.), *Communication and PR from a Cross-Cultural Standpoint, Practical and Methodological Issues*, pp. 15–26. Bruxelles: P.I.E. Peter Lang.

Rieder, R. (2013, Sep. 5). Storyful verifies social media video from Syria. *USA Today*. www.usatoday.com/story/money/columnist/rieder/2013/09/05/storyful-verifying-video-on-social-media-from-syria/2771029/

Schmitt-Beck, R. (2003). Mass Communication, Personal Communication and Vote Choice: The Filter Hypothesis of Media Influence in Comparative Perspective. *British Journal of Political Science 33*(2), 233–260.

Singer, J. B., Hermida, A., Domingo, D., Heinhonen, A., Paulussen, S., Quandt, T., Reich, Z., & Vojnovic, M. (2011). *Participatory Journalism, Guarding Open Gates at Online Newspapers*. Malden, MA: Wiley-Blackwell.

Slater, M. D., & Rouner, D. (1996). Value-affirmative and Value-Protective processing of Alcohol Education Messages That Include Statistical Evidence or Anecdotes. *Communication Research, 23*(2), 210–235.

Smith, B. G, & Place, K. R. (2013). Integrating Power? Evaluating Public Relations Influence in an Integrated Communication Structure. *Public Relations Research 25*(2), 168–187.

Soo-bum, L., & Youn-gon, K. (2013). A Frame Analysis on Korean Daily Newspapers' Coverage of Twitter: Focusing on the Perspective of Political Communication and Formation of Public Opinion. *Korean Journalism Review 7*(2), 51–77.

Stafford, T. (2005). Mobile Promotional Communication and Machine Persuasion: A New Paradigm for Source Effects? In M. R. Stafford & R. J. Faber (Eds.), *Advertising, Promotion, and New Media*, pp. 278–297. Armonk, NY: M.E. Sharpe.

Stewart, D. R. (Ed.) (2013). *Social Media and the Law, A Guidebook for Communication Students and Professionals*. New York, NY: Routledge.

Sundar, S. S., & Nass, C. (2001). Conceptualizing Sources in Online News. *Journal of Communication 51*(1), 52–72.

Tewksbury, D., & Rittenberg, J. (2012). *News on the Internet, Information and Citizenship in the 21st Century*. Oxford, UK: Oxford University Press.

Tuten, T. L. (2008). *Advertising 2.0, Social Media Marketing in a Web 2.0 World*. Westport, CT: Praeger.

Vaynerchuk, G. (2013). *Jab, Jab, Jab, Right Hook*. New York, NY: HarperCollins.

Waldman, K. (2013, September 4). I'm Here for Business Meetings with No Clothes. *Slate*. www.slate.com/articles/business/moneybox/2013/09/air_berlin_lost_luggage_the_german_airline_melts_down_on_social_media.single.html

Weeks, B. E., & Holbert, R. L. (2013, Summer). Predicting Dissemination of News Content in Social Media: A Focus on Reception, Friending, and Partisanship. *Journalism & Mass Communication Quarterly 90*(2), 212–232.

Zarrell, R. (2013, November 2). What Happens When You Dress as a Boston Marathon Victim and Post it on Twitter. *Buzzfeed*. www.buzzfeed.com/rachelzarrell/what-happens-when-you-dress-as-a-boston-marathon-victim

2   CMC, DIFFUSION AND SOCIAL THEORIES

"One of the most devastating relational developments in the world of social media is the 'status' bar on Facebook."

—*Tammy Nelson (@drtammynelson, 2012)*

Former Notre Dame linebacker and current NFL player Manti Te'o told a story about a dead girlfriend, allowed it to spread across traditional and social media during the 2013 college football bowl season ahead of the NFL draft, and then had to deal with the fallout (Sonderman, 2013). The online publication *Deadspin* titled their report, "Manti Te'o's Dead Girlfriend, The Most Heartbreaking and Inspirational Story of the College Football Season, Is a Hoax." People "were taken in" by what sounded like a great story. Te'o then released a statement, which read, in part:

> This is incredibly embarrassing to talk about, but over an extended period of time, I developed an emotional relationship with a woman I met online. We maintained what I thought to be an authentic relationship by communicating frequently online and on the phone . . . To realize that I was the victim of what was apparently someone's sick joke and constant lies was, and is, painful and humiliating . . .
> . . . To think that I shared with them my happiness about my relationship and details that I thought to be true about her just makes me sick . . . In retrospect, I obviously should have been much more cautious. If anything good comes of this, I hope it is that others will be far more guarded when they engage with people online than I was. (Burke & Dickey, 2013)

Te'o had apparently accepted the identity of a girlfriend named "Lennay Kekua." In the story, they met after a game and talked by telephone every night until she was in a car crash and later died of leukemia. National sports media latched onto the lie, and they repeatedly distributed it without checking. The university called it a "troubling matter" that appeared to be "a sad and very cruel deception to entertain its perpetrators." Online communication is sometimes compromised by a lack of authentic identity (Burke & Dickey, 2013).

Identity

Interpersonal communication researchers developed CMC as a way to describe the digital nature of mediated online communication as it developed in the 1980s and 1990s

Figure 2.1 This book's author held virtual classes in Second Life in 2008.

(Barnes, 2001; Negroponte, 1995; Turkle, 1995). In general, CMC addressed identity formation, presentation, distribution and other issues. Each of us has an online presence expressed by what we choose to share about others and ourselves. This happens through continuous and ongoing interaction with others. Self-presentation may be accurate in depiction or reflect virtual transportation to another "place" or ideal.

CMC examines how identities and interaction sometimes produce online communities. CMC may offer voice to groups seeking social change, cultural shifts and even political power. In this sense, CMC is connected to the historical development of the Internet as a revolutionary infrastructure that quickly spawned numerous useful communication tools. CMC began as message bulletin board systems (BBS) and email, and quickly grew through development of the World Wide Web (WWW) in the 1990s.

Barnes (2003) was among those categorizing CMC as interpersonal communication: "Internet interactivity occurs as interpersonal interactivity, informational interactivity, and **human-computer interaction (HCI)**" (p. 1). This approach includes everything from email to Web pages, and interactivity "supports message interest and involvement," as it "plays a central role in online social dynamics and group communication" (pp. 20–21). What we consider as social is a function of individual psychological development. "It's the natural consequence of having brains that were built to make sense of other brains and to understand everyone's place in the pecking order" (Lieberman, 2013, p. 302). CMC may also assist individuals in presenting identity in a way that seeks to be truthful (Bargh, 2002; Bargh & McKenna, 2004; Bargh, McKenna, & Fitzsimons, 2002). The social process of human-Internet interaction is found within social media communication.

Internet History

A 1960s military project called the Advanced Research Projects Agency Network (ARPANET) by the United States Department of Defense had a goal of connecting the east and west coasts of the United States with instantaneous computer communication. The earliest mainframe computers were at the Pentagon and on university campuses across the nation, but the computer networks did not connect. ARPANET demonstrated that data could be divided into labeled packets, sent and then re-assembled, and this **packet switching** model was also adopted as an efficient way to move messages on the Internet.

Early public systems, such as CompuServe, Prodigy, America Online and The WELL began to connect non-military users across the country during the 1980s and 1990s to telephone line dial-up chat rooms, information services and online games. At the same time, **early adopters** began to develop simple web pages. Some of the first online communities, such as Classmates.com, LiveJournal, Friendster, MySpace and LinkedIn, developed the concept of **user profiles** that contained personal information going beyond sharing an email address.

The concept of the SNS reflected the idea of extending interpersonal and face-to-face (f2f) networks into online spaces through creation of a personal profile and development of connection lists on a platform that offered the capability to view the activities of others and interact (Albarran, 2013; boyd & Ellison, 2008). Within this broad framework, numerous functions emerged—from **tagging** and sharing content to shopping and product reviews.

The basic idea was that people would have an interest in finding friends, communicating with them and sharing information. By the time Facebook, Twitter, Google+, Pinterest and other social networking sites had become popular, social networking was a mainstream form of online communication.

Social Network Site Definitions

CMC happens within the broad context of SNS. These are defined as:

> . . . web-based services that allow individuals to (1) construct a public or semi-public profile within a bounded system, (2) articulate a list of other users with whom they share a connection, and (3) view and traverse their list of connections and those made by others within the system. The nature and nomenclature of these connections may vary from site to site. (boyd & Ellison, 2008, p. 211)

This SNS definition avoids the word "networking," which may imply meeting strangers through online interaction. Instead, "frequently" the emphasis is on activating pre-existing offline "latent" social "ties" (p. 211). For example, Google's Gmail is a SNS that connects usually identifiable users with others across the Internet. Similarly, LinkedIn reconnects business contacts by offering current work status and other information. Of

BOX 2.1 SOCIAL MEDIA FUNCTIONS AND SITES

Form	Functions	Examples
Blogging: Personal Blogs	Storytelling and Commentary	WordPress, Blogger
Blogging: Professional	Storytelling and Commentary	HuffingtonPost, Slate, Salon, Daily Kos
Blogging: Micro-blogs	Content Sharing	Twitter, Tumblr, Pinterest, Weibo
Blogging: Aggregator	Content Aggregator	Storify, Telly, Story
Traditional News	Content Sharing	*The New York Times*, CBS, AP, ESPN
Social News	Curating and Tagging	Reddit, Digg, Flipboard, Fark, Delicious
Technology News	Tech Trends	Mashable, TechCrunch, Gizmodo
Social Cultural	Culture Sharing	Buzzfeed, Cracked, Upworthy
Social Entertainment	Celebrity Sharing	TMZ, KnowYourMeme, LOLCATS
Wikis	Collaborative	Wikipedia, Wikia Encyclopedia
Shopping and Reviews	Consumer Purchase	Amazon, Yelp, Viewpoints
Social SNS	Social Networking	Facebook, Google+, Snapchat
Business SNS	Social Networking	LinkedIn, MySpace, Yammer
SNS Search	Friend Crowdsourcing	Jelly, Reddit
Photographs	Photograph Sharing	Flickr, Instagram
Audio: Voice	Audio Sharing	Soundcloud, Cinch, Voxer
Audio: Music	Music Listening	Spotify, iTunes, Spreaker
Video	Video Sharing	YouTube, Vimeo, Vine, Tout
Video Streaming	Live Video	Ustream, Livestream, Streamcast

Geolocation	Location Based Services (LBS)	Foursquare, Waze, Find My Friends
Games	Social Gaming	Words With Friends, Candy Crush Saga
Virtual Reality (VR)	Avatar Interaction	Second Life, World of Warcraft, Minecraft
Dashboards	Management and Measurement	Hootsuite, Google Analytics, Topsy, Klout

course, new connections also are made, but they tend to reflect nearby mutual associations with other contacts.

What we call social networking happens within a cybercultural context (Bell, 2001; Benedikt, 1991). It is understood to frequently involve existing interpersonal friendships that move into somewhat fluid online spaces (Gasser, 2008; Berger, 2005). These global communities have varying levels of media richness (Williams, Caplan, & Xiong, 2007), and potential ambiguity in terms of self-disclosure and other psychological variables (Ramirez, 2007; Bernie & Horvath, 2006). It is not that the Internet is anonymous, but rather that identity can be altered. Some social media communication sites, such as Twitter, make it easier for a user to maintain an anonymous profile. Discussion boards, messaging and video conferencing sites offer highly interactive opportunities for user communication. At the same time, a user may broadcast produced messages through blogs, video blogs (**vlogs**), podcasts and other means.

Some of these are incredibly popular. The "vlogbrothers," created by brothers John (@realjohngreen) and Hank (@HankGreen) Green, began as a way to talk to each other and grew to over one million YouTube subscribers. It is about "nothing in particular, but the brothers share humorous exchanges to their followers, known as 'Nerdfighters.'" Their regular video posts attract hundreds of thousands of views.

Online users also enter virtual spaces through graphical or gaming environments hosted on SNS platforms. Of particular importance, an online user may have a virtual connection with others that mimics the feeling of travel to another location, such as with the Second Life site. Within virtual environments, teams may be able to collaborate online and need only limited face-to-face interaction. Common SNS characteristics include (boyd & Ellison, 2008, pp. 211–221):

- Profile user pages, which may include demographic and psychographic descriptions
- Relationships displayed as friends, followers, fans, contacts or other labels
- Public connection displays, which are a form of "impression management"
- Types of "self-presentation" that serve as "identity markers"
- Varying degrees of privacy through site and user settings

The early adoption of online communication tools was a foundation for development of social networks and broader use of social media. The study of how individuals interact in social settings has been the focus of research for more than 50 years. Tubbs and Moss (1983), for example, traced investigations in the nature of "popular" or "overchosen" and "unpopular" or isolated people (pp. 108–109). In describing social interaction between popular and unpopular people, they diagrammed through the "sociogram" how positive traits, such as enthusiasm and maturity, may be related to judgments about "sincerity" of another's conversation (p. 110). Information theory and models emphasize flow of messages through channels. The perception of communication depends upon situations, context and social conditions (Cole, 2003; Severin & Tankard, 2001; Bourdieu & Coleman, 1991). Heider's balance theory and Festinger's cognitive dissonance theory from the 1950s have been related to social judgment (Milburn, 1991). Burnett and Marshall (2003) linked communication models to Internet discussion:

> At the very core of the meaning of the Web is linkage and connection: it is fundamentally about modes of communication and presenting possibilities about how those modes might intersect. Thus the Web is simultaneously a mass-mediated *and* one-to-one form of communication. It is a site of incredible cultural consumption *and* cultural production and makes it harder to establish the boundary between these two activities. (p. 59)

CMC, then, depends upon online identity. Burnett and Marshall (2003) contend that "shifting boundaries" are moved by such factors as anonymity, language, narcissism and gender (pp. 78–80). Although users sometimes assume they are anonymous, as with memes posted on the mobile Whisper app, packet switching and **Internet Protocol (IP)** addresses guarantee that the original source of a message can be tracked and traced by government entities and others.

Within these contexts, social media communication may be observed and represented through visual graphs. Twitter users, for example, may be analyzed to identify "visual patterns found within linked entities" (Hansen, Shneiderman, & Smith, 2011, p. 32). Researchers have proposed and developed methods for analysis of structure and grouping of categories and clusters within a social network. One model is called Group-In-A-Box (GIB):

> One particularly important aspect of social network analysis is the detection of *communities*, i.e., sub-groups of individuals or entities that exhibit tight interconnectivity among the other wider population. For example, Twitter users who regularly re-tweet each other's messages may form cohesive groups within the Twitter social network. In a network visualization they would appear as clusters or sub-graphs, often colored distinctly or represented by a different vertex shape in order to convey their group identity. (Rodrigues, Milic-Frayling, Smith, Shneiderman, & Hansen, 2011, para. 2)

Some researchers call the network graph that is produced by analysis software a "sociogram," which has "vertices (also called nodes or agents) and edges (also called ties or connections)" (Hansen, Shneiderman, & Smith, 2011, p. 33). In social network analyses, lines in social space connect Twitter users. The maps represent the center of a group of people and the core of a network.

Network analyses are grounded in nearly 300 years of study in graph theory. In modern terms, "It is often useful to consider social networks from an individual member's point of view" (Hansen, Shneiderman, & Smith, 2011, p. 36). News and information diffuse either from one point to another, or from one point to many other points, and these may be visually displayed through computer-generated mapping. As early as the 1930s, researchers were developing hand-drawn "pictures of patterns of people and their partners" (p. 38). This theoretical perspective has influenced the modern study of relationships. For example, Heaney and McClurg (2009) applied social works to the study of American politics. They found social networks useful in understanding information flow, as well as collaboration within political organizations.

Garton, Haythornthwaite and Wellman (1997) describe social network analysts as examining relations:

> They treat the description of relational patterns as interesting in its own right— e.g., is there a core and periphery?—and examine how involvement in such *social networks* helps to explain the behavior and attitudes of *network members* . . . They use a variety of techniques to discover a network's densely-knit clusters and to look for similar role relations. (para. 3)

Communication theory also has been concerned with how networks relate to personal influence. Cooley (1909/1966) identified four factors: expressiveness, permanence, swiftness and diffusion of communication; he viewed the extension of messages as "enlargement" and "animation" (pp. 149–159).

> Social contacts are extended in space and quickened in time, and in the same degree the mental unity they imply becomes wider and more alert. The individual is broadened by coming into relation with a larger and more various life, and he is kept stirred up, sometimes to express, by the multitude of changing suggestions which this life brings to him. (p. 150)

Baran and Davis (2006) suggested that influence of opinion leaders may be understood through similar interests and social stratification of leaders and their followers. At the same time, however, the shift from interpersonal to mediated communication is likely to reduce feedback as people orient within a social network (Westley & MacLean, 1957). Influence may disperse from the center of a social network. This influence often accelerates when a leader is "stimulating" what have been called "**virtual communities**" (Koh, Kim, Butler, & Bock, 2007, p. 70). In order to be sustainable, the researchers contend that four principles must exist: clear purpose/vision, clear member role definition, moderator leadership, and online/offline events (p. 70–71). Events, in fact, play a key role in strengthening member identification within a social network.

In one pilot study by our Omaha research team, an event demonstrated that a local conference may have a reach that extends well beyond about 400 registered participants. This may produce a relatively large and complex social network, in this case with an international reach on Twitter of about 96,000 users. At the center of the social network for the technology conference were its organizers, as reflected through the @Omaha101010 account, the @unomaha campus account, and the @cariador social media director's account. Five conference panelists were among the top ten participants within the social network. Online, some participants may take on the role of opinion leader, but others outside of the event may also play important roles through tweeting and re-tweeting to their followers. The leaders at the center of the Twitter social network were seen as key in spreading the conference message beyond those at the site by bridging to other users. Participants at the center of a social network link both to opinion leaders external to the conference as well as directly to the more casual followers.

In our second test of social networking, a college hockey game produced a singular network of over one thousand Twitter participants. The event sponsor, a university athletic department, had its @OMavs Twitter account near the center of the social network. In this social network, the center was more dispersed than the technology conference. Instead, this social network took on the characteristics of a large mass media audience in which members were communicating with each other instead of those media at the center. Within a large social network, there tend to be user clusters. Although the athletic department was near the center of the network, they were displaced from the core by some local media and hockey boosters. A *media cluster* involving three local newspapers and a local television station were among those Twitter accounts at the social network center. The hockey game, with its thousands in attendance, also had Twitter followers beyond the arena obtaining information from media sources and interacting with fans.

In contrast, the 2011 Association for Education in Journalism and Mass Communication (AEJMC) international conference of journalism educators in St. Louis is an example of a tightly clustered social network. The existence of social relationships produced a social network map that resembled a smaller version of the technology conference example. At the center were a majority of the 81 participants. A small group of educators emerged as most central to the larger social network. The sponsoring organization was at the center of the social network, along with other very active Twitter users and researchers focused on online studies.

Social network analyses continue to evolve as scholars refine methods (Butts, 2008). In particular, the methods used to define social network centrality and boundaries are open to discussion. As additional events are analyzed, it should be possible to begin to predict participation behavior (Howard, 2008; Wright, 2011).

Early communication studies demonstrated an understanding about group behavior, sharing, socialization, entertainment, and following (Schramm, 1972). Social networks have introduced new communication questions about leadership, behavior, and online social influence (Huffaker, 2010; Greenhow & Robelia, 2009). Researchers need to extend existing communication theories to the social networking landscape. By performing future systematic content analyses of language used in online interaction, it may be possible to discover emerging patterns of interaction and engagement. Such research should strengthen understanding about the nature of popularity, social isolation, opinion diffusion and social network leadership.

Interaction

At the heart of the social media communication shift is the desire to use the online network to connect with others and broaden social networks. Since the beginning of the change in the 1990s, there has been tension between the desire of governments to regulate online interaction and those that see the Internet as fundamentally different. John Perry Barlow (@JPBarlow), who once wrote music lyrics for the Grateful Dead and joined The WELL (an early online community in the 1980s), helped define the independent attitude of users through his writings. Following passage of the *Communications Decency Act of 1996*, Barlow responded with *A Declaration of the Independence of Cyberspace*, distributed via email.

📱 BOX 2.2 A DECLARATION OF THE INDEPENDENCE OF CYBERSPACE

```
Date: Fri, 9 Feb 1996 17:16:35 +0100
To: barlow@eff.org
From: John Perry Barlow <barlow@eff.org>
Subject: A Cyberspace Independence Declaration
```

Yesterday, that great invertebrate in the White House signed into the law the Telecom "Reform" Act of 1996, while Tipper Gore took digital photographs of the proceedings to be included in a book called "24 Hours in Cyberspace."

I had also been asked to participate in the creation of this book by writing something appropriate to the moment. Given the atrocity that this legislation would seek to inflict on the Net, I decided it was as good a time as any to dump some tea in the virtual harbor.

After all, the Telecom "Reform" Act, passed in the Senate with only 5 dissenting votes, makes it unlawful, and punishable by a $250,000 to say "shit" online. Or, for that matter, to say any of the other 7 dirty words prohibited in broadcast media. Or to discuss abortion openly. Or to talk about any bodily function in any but the most clinical terms.

It attempts to place more restrictive constraints on the conversation in Cyberspace than presently exist in the Senate cafeteria, where I have dined and heard colorful indecencies spoken by United States senators on every occasion I did.

This bill was enacted upon us by people who haven't the slightest idea who we are or where our conversation is being conducted. It is, as my good friend and Wired Editor Louis Rossetto put it, as though "the illiterate could tell you what to read."

Well, fuck them.

Or, more to the point, let us now take our leave of them. They have declared war on Cyberspace. Let us show them how cunning, baffling, and powerful we can be in our own defense.

I have written something (with characteristic grandiosity) that I hope will become one of many means to this end. If you find it useful, I hope you will pass it on as widely as possible. You can leave my name off it if you like, because I don't care about the credit. I really don't.

(continued)

But I do hope this cry will echo across Cyberspace, changing and growing and self-replicating, until it becomes a great shout equal to the idiocy they have just inflicted upon us.

I give you . . .

A Declaration of the Independence of Cyberspace

Governments of the Industrial World, you weary giants of flesh and steel, I come from Cyberspace, the new home of Mind. On behalf of the future, I ask you of the past to leave us alone. You are not welcome among us. You have no sovereignty where we gather.

We have no elected government, nor are we likely to have one, so I address you with no greater authority than that with which liberty itself always speaks. I declare the global social space we are building to be naturally independent of the tyrannies you seek to impose on us. You have no moral right to rule us nor do you possess any methods of enforcement we have true reason to fear.

Governments derive their just powers from the consent of the governed. You have neither solicited nor received ours. We did not invite you. You do not know us, nor do you know our world. Cyberspace does not lie within your borders. Do not think that you can build it, as though it were a public construction project. You cannot. It is an act of nature and it grows itself through our collective actions.

You have not engaged in our great and gathering conversation, nor did you create the wealth of our marketplaces. You do not know our culture, our ethics, or the unwritten codes that already provide our society more order than could be obtained by any of your impositions.

You claim there are problems among us that you need to solve. You use this claim as an excuse to invade our precincts. Many of these problems don't exist. Where there are real conflicts, where there are wrongs, we will identify them and address them by our means. We are forming our own Social Contract. This governance will arise according to the conditions of our world, not yours. Our world is different.

Cyberspace consists of transactions, relationships, and thought itself, arrayed like a standing wave in the web of our communications.

Ours is a world that is both everywhere and nowhere, but it is not where bodies live. We are creating a world that all may enter without privilege or prejudice accorded by race, economic power, military force, or station of birth.

We are creating a world where anyone, anywhere may express his or her beliefs, no matter how singular, without fear of being coerced into silence or conformity.

Your legal concepts of property, expression, identity, movement, and context do not apply to us. They are based on matter, There is no matter here.

Our identities have no bodies, so, unlike you, we cannot obtain order by physical coercion. We believe that from ethics, enlightened self-interest, and the commonweal, our governance will emerge. Our identities may be distributed across many of your jurisdictions. The only law that all our constituent cultures would generally recognize is the Golden Rule. We hope we will be able to build our particular solutions on that basis. But we cannot accept the solutions you are attempting to impose.

In the United States, you have today created a law, the Telecommunications Reform Act, which repudiates your own Constitution and insults the dreams of Jefferson, Washington, Mill, Madison, DeToqueville, and Brandeis. These dreams must now be born anew in us.

You are terrified of your own children, since they are natives in a world where you will always be immigrants. Because you fear them, you entrust your bureaucracies with the parental responsibilities you are too cowardly to confront yourselves. In our world, all the sentiments and expressions of humanity, from the debasing to the angelic, are parts of a seamless whole, the global conversation of bits. We cannot separate the air that chokes from the air upon which wings beat.

In China, Germany, France, Russia, Singapore, Italy and the United States, you are trying to ward off the virus of liberty by erecting guard posts at the frontiers of Cyberspace. These may keep out the contagion for a small time, but they will not work in a world that will soon be blanketed in bit-bearing media.

Your increasingly obsolete information industries would perpetuate themselves by proposing laws, in America and elsewhere, that claim to own speech itself throughout the world. These laws would declare ideas to be another industrial product, no more noble than pig iron. In our world, whatever the human mind may create can be reproduced

(continued)

and distributed infinitely at no cost. The global conveyance of thought no longer requires your factories to accomplish.

These increasingly hostile and colonial measures place us in the same position as those previous lovers of freedom and self-determination who had to reject the authorities of distant, uninformed powers. We must declare our virtual selves immune to your sovereignty, even as we continue to consent to your rule over our bodies. We will spread ourselves across the Planet so that no one can arrest our thoughts.

We will create a civilization of the Mind in Cyberspace. May it be more humane and fair than the world your governments have made before.

Davos, Switzerland

February 8, 1996

****

John Perry Barlow, Cognitive Dissident Co-Founder, Electronic Frontier Foundation

Home(stead) Page: www.eff.org/~barlow

Message Service: 800/634-3542

Barlow in Meatspace Today (until Feb 12): Cannes, France

Hotel Martinez: (33) 92 98 73 00, Fax: (33) 93 39 67 82

Coming soon to: Amsterdam 2/13-14, Winston-Salem 2/15, San Francisco 2/16-20, San Jose 2/21, San Francisco 2/21-23, Pinedale, Wyoming

In Memoriam, Dr. Cynthia Horner and Jerry Garcia

****

It is error alone which needs the support of government. Truth can stand by itself.

    —Thomas Jefferson, Notes on Virginia

Source: Barlow, J. P. (1996). A Cyberspace Independence Declaration. http://w2.eff.org/Censorship/Internet_censorship_bills/barlow_0296.declaration

Barlow suggested that governments should have "no sovereignty" over "cyberspace" and its users: "On behalf of the future, I ask you of the past to leave us alone." This idealistic view of online life attempted to separate it from the physical world and its limitations. Still, Barlow's **Electronic Frontier Foundation (EFF)** since the 1990s has remained active in fighting government regulation and intrusion, such as the National Security Agency (NSA) collection of online and telephone data.

Another CMC pioneer, Howard Rheingold (@HRheingold), observed that virtual communities involve creation of social groups and relationships over time: "You can't kiss anybody and nobody can punch you in the nose, but a lot can happen within those boundaries" (Rheingold, 1993, p. 3). Rheingold, also an early member of The WELL, imported 1960s hippie culture into online, Web and social media communication.

CMC involves social experimentation: "Social isolation becomes a difficult proposition for any contemporary community" (Jones, 1998, p. 17). It is often assumed that computers "break down boundaries" or "break down hierarchies" in cyberspace: "And yet computers can just as easily create boundaries and hierarchies" (p. 27). When it comes to social media communication, individuals present themselves online, and use constructed identity for impression management in relationships. "Social networking sites, such as Facebook, are particularly interesting to communication researchers because they are dedicated specifically to forming and managing impressions, as well as engaging in relational maintenance and relationship-seeking behaviors" (Rosenberg & Egbert, 2011, p. 2).

Community

Online community emerges from the development of individual social identities and realistic relationships between people (Bugeja, 2005; Lindlof & Taylor, 2002; Raacke & Bonds-Raacke, 2008). Chen and Persson (2002) found that older Internet users tended to score higher on measures of personal growth and life purpose. "In a sense, older Internet users were more like young adults than non-users" (p. 741). That is, people spending time online share common characteristics that separate them from those less likely to participate. Social media communication platforms create symbolic environments in which metaphors, such as the Facebook "wall" or the Pinterest "board," construct shared meaning and understanding. Mediated interpersonal communication develops when online communication begins to function as it would in a face-to-face environment. Individual relationships are unique, interdependent and rich with sharing and disclosure. Social media tend to emphasize sharing more than disclosure. When people say that there is a need for more engagement within social media, they may not understand that stronger relationships are built upon transparency.

Diffusion of New Ideas

The adoption and spread of new ideas, new technologies and new practices follow somewhat predictable patterns. Although the United States experienced dramatic growth of Internet and social media communication technologies over two decades, diffusion is uneven, and much of the world is slower to change (Bargh & McKenna, 2004). At the same time, however, in India, China and other rapidly developing countries, adoption of computers, mobile media and social media communication has advanced quickly in recent years. Rogers' (1995) model has been used to study change within a variety of contexts. It labels types of adopters within categories and allows us to track diffusion using a S-shaped curve over time. Social media communication began with adoption of personal, home computers that were relatively simple to use, offered increasing computing power and were priced less expensively over time: "home computers became more user friendly, and their rate of adoption rose gradually" (Rogers, 1995, p. 243).

Internet and social media users tend to be early adopters of an innovative communication technology. The adoption process involves five major stages: awareness, interest, evaluation, trial and then adoption (Lowery & DeFleur, 1995, p. 128). Rogers' model proposed five groups that roughly fit a normal curve distribution.

📱 **BOX 2.3 THE DIFFUSION MODEL**

- *Innovators*: the earliest people experimenting with the change (2.5%).
- *Early adopters*: those swayed by the innovators to jump on board of what is obviously a new trend (13.5%).
- *Early majority*: the first wave of mass appeal (34%).
- *Late majority*: the last wave of mass appeal (34%).
- *Laggards*: the remaining people who are either slow to come to the change, or resist it entirely (16%)

Source: Lowery, S.A., & DeFleur, M.L. (1995). *Milestones in Mass Communication Research, Media Effects, third edition*. White Plains, NY: Longman, p. 130.

Uses and Gratifications

Social media offer a nearly unlimited range of potential uses, and these may or may not meet user expectations for new need gratification (Sundar & Limperos, 2013). Large amounts of time online have been shown to increase overall satisfaction: "For those individuals who spend less time on the Internet, the supportive relationships may be perceived as too insignificant to exhibit costs or rewards" (Wright, 2000, p. 115). While social media offer the hope of breaking down traditional social barriers, communication theory suggests that this was not the case with use of traditional mass media: "Open and easy communication as a basis for social solidarity between peoples becomes *more difficult* because of social differentiation, impersonality and distrust due to psychological alienation, the breakdown of meaningful social ties, and increasing anomie among the members" (Lowery & DeFleur, 1995, p. 12). In a sense, social media are the current test for our ability to create meaningful online communities, relationships and social movements.

Online communication also follows traditional media use patterns in terms of motivations. People use CMC for information about the world around them, relaxation, entertainment, excitement, and as an escape from the stresses of daily life (Perse & Dunn, 1995). Early research offered clues as to why social media has emerged, as national surveys found that computer use was connected with friends and family activities, a vehicle to avoid loneliness and development of new habits. A 2011 Edelman U.S. national survey also confirmed that a majority view social media as entertainment, with a whopping 70% doing so among 18- to 29-year-olds.

One concern is the willingness of people to speak out about issues while online. Yun and Park (2011) considered the potential for there to be fear of isolation, as suggested by the spiral of silence (Noelle-Neumann, 1984) media theory:

> Since online forums technically guarantee anonymity, there is no reason for participants to experience the fear of isolation. However, it appears that it is inevitable for human beings to have a certain degree of fear of isolation whether online or offline. It is possible that people may bring their norms and habits of offline social interaction to their online communications. A difference in the level of the trait fear of isolation was also observed between message posters and lurkers. People with low fear of isolation were more likely to post a message than people with high fear of isolation. (p. 216)

CMC has explored the influence of media technology in creating interaction, online communities and a sense of identity for various groups (Barnes, 2001). Personal and family web usage allows people to share information over great distances (Barnes, 2003). Ferguson and Perse (2000) suggested that the Web was becoming a functional alternative to TV for many. *or social model?*

Media technology uses (Pavlik, 1996) and gratifications (Lin, 1993), address the cultural importance (Stevenson, 1995) of cyberculture, online communities and individual identities (du Gay, Evans, & Redman, 2000; Bell, 2001). Social media communication represents an evolution of individual, social and cultural desires to connect with new people.

((•)) BOX 2.4 THOUGHT LEADER LILI BOSSE

Social media played a significant role when I ran for office, as it was a fabulous no-cost method of reaching my constituents with my message. I currently use it as a way to let residents know what is happening in our city on a daily basis. It allows for me to be accessible, which is very important to me as an elected official.

The biggest issue ahead is the balance of private and public life as an elected official. With social media now, everything is public. The challenge will be how to be an effective leader by being very transparent and open, however balancing the importance of one's personal and private life will be the challenge.

The largest opportunity will be reaching more and more people by providing an easy way to be an accessible and open communicator. Social

Figure 2.2 @LiliBosse1.
Photograph by Vince Bucci, courtesy Lili Bosse.

(continued)

media is the most effective tool to reach a whole new younger voting demographic and allows for transparency and the ability to create back-and-forth dialogue between the constituents and public officials.

Lili Bosse is leading Beverly Hills as mayor during the city's Centennial year. She previously served as vice mayor and city council member since 2011. She also served on the Beverly Hills Planning Commission, Fine Art Commission, and Traffic and Parking Commission. Bosse, a Rotary Club member, has been active on community education and religious boards. lbosse@beverlyhills.org

Online Culture and Power

Social media communication happens within a cultural context of values, ritual and even "chaos" (Carey, 1992, p. 34). Carey theorized that words *reshape* "our common culture" (p. 35), and the emerging social media culture is full of new words and developing social relationships. While some use social media in an effort to maintain existing power, others use it to try to grab new power. Social media extend the shifting emphasis toward the importance of communication "through which experience is described, shared, modified, and preserved" (Williams, 1966, p. 18). Media technology uses narrative storytelling techniques to make sense of practices within communities. Within this context, Stevenson (1995) suspected that new communication tools functioned in the service of socially reproducing status quo rather than real change. In the context of social media communication, there is an ongoing fear that virtual spaces confuse reality, representing myth and ritual as truth.

CMC and Social Media

Computer-mediated communication began with interest decades ago in discussion boards and email communication. The earliest concerns related to CMC as a tool to recreate communities of interest online, as well as its limitations. CMC did not offer communication that was as rich as face-to-face communication, and the lack of understanding resulted in negative experiences, such as "flame war" online fights. CMC, though, also allowed people to overcome physical and psychological limitations (Amichai-Hamburger, Wainapel, & Fox, 2002). Some negative communication consequences, however, have been related to a preference for online social interaction, psychosocial depression, loneliness and problematic Internet use (Caplan, 2003). Research has supported the idea that ". . . preference for online socialization is a key contributor to the development of problematic Internet use," and there appeared to be "a significant relationship between psychosocial health and preference for online socialization" (p. 638). In other words, CMC is a tool that may lead people with problems to take these into online environments, rather than, as is often assumed, the negative effects being caused by online usage.

In the case of so-called massively multiplayer online (MMOs) games, research has studied the boundaries between game play and life in the formation and maintenance of relationships and romance (Huynh, Lim, & Skoric, 2013): "The typology of players differentiated by their construction of the play/life boundary indicates that they are active participants in creating and appraising the play experience and determining how it should be transformed" (p. 261).

CMC also helps us understand the spread of Internet memes, which are "commonly applied to describe the propagation of content items such as jokes, rumors, videos, or websites from one person to others" and "may spread in its original form, but it often also spawns user-created derivatives" (Shifman, 2013, p. 362). Readers may be familiar with the use of memes on social media sites, such as Facebook. Shifman (2013), drawing from Richard Dawkins' 1976 invention of the term as linked to "melodies" and "catch-phrases," sees memes as "abstract beliefs" (p. 363). In a process similar to genetic evolution, memes are thought to compete for attention through imitation and iteration (pp. 364–365):

1. Memes are "understood as cultural information that passes along from person to person, yet gradually scales into a shared social phenomenon."
2. They "reproduce by various means of imitation."
3. They are interesting because of "their diffusion through competition and selection."

Although online users have freedom, research indicates the existence of cultural boundaries. "This pattern suggests that the ostensibly chaotic world (wide web) may in fact follow more organized cultural trajectories than meets the eye" (p. 372).

A paradox may be found within social media that they may have both a tendency to trigger silence on controversial issues, but users also may feel liberated to express opinions (Gearhart & Zhang, 2014). Spiral of silence theory, which suggests people assess climate of opinion before responding, appears to be active within online public opinion. Gearhart and Zhang (2014) recently discovered that on social media sites—Facebook, Twitter, LinkedIn and YouTube—experiments reveal monitoring behavior:

> Practitioners should note that seemingly nonactive users are actively engaged in this medium by observing the SNS opinion climate. SNS users in the current study demonstrate this by indicating that although they may not publicly comment themselves, they would read the comments in both conditions and some indicate they would tell others offline about the situation. Further, no groups are more likely to ignore the story and comments completely. Practitioners should consider this form of engagement when developing new methods of interaction and/or methods of user tracking in this medium. (p. 16)

CMC helps us to better understand online communication and the foundations of social media. It also is a framework for understanding social media application in fields, such as journalism, public relations, advertising and marketing.

■ DISCUSSION QUESTIONS: STRATEGIES AND TACTICS

1. How has CMC influenced the way we form relationships? How may it blur the lines between reality and fantasy?
2. How would a visualization of your social networks depict communication patterns and relationships? How could this be used to influence future online behavior?
3. Describe your favorite Internet meme: Why do you like it? How does it transfer cultural understandings from one person to another?

References

Albarran, A. B. (2013). Introduction. In Alan B. Albarran (Ed.) *The Social Media Industries*, pp. 1–15. New York, NY: Routledge.

Amichai-Hamburger, A., Wainapel, G., & Fox, S. (2002). On the Internet No One Knows I'm an Introvert: Extroversion, Neuroticism, and Internet Interaction. *CyberPsychology & Behavior* 5(2), 125–128.

Baran, S. J., & Davis, D. (2006). *Mass Communication Theory, fourth edition.* Belmont, CA: Thomson Wadsworth.

Bargh, J. (2002). Beyond Simple Truths: The Human-Internet Interaction. *Journal of Social Issues, 58*(1), 1–8.

Bargh, J., & McKenna, K. (2004). The Internet and Social Life. *Annual Review of Psychology* 55(1), 573–590.

Bargh, J., McKenna, K., & Fitzsimons, G. (2002). Can You See the Real Me? Activation and Expression of the "True Self" on the Internet. *Journal of Social Issues 58*(1), 33–48.

Barlow, J. P. (1996). A Cyberspace Independence Declaration. http://w2.eff.org/Censorship/Internet_censorship_bills/barlow_0296.declaration

Barnes, S. B. (2001). *Online Connections: Internet Interpersonal Relationship.* Cresskill, NJ: Hampton Press.

Barnes, S. B. (2003). *Computer-Mediated Communication, Human-to-Human Communication Across the Internet.* Boston, MA: Allyn and Bacon.

Bell, D. (2001). *An Introduction to Cybercultures.* London, UK: Routledge.

Benedikt, M. (1991). Cyberspace: Some Proposals. In M. Benedikt (Ed.), *Cyberspace: First Steps,* pp. 119–124. Cambridge, MA: Massachusetts Institute of Technology Press.

Berger, C. (2005). Interpersonal Communication: Theoretical Perspectives, Future Prospects. *Journal of Communication 55*(3), 415–447.

Bernie, S., & Horvath, P. (2006, June). Psychological Predictors of Internet Social Communication. *Journal of Computer Mediated Communication 7*(4). http://onlinelibrary.wiley.com/doi/10.1111/j.1083–6101.2002.tb00154.x/full

Bourdieu, P., & Coleman, J. S. (1991). *Social Theory for a Changing Society.* Boulder, CO: Westview Press.

boyd, d. m., & Ellison, N. B. (2008). Social Network Sites: Definition, History and Scholarship. *Journal of Computer-Mediated Communication 13*(1), 210–230.

Bugeja, M. (2005). *Interpersonal Divide.* New York, NY: Oxford University Press.

Burke, T., &. Dickey, J. (2013, January 16). Manti Te'o's Dead Girlfriend, The Most Heartbreaking and Inspirational Story of the College Football Season, Is a Hoax. *Deadspin.* http://deadspin.com/manti-teos-dead-girlfriend-the-most-heartbreaking-an-5976517

Burnett, R., & Marshall, P. D. (2003). *Web Theory: An Introduction.* London, UK: Routledge.

Butts, C. T. (2008). Social Network Analysis: A Methodological Introduction. *Asian Journal of Social Psychology 11*, 13–41.

Caplan, S. (2003). Preference for Online Social Interaction: A Theory of Problematic Internet Use and Psychosocial Well-Being. *Communication Research 30*(6), 625–648.

Carey, J. W. (1992). *Communication as Culture, Essays on Media and Society.* New York, NY: Routledge.

Chen, Y., & Persson, A. (2002). Internet Use Among Young and Older Adults: Relation to Psychological Well-Being. *Educational Gerontology 28*(9), 731–744.

Cole, J. I. (2003). *The UCLA Internet report, Surveying the Digital Future, Year Three.* Los Angeles, CA: UCLA Center for Communication Policy. www.ccpa.ucla.edu

Cooley, C. H. (1909/1966). The Significance of Communication. In B. Berelson & M. Janowitz (Eds.), *Reader in Public Opinion and Communication, second edition*, pp. 147–155. New York: Free Press.

du Gay, P., Evans, J., & Redman, P. (Eds.) (2000). *Identity: A Reader*. London, UK: Sage.

Ferguson, D. A., & Perse, E. M. (2000). The World Wide Web as a Functional Alternative to Television. *Journal of Broadcasting & Electronic Media 44*(2), 155–174.

Garton, L., Haythornthwaite, C., & Wellman, B. (1997, June). Studying Online Social Networks. *Journal of Computer-Mediated Communication, 3*(1). http://onlinelibrary.wiley.com/doi/10.1111/j.1083–6101.1997.tb00062.x/full

Gasser, H. (2008). Being Multiracial in a Wired Society: Using the Internet to Define Identity and Community on Campus. *New Direction for Student Services 23,* 63–71.

Gearhart, S., & Zhang, W. (2014). Gay Bullying and Online Opinion Expression: Testing Spiral of Silence in the Social Media Environment. *Social Science Computer Review 32*(1), 18–36.

Greenhow, C., & Robelia, B. (2009, July). Old Communication, New Literacies: Social Network Sites as Social Learning Resources. *Journal of Computer-Mediated Communication, 14*(4), 1130–1161.

Hansen, D. L., Shneiderman, B., & Smith, M. A. (2011). *Analyzing Social Media Networks with NodeXL*. Burlington, MA: Elsevier.

Heaney, M. T., & McClurg, S. D. (2009, September). Social Networks and American Politics. *American Politics Research, 37*(5), 727–741.

Howard, B. (2008, November). Analyzing Online Social Networks. *Communications of the ACM, 51*(11), 14–16.

Huffaker, D. (2010, October). Dimensions of Leadership and Social Influence in Online Communities. *Human Communication Research, 36*(4), 593–617.

Huynh, K. P., Lim, S. W., & Skoric, M. M. (2013). Stepping Out of the Magic Circle: Regulation of Play/Life Boundary in MMO-Mediated Romantic Relationship. *Journal of Computer-Mediated Communication 18*(3), 251–264.

Jones, S. G. (1998). *Cybersociety 2.0, Revisiting Computer-Mediated Communication and Community*. Thousand Oaks, CA: Sage.

Koh, J., Kim, Y.-G., Butler, B., & Bock, G.-W. (2007, February). Encouraging Participation in Virtual Communities. *Communications of the ACM, 50*(2), 69–73.

Lieberman, M. D. (2013). *Social, Why Our Brains Are Wired to Connect*. New York, NY: Crown Publishers.

Lin, C. A. (1993). Adolescent Viewing and Gratifications in a New Media Environment. *Mass Comm Review 20*(1–2), 39–50.

Lindlof, T., & Taylor, B. (2002). *Qualitative Communication Research Methods*. Thousand Oaks, CA: Sage.

Lowery, S. A., & DeFleur, M. L. (1995). *Milestones in Mass Communication Research, Media Effects, third edition*. White Plains, NY: Longman.

Milburn, M. A. (1991). *Persuasion and Politics*. Belmont, CA: Wadsworth.

Negroponte, N. (1995). *Being Digital*. New York, NY: Alfred A. Knopf.

Noelle-Neumann, E. (1984). *The Spiral of Silence, Public Opinion – Our Social Skin*. Chicago, IL: University of Chicago Press.

Pavlik, J. V. (1996). *New Media Technology, Cultural and Commercial Perspectives*. Boston, MA: Allyn and Bacon.

Perse, E. M., & Dunn, D. G. (1995). *The Utility of Home Computers: Impact of Multimedia and Connectivity*. Paper presented to the Association for Education in Journalism and Mass Communication, Washington, DC, August.

Raacke, J., & Bonds-Raacke, J. (2008). Myspace and Facebook: Applying the Uses and Grati-fications Theory to Exploring Friend-Networking Sites. *CyberPsychology & Behavior, 11*(2), 169–174.

Ramirez, A. (2007). The Effect of Anticipated Future Interaction and Initial Impression Valence on Relational Communication in Computer-Mediated Interaction. *Communication Studies, 58*(1), 53–70.

Rheingold, H. (1993). *The Virtual Community.* Ontario: Addison-Wesley.

Rodrigues, E. M., Milic-Frayling, N., Smith, M., Shneiderman, B., & Hansen, D. (2011). *Group-In-A-Box Layout for Multi-Faceted Analysis of Communities.* http://hcil.cs.umd.edu/trs/2011–24/2011–24.pdf

Rogers, E. M. (1995). *Diffusion of Innovations, fourth edition.* New York, NY: Free Press.

Rosenberg, J., & Egbert, N. (2011). Online Impression Management: Personality Traits and Concerns for Secondary Goals as Predictors of Self-Presentation Tactics on Facebook. *Journal of Computer-Mediated Communication 17*(1), 1–18.

Schramm, W. (1972). Nature of Communication Between Humans. In W. Schramm & D. F. Roberts (Eds.), *The Process and Effects of Mass Communication, revised edition*, pp. 8–32. Urbana, IL: University of Illinois Press.

Severin, W. J., & Tankard, Jr., J. W. (2001). *Communication Theories, fifth edition.* New York, NY: Longman.

Shifman, L. (2013). Memes in a Digital World: Reconciling with a Conceptual Troublemaker. *Journal of Computer-Mediated Communication 18*(3), 362–377.

Sonderman, J. (2013, January 17). Notre Dame Football Player Te'o Girlfriend Hoax "Became Truth through the Media." *Poynter.* www.poynter.org/latest-news/mediawire/200919/notre-dame-football-player-teo-girlfriend-hoax-became-truth-through-the-media/

Stevenson, N. (1995). *Understanding Media Cultures, Social Theory and Mass Communication.* London, UK: Sage.

Sundar, S. S., & Limperos, A. M. (2013). Uses and Grats 2.0: New Gratifications for New Media. *Journal of Broadcasting & Electronic Media 57*(4), 504–525.

Tubbs, S. T., & Moss, S. (1983). *Human Communication, fourth edition.* New York, NY: Random House.

Turkle, S. (1995). *Life on the Screen: Identity in the Age of the Internet.* New York: Simon and Schuster.

Westley, B. H., & MacLean, Jr., M. S. (1957). A Conceptual Model for Communications Research. *Journalism Quarterly, 34*(1), 31–28.

Williams, D., Caplan, S., & Xiong, L. (2007). Can You Hear Me Now? The Impact of Voice in an Online Gaming Community. *Human Communication Research, 33*(4), 427–499.

Williams, R. (1966). *Communications.* London: Chatto & Windus.

Wright, A. (2011, May). Web Science Meets Network Science. *Communications of the ACM, 54*(5), 23.

Wright, K. (2000). Computer-Mediated Social Support, Older Adults, and Coping. *Journal of Communication 50*(3), 100–118.

Yun, G. W., & Park, S.-Y. (2011). Selective Posting: Willingness to Post a Message Online. *Journal of Computer-Mediated Communication. 16*(2), 201–227.

3   SOCIAL MEDIA IN JOURNALISM

"Journalism is meant to give people a true sense of their world, so they can participate and have a voice in how their world is structured."
—*Arianna Huffington (@ariannahuff, 2013)*

As president and editor in chief of *The Huffington Post* and its media group, Arianna Huffington has been at the forefront of redefining journalism through an online business model. When asked to define journalism by *Columbia Journalism Review (CJR)*, Huffington was not alone in moving beyond the traditional who, what, when, where, why and how listing of questions. Alexander Jutkowitz (@GroupSJR), Group SJR managing partner, said that the digital age affords people and organizations a way to share:

> Journalism happens when someone tells a compelling true story. Period. The practice need not be limited to an elite group of professionals called "journalists," but those who attempt it must tell great stories and share knowledge. A tongue-in-cheek essay, an infographic that makes a complicated topic instantly accessible, or an in-depth piece of reporting that teaches, inspires, or reveals— all of these things make people smarter and better able to navigate the world. That, in turn, makes societies better. (CJR, 2013, para. 2)

David Cohn (@Digidave), editor of mobile news startup Circa, added that social media may be considered a buzz word because traditional media also were social: "To be a journalist is to collect, filter, and distribute information that serves as social glue for a community" (para. 16).

Journalism is changing because of the use of social media and rapid mobile media adoption. The social media shift is impacting all aspects of the industry—from the newsroom to advertising and management. For content managers at newspapers, for example, **content management systems (CMS)** increasingly make it easier to share news content across traditional and social media platforms. Facebook has been a popular tool for news sharing, but Twitter continues to grow. News managers, armed with the latest industry data, urge reporters to not only share links to their stories, but also to engage with audience members using interesting and useful content.

Journalism is a distinct type of content. Craft and Davis (2013, p. 11) identified five democratic needs:

1. Journalism informs, analyzes, interprets and explains.
2. Journalism investigates.

3. Journalism creates public conversation.
4. Journalism helps generate social empathy.
5. Journalism encourages accountability.

Within a social media context, journalism is often, though not exclusively, the first to break news on sites, such as Twitter. Shared links lead readers to more in-depth stories that may provide analysis, interpretation and explanation. A less common but important function of journalism is independent investigation of the political system. We sometimes speak of journalists playing a watchdog role over public officials. Increasingly, the sharing of news through social media is a spark for public conversation in online spaces. The idea of "vertical" accountability through journalism is perhaps the most difficult, as "horizontal" checks and balances within government provide the most formal accountability (Craft & Davis, 2013, pp. 19–20). Still, it is fair to say that by sparking online public conversation that often includes public officials, journalists and the public have the potential to press for a measure of accountability in government.

((*)) BOX 3.1 THOUGHT LEADER AMY GUTH

What has changed? Reader behavior, really. Nobody waits around loyally to get a story from the local paper; people want immediate information, regardless of the medium. In newsrooms, we've seen this manifest even quite simply, such as in the importance of breaking news desks monitoring social media to help surface stories as they are happening. Nobody picks up the phone and calls the breaking news editor anymore; people just whip out a phone, take a photo and post it. Done.

Figure 3.1 @amyguth.

Within the industry, the most significant change has been that it's not enough to simply file your story and go home anymore. We must be proactive and build networks. Some bemoan that and are reluctant to embrace the change. Personally, I think the shift has been exciting. It's always better to be able to steer your own ship, so to speak.

I remember very clearly when I saw the writing on the wall. We'd just seen major digital disruption hit the music industry and there were some who dug in their heels and stuck to doing things the traditional way and there were those who realized change was coming with or without them and chose to be open and adapt. The adapters were thrown into a time of incredible creativity and creation, which was cool to watch. Because the music industry's disruption was about two years ahead of publishing, we had the luxury of learning from them and being ready to surf the wave when the time came.

It is my hope that media literacy takes a bigger share of the spotlight in the years to come. While our access to information is greater than ever before, the importance of being able to discern between a story reported by a trained journalist (regardless of medium of delivery) and conjecture or speculation will hopefully become more and more of an area of discussion.

What I predict is a move to follow individuals as sources of content, rather than the publications of their employment, so for journalists, building a personal "brand" will be essential and an exciting way to take an internal locus of control approach to one's career. I'm also still very excited about location-based tools. I think we've really just scratched the surface there.

Amy Guth, RedEye/Metromix general manager, developed social media best practices in the *Chicago Tribune* newsroom. She tracked Occupy Chicago protesters on Twitter during the NATO Summit and went on to a management position with Tribune Media that included managing search engine optimization and social media. She is president of the Association for Women Journalists Chicago, author of *Three Fallen Women*, and contributor of WGN radio and television. She also has been on air at WBEZ radio. She founded Pilcrow, a small literary festival. She studied anthropology, literary anthropology and sociology at the University of Texas at Arlington.

McCombs, Holbert, Kiousis, and Wanta (2011) described a "changing environment" for news and public opinion because of the online shift and emphasis of entertainment within media:

> The age of media convergence has brought together media genres that used to be seen as quite disparate. Diana Mutz has argued that it is futile to speak of a distinction between news and entertainment within the present media landscape because it is increasingly difficult to tell where the news begins and the entertainment ends and vice versa . . . This will become all the more the case in the coming years. (p. 25)

Journalists have learned to become generalists by writing for the Web, blogging, developing digital photography skills, audio/video techniques, programming and social networking (Luckie, 2011): "Many social networkers use the sites to share and comment on news stories and by doing so have transformed the way journalism is distributed on the web" (p. 169). Twitter, for example, can also involve either a "back-and-forth exchange" or private **direct message (DM)** between two followers (p. 172). Journalists must make decisions about how much audience engagement serves the goals of their personal and company brands.

Journalists are very active on Twitter, especially during breaking news events. They are being encouraged to not only share story links, but also rich media—photographs, videos and source links—using mobile apps, such as Instagram, Tumblr, Vine, Tout and Jelly. Media groups, though, face unique circumstances in each market. In smaller towns, for example, Twitter may not be as popular as in larger cities. As news managers become more sophisticated about social media, they want to be able to demonstrate ROI of time and resources.

What began as a digital media revolution two decades ago has morphed into a social media landscape. Journalists have been required to adopt new tools, such as smartphones, in order to participate in a developing form that places value on interactivity and is "transparent" and "collaborative" (Briggs, 2010, p. 7).

Although social media are seen as a path to news content once dominated by Google searches, SEO remains an important concern. CMS systems now prompt the user to use SEO-friendly words for headlines and tags. In a highly competitive news environment, any advantage to attract potential audience members is seen as important. The issue for many newsrooms is how to identify important local social media conversation. By practicing effective conversation monitoring, it is possible for newsrooms to attempt to "capture" engagement topics and participate as opinion leaders. Every local community has influencers, and newsrooms must engage them and offer valuable content within their social networks.

At newspapers, one important tactic has been to add video to their websites. Local newspapers, many now with a **paywall** that limits some reader access to subscriber use only, often compete with free television news sites. As video compression and Internet speeds have made it easier to view and share video, it has become a way to increase the amount of time users spend on specific news pages.

NDN is a national U.S. video network that includes newspaper and television sites. The company offers traditional online video syndication and so-called "content verticals" in key topic areas—sports, arts and entertainment, men, women, lifestyles, home décor, business and technology, and news and politics. By selling national and local advertising pre-roll video of 15 or 30 seconds, NDN and the news organizations are able to increase online revenues. For newspapers, this is crucial because offline subscriptions, advertising and revenue have been in steady decline for many years. Editors retain control over which stories are selected for their site, but each item carries with it a potential pre-roll advertising spot. NDN also builds in social media sharing, so that users push out video content to their social networks. The potential broad reach of pre-roll advertising attached to the videos has attracted large national advertisers, from American Express to NBC and Walmart. Every news video creates inventory to be sold to advertisers, and pricing has been developed using a traditional media **cost per thousand (CPM)** basis. For example, an advertiser might be charged $25 per 1,000 viewers of a video. The video system generates both page views and revenue for each media company within the NDN network.

At the same time, media companies seek to measure all activity on their sites. They have attempted to move beyond page views and unique viewers to use advanced Google Analytics that track traffic coming from social media sites, as well as engagement reflected by amount of time on sites. Social media influencers are increasingly seen as important because their sharing and discussing of news media content may trigger additional interest. In this sense, news media are now interested more than ever in what audience members and their friends are talking about.

Even as social media grow, a substantial chunk of the news audience remains traditional media users. Newspapers, for example, are not going away any time soon. Scarborough Research and the Newspaper Association of America reported that 69% of American adults, about 164 million people, are regular readers of a print, online or mobile newspaper edition. The addition of a newspaper paywall designed to force paid subscription for content may be beginning to have a negative effect, as access is removed in some cases. The Scarborough study found that 54% of readers in the coveted 18- to 24-year-old demographic group either read a printed newspaper or access sites via a desktop computer, and only 17% of all mobile users are considered mobile-only readers. Print-only readers are on average 11 years older (median age of 54) than online-only (median age 43), and they are 21 years older than the mobile-only crowd (median age 33) (Newspaper Association of America, 2013).

Journalism Theories

The introduction of social networking sites and social media continued to fundamentally change journalism. Tewksbury and Rittenberg (2012) conclude: "The shift from a top-down media system to one that features more horizontal interaction of people and news represents a change in the relationship that citizens and others in a nation have with information" (p. 5), and:

> . . . private citizens creating content online . . . are redefining the nature of news. They are adding to the flow of information online—be it opinion, links to related concepts, images, or other content—and they are contributing to the social and political lives of nations . . . The trend of information control shifting away from a few powerful entities toward smaller outlets and even citizens is a type of information democratization. (p. 11)

The historic paradigm that news agenda-setting influences what people think about (McCombs & Shaw, 1972) may be weakened by the increasing importance of social media effects on media and public discussion (Jacobson, 2013). A Pew Research Center and Knight Foundation study found that nearly half of Facebook users, or about one-third of the population, consume news on the largest social media platform (Mitchell, Kiley, Gottfried, & Guskin, 2013). The major conclusion was that "news is a common but incidental experience" (para. 1). While users went on the social network for other purposes, they often found news.

> Most U.S. adults do not go to Facebook seeking news out, the nationally representative online survey of 5,173 adults finds. Instead, the vast majority of Facebook news consumers, 78%, get news when they are on Facebook for other reasons. And just 4% say it is the most important way they get news. As one respondent summed it up, "I believe Facebook is a good way to find out news without actually looking for it." (para. 3)

News shared on Facebook appeared particularly important among those who do not otherwise follow news. The often-cited excuse of not having time to keep up with news continues to be the case in the social media era. One-third (34%) of Facebook news consumers were young adults 18–29—a group traditionally too busy to follow news.

For news professionals, Facebook has become an important way to reach younger readers because this group looks to social media for information:

> . . . these 18- to 29-year-olds get news on Facebook across topics at roughly the same levels as older age groups, turn there as often for breaking news and deem the site as important a source of news. (para. 6)

In other ways, news consumers on Facebook tend to mirror the larger population, although they tend to be more active as Facebook site users. More than three-fourths (77%) visit Facebook to check on friends, with two-thirds (65%) visiting multiple times per day. According to the Pew study, the most popular topics on Facebook are: Entertainment (73%), People & events in my community (65%), Sports (57%), National politics & government (55%), Crime (51%), Health & medicine (46%), Local government & politics (44%), Local weather & traffic (42%), International news (39%), Science & technology (37%), Business (31%), and Breaking news (28%). Respondents said they most often clicked on links because they were interesting, entertaining or unexpected.

The Pew research identified a group of active news sharers that distribute links they think others should know about. Some of the people who share also are seeking to spark conversation or make a statement. At least some do it just to be able to find the item later.

A majority of Facebook news consumers were found to engage in the content by liking it or clicking on a link, while less than half shared news. Still, news was far less important to users than the social reasons to visit and engage on Facebook. The Pew Research Center reported that 64% of U.S. adults used Facebook, which made it the largest social media site in 2013. In a survey with the John S. and James L. Knight Foundation of 5,173 respondents, nearly half sometimes went looking for news on Facebook, and 78% saw news while there looking for something else.

Facebook remains mostly a social networking platform to connect with friends and family. Often, photographs and videos drive interest—whether it is to share or view what others have offered. Three areas—personal updates, news and games—are mentioned, but as much less important than the core reasons for Facebook engagement. A majority (57%) responded that Facebook is not a very important way to get news. Social news appears to be built upon the larger social experience and context (Pew 2012).

Social media reflect convergence of media content, as social networking sites attract professional journalists from around the globe. The growing appetite for mobile news content also may encourage engagement between journalists and their international readers (Westlund, 2008): "These people are always connected and appreciate access to news independent of time and space" (p. 460). Journalists may be pressured to post rapid news updates, and this could damage long-term credibility with audience members (Johnson & Kaye, 2010). However, perceived credibility of information increases when writer information and a hyperlink are part of the post (Johnson & Wiedenbeck, 2009).

News organizations see social media, in part, as new tools for promotion and even profit. Kerrigan and Graham (2010) treat social media spaces as settings for buyer and seller interaction. If news people are selling their stories, then social marketing comes into play. The relationships also may foster the selling of story ideas to journalists participating in social media interaction.

Citizen Journalism

Journalism shifted from being largely one-way mass communication to participatory work that includes some **user-generated content (UGC)**. Paulussen and Ugille (2008) examined UGC influence on mainstream media and identified a shift in interest toward collaboration with audience members. Professional characteristics within a particular newsroom are seen as important variables (Domingo, 2008; Wardle & Williams, 2010). The organizational context, including editorial staff and information technology (IT) staff cultures, may reflect either tension or conditions more favorable to IT collaboration. In the end, deadline pressures and the need for reliable and trusted sources may limit use of UGC: "Therefore, it can be expected that professional journalists will make rather limited use of user generated content, because they somewhat routinely and passively rely on a number of official suppliers of information" (Paulussen & Ugille, 2008, p. 34). When their content is ignored, as might be expected, citizen journalists express frustration about editorial decisions to use professional content:

> As journalists have to work under high pressure, they tend to rely heavily on well-known routines and hold on to their core task, which they still define in terms of gatekeeping. There is indeed a strong belief that the primary role of journalism lies in the selection stage of the news making process. Their gatekeeping skills are among the major traits through which professionals distinguish themselves from amateur journalists." (p. 38)

The assessment, based upon observations in Europe, reflects a degree of realism about the historic sociology within newsrooms. For more than a decade, there has been interest in and enthusiasm for the idea of citizen journalism with stronger social ties to communities and access to publishing via blogs and other online methods (Matheson, 2004). News can be seen as a product that is in need of re-articulation based upon the creation of online blogs.

Crowdsourcing

During a breaking news event, users may provide information not yet available to professional journalists. In an era in which most people carry smartphones with high-quality cameras with them almost everywhere, photographs appear almost instantaneously on Twitter from the sites of most breaking news events.

📱 **BOX 3.2 THE ANDY CARVIN METHOD**

Andy Carvin was a journalism innovator at National Public Radio (NPR) during the Arab Spring uprisings in the Middle East beginning in 2009 until he was offered a contract buy-out at the end of 2013. He joined First Look Media in 2014 to launch a newsroom funded by the eBay founder and built around social media.

(continued)

At NPR, Carvin used the live tweet method during several Middle East political revolutions, including Libya, Egypt and Syria. Carvin told *The Guardian* in 2011 that his work is "a form of situational awareness." During the Libyan uprising, Carvin tweeted 1,200 times over a two-day period. He told *The Guardian* that by using known sources or observing online behavior, he filters those messages that may be credible. His followers helped verify information. Carvin called this "open source journalism," even though his "Real-time Informational DJ & occasional journalist" approach included private communication. His work was grounded in activism and technology, rather than extensive, formal journalism training.

In Carvin's book *Distant Witness*, he described how social media helped loosen control over news. "I'm a storyteller who works at a news organization who commits acts of journalism," Carvin told NPR's program *On the Media*. He differentiated what was happening on Twitter from traditional news practices.

"Instead, if I just share more openly what I know and what I don't know, someone out there will probably come out and have an answer," Carvin said. This may include sharing information that turns out to be untrue or more graphic than would normally be accepted by mainstream media. "I made a decision early on that I wasn't going to censor myself simply because it was graphic, and I had a lot of people complain about that," Carvin said. "My Twitter followers and I, just by talking to each other," figure things out.

There can be a problem with source credibility. "Well, it certainly helps if you know someone on the ground to start with," Carvin told NPR's Brooke Gladstone. He was not concerned about balance of viewpoints,

Figure 3.2 National Public Radio (NPR) has a new headquarters in Washington, DC, as seen in this 2013 photograph.

instead presenting information from those online with him. "I'm trying to capture their stories," he said. The live tweeting method is to ask sources for assertions and confirmation. This can be in opposition to cultural norms, as it was in Yemen. "I had to back off a little," he said.

Media critic Michael Wolff challenged Carvin's "overreach" during live tweeting of the Newtown shootings. The crowdsourcing on Twitter generated false reports about a purple van, a second shooter and a fake letter. "While the guise is to re-tweet in order to verify," Wolff wrote, "the effect is to propagate." Carvin directly responded to Wolff's column by rejecting the label of "social media promoter" on Twitter:

> I'm not sure what you mean by social media promoter. I use social media a lot because my day job is to experiment with new tools to see if they can improve the quality and diversity of our reporting. If anything, I'm a promoter of NPR and the importance of public media in our society. Social media is just an aspect of it.

Carvin insisted one of his jobs was to monitor mainstream media reports and ask questions. He asked "people to figure" out whether or not reports are true or false. Carvin's methods, though, were in stark contrast to those of traditional NPR journalists. While crowdsourcing may unearth facts during a breaking news story, Carvin's methods are particularly shaky when applied to reporting within other cultural contexts.

Sarar Mohamed Khamis, University of Maryland professor and Arab media expert, says a YouTube video may be viewed as blasphemy in the Middle East, which produces violent reactions in the Muslim world. "There is a very, very high level of respect to all religious symbols and all the messages of God," she said. "This is a very, very sensitive topic for any Muslim—we are always really required to . . . show the utmost respect possible to all religious figures, symbols, prophets and messengers . . . and not to treat them in any way that could be not only defamatory or negative, but even treats them as just ordinary human beings is considered offensive let alone portraying them in negative cartoons, or some kind of video, or some kind of media representation that is hurtful."

"This is really intolerable to Muslims worldwide," she added, because of cultural and religious contexts and lack of understanding. "Everyone has the right to freedom of opinion and expression; this right includes freedom to hold opinions without interference and to seek, receive and impart information and ideas through any media and regardless of frontiers."

"Freedom of expression is a fundamental human right," University of Minnesota Professor Jane Kirtley said. "It's not uniquely American—we like to think that we've been moving toward perfecting it, but this is not an example of America trying to impose its values."

"We're talking about apples and oranges, coming from different perspectives," Khamis said. "Different cultural, religious [and] social backgrounds, political contexts, then what constitutes freedom of expression?"

(continued)

In this view, the "borderless Internet" across languages, cultures and religions is seen as a problem because of anonymity, hate speech, attacks and lack of representation of religious leaders. "If it is not really somehow 'regulated' . . . somehow put in the right perspective, it can go out of hand," Khamis said.

Carvin, however, echoed the decidedly Western view on free speech. "Social media has the word 'social' in front of it for a reason because you have human beings interacting with each other . . . everything from talking about the news to sharing their latest cat videos, and I think all of it is valid and all of it is important."

The contrast between Carvin's use of social network "bonds" with followers and the traditional media audience perspective presents a challenge going forward. Carvin "realized early on the worst thing I could do on Twitter is act like a broadcaster journalist," and instead he "acts like a person." This is his personal brand. The organizational brand of NPR and other traditional journalists instead continues to exercise caution in reporting—especially during developing stories abroad.

On the one hand, promoting transparent journalistic methods is a healthy outcome from Carvin's experiments on Twitter. On the other hand, trusting anonymous sources to publicly judge information in real time does not always seem responsible within the context of a dangerous and unstable world.

Sources:

Lipschultz, J. H. (2013, August 20). Live Tweets, Journalism, Middle East Culture and NPR Branding. Media. *The Huffington Post*. www.huffingtonpost.com/jeremy-harris-lipschultz/live-tweets-journalism-mi_b_3779940.html

Ingram, M. (2014, February 4). Andy Carvin, A Pioneer in Using Twitter for Real-Time Journalism, Joins Omidyar's First Look Media. *Gigaom*. http://gigaom.com/2014/02/04/andy-carvin-a-pioneer-in-using-twitter-for-real-time-journalism-joins-omidyars-first-look-media/

Micro-blogging

Most newsrooms are happy to have journalists using micro-blog sites, such as Twitter, to push out links to stories and engage with audience members. Some sensational stories, however, may be seen as "click-bait" (designed to simply drive user traffic to a site), as was the case when publicity for a book featured a claim that President Obama once told staff that he was "really good at killing people" (Cantor, 2013, para. 1).

The micro-blogging influence of Twitter goes beyond early adopters to news media that use it for content sharing (Schmierbach & Oeldorf-Hirsch, 2012). The research suggests that journalists continue to use Twitter more for sharing than engagement and interaction with followers. An ongoing issue is that information on Twitter is generally viewed as less credible and trustworthy than the mainstream sites. This may help explain why journalists remain cautious in using social media for engagement:

> In contrast to many studies of online credibility, this study shows that even somewhat regular users of Twitter do not see it as providing more credible information, and the population as a whole is unusually skeptical of Twitter relative to other means of distribution. . . . The exact mechanisms are unclear. . . . On the surface, however, it is noteworthy simply because unlike traditional blogs, Twitter here is not serving as a selective source. . . .Yet participants still viewed the content on Twitter differently . . . Perhaps the positive responses to other selecting sources are also due to cues, and not to reasoned evaluations about the benefits of custom-selected material. At an applied level, this study suggests the need for caution in the use of Twitter as a way to distribute news. (Schmierbach & Oeldorf-Hirsch, 2012, p. 333)

Even when the news distributor was a large organization, such as *The New York Times*, the research suggests less trust attached to tweets. The "trust of news information" is theoretically distinct from "trust of those who deliver the news" and "trust of media corporations" (Williams, 2012, p. 117). These can be seen as "informational," "interpersonal" and "institutional" trust (p. 119). News is "increasingly produced and disseminated by individuals and agencies that act outside of traditional media establishments," and "it is particularly important for media practitioners to remain attentive to changes in news audiences' attention patterns and assessments of media trustworthiness" (p. 127). However, it is not clear what happens to trust when journalists release editorial control through social media.

User-generated content, also called participatory journalism, is one way to reflect "the idea of collaborative and collective—not simply parallel—action" (Singer et al., 2011, p. 2). In this view, social networking sites are seen as one of many online forms (including blogs, comments and polls) that allow for great participation (p. 17). The active audience selects, filters and even creates content through what has been called citizen journalism. To the extent that audience members take on this quasi-journalist role, they challenge the traditional professional journalism news gatekeepers who sifted and edited for them. The public may serve as "eyewitnesses," "experts" through their comments, "commentators," "pulse-takers," "guardians of quality," "ancillary reporters," or independent journalists (pp. 38–44). The level of audience activity varies widely, and it is most often the case that audience members remain passive consumers. CMC theorizes a desire to create and participate in online communities, though these tend to exist within specialized interest areas.

Journalism Case Studies

To some extent, the WikiLeaks site represents the most dramatic example of participatory journalism, by becoming "networked into mainstream media across the globe as it shifted from isolated whistle-blower to collaborative investigator and publisher" (Beckett, with Ball, 2012, p. 9). By publishing raw material that publicly accuses wrongdoing, the site has worked both with news organizations and independently. Here, too, we see signs of fundamental redefinition of journalism and political power:

> Political media once had a defined structure that created a limited product. They had quite a specific function in liberal democracies as the conduit of information between power and the people. The Internet and digital communications have the

capacity to change that relationship . . . The scale of the leak, and the ability to spread it globally, are enabled by the new technology and the Net . . . WikiLeaks is a network exploit that uses the Internet in a radical way to gather material, protect itself and to tap into other networks, including mainstream media. (p. 13)

That said, WikiLeaks has not been entirely protected in recent years from responses by formal governmental powers. Australian Julian Assange, founder and editor-in-chief of WikiLeaks, was facing a European Arrest Warrant, but he was granted diplomatic asylum at Ecuador's embassy in London. Chelsea (previously Bradley) Manning, a U.S. Army private who provided information to WikiLeaks, was convicted of violating the Espionage Act and faces up to 35 years in prison. Assange could be charged as a co-conspirator in the theft of documents.

Successes

Social media "democracy of distribution" has changed the news-making process (Ingram, 2011, para. 1). During the 2011 Tunisian and Egyptian revolutions, for example, groups included a number of key actors:

- Activists
- Mainstream media outlets
- Journalists

(((•))) BOX 3.3 THOUGHT LEADER JASON COLLINGTON

Social media lets us back into the party. The party where the cool kids are. The party that doesn't let just anyone in. Social media done right lets us get back into the parties where friends come together and share what's important to them. Social media also has allowed us to reconnect to those who used to have or never ever had access to our content. It has allowed us to do what journalists were put here to do: build community and inform that community. Without social media, the Internet is 1,000 oceans.

We need to be popular as well as authentic to our media company's mission at the same time. Just like any party, you don't want to be the guy who tries to date every gal. We

Figure 3.3 @jasoncollington. *Photograph by the* Tulsa World, *courtesy Jason Collington.*

need to continue to find our place in the conversations and lives of our current audiences and make changes to be included in the conversations and lives of our potential audiences. We also have to acknowledge that the creators of social media have many of the same goals as we do. We all want to create the personalized newspaper. We have to innovate and learn what we can leverage, so that we do it first.

We need to become even more relevant to more people. I think people are going to filter their content even more over the next five years. We have to hurry and prove we belong in their social media. If we don't make the cut, they are going to build their community without us.

Jason Collington is web editor at the *Tulsa World*, where he has written and edited since 1999. Tulsa, Oklahoma, is the 46th largest U.S. city, and the newspaper there was acquired by billionaire Warren Buffett's BH Media Group. The chain of newspapers is emphasizing engagement with readers. His journalism degree is from Oklahoma State University, and he has been a Lecturer there for four years. The AP and SPJ in Oklahoma have repeatedly recognized Tulsaworld.com as one of the state's top news websites.

Bloggers

Blogging became popular online early in the new century. Independent bloggers were able to use new tools to reach large audiences. Commercial sites, such as *The Huffington Post*, were launched and became successful challengers to traditional media. Most local and national media now have active bloggers offering opinion and interpretation.

📱 **BOX 3.4 *HUFFPOST* BLOGGER TERMS AND GUIDELINES**

Bloggers for *The Huffington Post* (the author of this book is one) are governed by an extensive set of rules and guidelines. "By submitting blog posts for publication on the HuffingtonPost.com website or on any other site owned or operated by The Huffington Post.com or AOL Inc. (collectively, "Huffington Post")." Bloggers are told to not submit posts if they do not agree.

A blogger is treated as "an independent contractor" rather than as a paid employee. *The Huffington Post* specifies that bloggers do not receive any pay or benefits. Bloggers are offered "a large, diverse audience" in which other works, such as this book, may be promoted. Bloggers are encouraged to use Twitter and Facebook and share content across social networks.

As an independent contractor, a blogger is not "under the direction or control" of the site. "You can write about anything you want," but there are no publication guarantees. The work may or may not be accepted, and *HuffPost* bloggers may not identify themselves at events as a representative. Content submissions must be original or "properly licensed content." Beyond copyright, it must not be "objectionable, inaccurate or inflammatory," "obscene, defamatory, threatening, pornographic, harassing, hateful, racially or ethnically offensive," and "not an advertisement or solicitation of business or contributions."

(continued)

The Huffington Post may remove content that violates the rules. An important aspect that will be discussed later in the book is disclosure, and *HuffPost* urges bloggers to be transparent: "*HuffPost* bloggers should disclose any financial conflicts of interest." Where there may be an issue, "that information should be disclosed at the bottom of the applicable blog post."

Bloggers also must make corrections with 24 hours of a notice. Corrections or clarifications are noted at the bottom of a post. In the case of a defamation complaint, the correction "must be posted in as prominent a location as the defamatory content."

While bloggers retain content copyright, *The Huffington Post* retains "a non-exclusive, worldwide, royalty-free, irrevocable, perpetual license to exercise all rights under copyright law." *The Huffington Post* also provides style guidelines used to edit blogger submissions.

All site users, including bloggers and readers commenting, also are subject to Terms and Conditions. *The Huffington Post* may discontinue, suspend or terminate usage. By being on the site, users grant rights:

> By posting or submitting content on or to our site (regardless of the form or medium with respect to such content, whether text, videos, photographs, audio or otherwise), you are giving us, and our affiliates, agents and third party contractors the right to display or publish such content on our site and its affiliated publications (either in the form submitted or in the form of a derivative or adapted work), to store such content, and to distribute such content and use such content for promotional and marketing purposes . . .
>
> . . . we may, or may permit users to, based solely on functionality provided and enabled by our website, compile, re-edit, adapt or modify your video submission, or create derivative works therefrom, either on a stand-alone basis or in combination with other video submissions, and (unless you and we agree otherwise) you shall have no rights with respect thereto and we or our licensees shall be free to display and publish the same (as so compiled, re-edited, adapted, modified or derived) for any period.

The site discloses that they may be required by law to provide law enforcement or government with user information, their liability to users is limited, and disputes are governed by New York law.

Sources:

Terms and Conditions. (2014). *The Huffington Post*. www.huffingtonpost.com/terms.html

Blogger Guidelines. (2010). *The Huffington Post*.

Most blog posts tend to be 500 to 1,000 words, as online readers are more likely to consume short rather than long reads. At the same time, online sites tend to have fewer editors than traditional publications. Longer posts may not be edited as quickly. Sites vary in terms of style rules, such as capitalization, use of SEO words and phrases, and quotation style. *The Huffington Post*, for example, uses block quotes, but these tend to be short. Sites also vary in use of italics and quotation marks for references to book titles. Blogging sites tend to encourage use of **hyperlinks** as references to content that is discussed, as shorthand for those interested in reading more about the topic.

Use of images and video links varies across blog sites. Most editors want stories that are visually appealing and keep readers at the site for as long as possible. Some CMS systems, though, are easier to use than others for sizing images and embedding video links. From an SEO standpoint, the Google algorithm rules keep changing, but bloggers use tags and **keywords** entered on the CMS system to make it easier to find the post through online search. Social media communication has impacted this, as authors are encouraged to push their content out on the social Web. This is encouraged through email lists, Facebook and Twitter posts, contacting other bloggers, responding to all comments at the blog and social sites, leveraging friends and online fans, and generally engaging within social networks.

Social Media Celebrity

There has been a blurring of the lines, as some of those active on Twitter cut across these traditional categories. For example, Jillian York (@jilliancyork), director for International Freedom of Expression at the Electronic Frontier Foundation, is also a blogger who was active during the Arab Spring. Visualization of social networking revealed that she was an important hub for information. She now has more than 100,000 tweets and nearly 34,000 Twitter followers.

Social media also were an influential place for conversation about gun laws following the 2012 school shooting in Newtown. Pew (2012) found that 64% of Twitter assertions were calls for stricter gun control (p. 1):

> From the news of the shooting on Friday afternoon through noon on Monday, the discussion on blogs and Twitter paralleled each other closely. The discussion about our country's gun laws ranked first on each platform, accounting for 28% of the overall conversation about the tragedy. And, the focus remained remarkably steady over the course of the three days, already registering at a quarter of the conversation on each platform by midnight on Friday. (p. 2)

The gun reform discussion was slightly higher than expression of sympathy and prayers (25%) on Twitter. So-called "straight news" represented only 13% of the Twitter talk during the period.

The "Kony 2012" viral video (www.youtube.com/watch?v=Y4MnpzG5Sqc) is an example of media content becoming its own media event: "The next 27 minutes are an experiment, but in order for it to work you *have* to pay attention." The YouTube video about Ugandan warlord Joseph Kony rapidly attracted the attention of young adults, which is a group that does not tend to pay as much attention to traditional news as older groups. The 30-minute video, though, had nearly 80 million views in just 10 days (Choney, 2012). A year later, it had more than 98 million views worldwide. Unlike a typical entertainment video that goes viral, such as the "Gangnam Style" music video (with more than 2 billion views), Kony 2012 was a **Non-Governmental Organization (NGO)** Invisible Children advocacy video (Harsin, 2013).

To begin with, no theory has so far convincingly explained the video's virality yet failure to mobilize people to "cover the night." Roughly, theories emphasize production quality and narrative to explain its popularity; then, credibility problems, filmmaker (Jason) Russell's breakdown, and lazy "clicktivism" (p. 265) to explain its failure to prompt action. So-called clicktivism is a way to explain how simple it is to click in support of an online cause without doing anything else. One explanation for the video's simultaneous success and failure is the role celebrities played in using social media to spread the video. "Oprah's tweet alone spiked its visibility by 15 percent" (p. 266). It would seem that opinion leadership and interest in entertainment came together to help push the media content. Oprah is trustworthy, and the promotion of a video essentially manufactures a news event. In an international context, breaking news events present both mainstream journalism and social media challenges. Trust in content often comes down to judging media source credibility, which can be a product of media bias, gatekeeping bias, coverage bias and statement bias (Tian & Chao, 2012). Social media content may have a life of its own online, but there is no guarantee that engagement and conversation translates to offline action. The Kony 2012 project raised awareness in 2012, but the warlord remained on the run from an international criminal indictment, as interest faded.

Failures

The most significant challenge facing journalism in the social media age is paying for the enterprise. Major newspapers responded to declining subscriptions, revenue loss due to online competition and new technologies with waves of layoffs. Traditional journalists have been replaced with younger, online-experienced employees. Some are journalists, but others are computer programmers and social media specialists. The timing of the 2008–09 global economic recession further impacted direction of all mainstream media toward a "leaner" business model. At this writing, even college media were facing financial difficulties. As those in government and business use the Internet to directly communicate with the public, there is "a continued erosion of news reporting resources" for quality journalism: "This adds up to a news industry that is more undermanned and unprepared to uncover stories, dig deep into emerging ones or to question information put in its hands" (Pew, 2013, p. 3):

> In circumventing the media altogether, one company, Contently, connects thousands of journalists, many of them ex-print reporters, with commercial brands to help them produce their own content . . . Fortune took that step, launching a program for advertisers called Fortune TOC—Trusted Original Content—in which Fortune writers, for a fee, create original Fortune-branded editorial content for marketers to contribute exclusively on their own platforms." (p. 4)

The Pew Research Center (2013, pp. 5–6) has identified six important trends, including "advertorials" that are advertisements packaged as news editorial content:

1. Public awareness of effects from newsroom cutbacks
2. News industry failure to capture the bulk of new digital and mobile advertising
3. Increasing amount of native advertising—advertorial content, sponsored tweets, etc.—running the risk of reader confusion
4. Paid digital experiments, including use of paywalls for user-paid content

5. Potential for digital impact to challenge local television news revenues
6. Social media and word-of-mouth origination of news instead of through news media sources

In a 2013 Pew survey, 72% of adults talked with friends and family as the most common way to receive news through word of mouth (WOM). But there is a growing number (15%) using social networking sites (SNS) to get news from friends and family, and this is even larger among 18- to 25-year-olds (24%).

About one-fourth of 18- to 29-year-olds, a key demographic group, reports relying upon social media for news. All of this adds up to both a challenge to and opportunity for professional journalists and news organizations.

Lessons

Once the dream of every journalism student was to someday write for *The New York Times*, but social media have helped change the landscape. Former *Times* technology columnist David Pogue, who wrote a book full of Twitter tweets, left the newspaper after 13 years in 2013 to join Yahoo. On his Tumblr blog, he told readers:

> It's not easy leaving the Times, especially when you admire it as much as I do. No matter what happens to prose on paper, the Times itself, as a gatherer and curator of news, will always be necessary and important. The culture may be changing, and the readership may be shifting, but this paper steadfastly focuses on responsible journalism, ironclad ethics and superb writing. I'll always be a loyal ally. (Pogue, 2013, para. 3)

Pogue noted that his work at the *Times* had been an amazing period of more than a decade that featured development of the Web, social media, e-books, smart-phones and tablet technologies. While technological innovation drives change, social uses of new technology products surprised even the inventors and innovators.

U.S. journalists trained in the last century were infused with the ideal of objectivity. It was sometimes suggested that journalism should strive for balance and fairness by telling two or more sides to a story and letting audience members be the judge. The norm of objectivity, which has spread globally to many cultural contexts, remains a topic of contentious debate (Maras, 2013). The search for truth or reality, at least one devoid of personal opinion, is nearly impossible within a social media world that is flooded with bloggers and tweets. Maras (2013) observed that a group of gate-watching bloggers monitors mainstream media: "The concept serves as a 'pretence' for quality journalism at a time when social media is opening up new possibilities for collaborative news creation" (p. 190, citing Rettberg, 2008, p. 310). In fact, as mentioned early in this chapter, social media have challenged the very definition of journalism:

> This is not to suggest this is a zone without issues, and media organizations are faced with new decisions around working with citizen journalists and online communities . . . a different but no less serious set of reputational issues arise from staff reporters using social media such as Twitter, which demands a style of writing and opinion very different from that encountered in most news articles. (Maras, 2013, pp. 191–192)

This suggests that by engaging in collaborative communities, journalists must release some editorial control and enter into a state of negotiation with the public over facts and opinions. In this sense, news organizations that "face their critics" through social media engagement may encourage fairness through an ongoing listening process (Nunnelley, 2006, p. 53). This transformation of journalism is a work in process.

The art of storytelling, across a variety of media platforms, is transforming journalism and media education. Hart (2011) has focused upon "**narrative** possibilities" within passionate storytelling:

> Story makes sense out of a confusing universe by showing us how one action leads to another. It teaches us how to live by discovering how our fellow human beings overcome the challenges in their lives. And it helps us discover the universals that bind us to everything around us. (p. 5)

Story, to Hart, is universal because a good story has no print and broadcast division. In this sense, there are essential principles—a sequence of actions, a sympathetic character, a complication, and a resolution. Hart (2011) challenges the reader to consider decisions about stance, distance and the ladder of abstraction, which he sees as "one of the most useful concepts for any writer" (p. 55). Thornburg (2011) views online news as a different animal that must conform to the changing rules of social media:

> As an online journalist, you'll still work with the traditional elements and values of news. But you'll also take advantage of the three attributes of online communication that make reporting, producing and distributing your stories via the Internet fundamentally different from working in any other medium. (p. 8)

Thornburg (2011) divides the terrain into multimedia ("a variety of choices about how to combine storytelling techniques"), interactive and on-demand. Journalists within a social media environment are audience-centered, conscious of keywords and SEO, unafraid of marketing and ready for continuous engagement:

> The interactivity of the Web has brought an end to one-way flow. Reporters are now answering questions from the audience. Politicians, businesspeople and celebrities are now speaking directly to the audience, without a reporter as an intermediary. And the audience is now demanding explanations, both from reporters and directly from sources. It is getting harder to tell who is the reporter, who is the source and who is the audience. (pp. 306–307)

The *conversation* of journalism today leads Thornburg (2011) to argue for "Remixing the News" (p. 333). He describes a type of journalism filled with data distribution, nonlinear narratives, chunks, links and filters.

Some journalists remain skeptical of the long-term value for social media. They point, for example, to a study showing that the average Twitter account has only one follower (Reuters, 2013). On the other side of the argument, however, *The New York Times* continues to build the size of their social media team to cater to millions of followers (Roston, 2014). Twitter followers who track breaking news in the moment expect speed, but newspapers' social media desks have also learned that some enterprise stories are worthy of repeating multiple times during the week. As experience grows, a set of journalism best practices is emerging.

■ DISCUSSION QUESTIONS: STRATEGIES AND TACTICS

1. How do you define journalism? How do you think traditional definitions of the work of journalists are being altered through participation in social media? What can working journalists do to maintain professionalism?

2. What must journalists do to be relevant to young people? What role should entertaining video play in attracting new audiences to journalism? Are there other tactics journalists can use have a positive effect on business economics?

3. Does the norm of objectivity remain important within your definition of journalism? Are there other strategies journalists need to adopt to be considered as a trusted source for fair information within their communities?

References

Beckett, C., with Ball, J. (2012). *WikiLeaks, News in the Networked Era*. Cambridge, UK: Polity Press.

Briggs, M. (2010). *Journalism Next*. Washington, DC: CQ Press.

Cantor, M. (2013, November 3). Book: Obama Claimed to Be 'Really Good at Killing People.' *Newser*. www.newser.com/story/176961/book-obama-claimed-to-be-really-good-at-killing-people.html?utm_source=twitterfeed&utm_medium=twitter

Choney, S. (2012, March 15). Kony Video Proves Social Media's Role as Youth News Source: Pew. TECHNOLOG. NBC News. www.nbcnews.com/technology/kony-video-proves-social-medias-role-youth-news-source-pew-455365

CJR (2013, September 3). Who, What, When, Where, Why, and How. CJR Asks the Question: What Is Journalism for? *Columbia Journalism Review*. www.cjr.org/cover_story/who_what_when.php

Craft, S., & Davis, C. N. (2013). *Principles of American Journalism: An Introduction*. New York, NY: Routledge.

Domingo, D. (2008). Interactivity in the Daily Routines of Online Newsrooms: Dealing with an Uncomfortable Myth. *Journal of Computer-Mediated Communication 13*, 680–704.

Harsin, J. (2013). WTF Was Kony 2012? Considerations for Communication and Critical/Cultural Studies (CCCS). *Communication and Critical/Cultural Studies 10*(2–3), 265–272.

Hart, J. (2011). *Story Craft: The Complete Guide to Writing Narrative Nonfiction*. Chicago, IL: University of Chicago Press.

Ingram, M. (2011, December 21). News as a Process: How Journalism Works in the Age of Twitter. GIGAOM. http://gigaom.com/2011/12/21/news-as-a-process-how-journalism-works-in-the-age-of-twitter/

Ingram, M. (2014, February 4). Andy Carvin, A Pioneer in Using Twitter for Real-Time Journalism, Joins Omidyar's First Look Media. *Gigaom*. http://gigaom.com/2014/02/04/andy-carvin-a-pioneer-in-using-twitter-for-real-time-journalism-joins-omidyars-first-look-media

Jacobson, S. (2013). Does Audience Participation on Facebook Influence the News Agenda? A Case Study of *The Rachel Maddow Show*. *Journal of Broadcasting & Electronic Media 57*(3), 338–355.

Johnson, K. A., & Wiedenbeck, S. (2009). Enhancing Perceived Credibility of Citizen Journalism Web Sites. *Journalism & Mass Communication Quarterly 86*(2), 332–348.

Johnson, T. J., & Kaye, B. K. (2010). Choosing Is Believing? How Web Gratifications and Reliance Affect Internet Credibility Among Politically Interested Users. *Atlantic Journal of Communication 18*(1), 1–21.

Kerrigan, F., & Graham, G. (2010). Interaction of Regional News-media Production and Consumption through the Social Space. *Journal of Marketing Management 26*(3/4), 302–320.

Lipschultz, J. H. (2013, August 20). Live Tweets, Journalism, Middle East Culture and NPR Branding. Media. *The Huffington Post*. www.huffingtonpost.com/jeremy-harris-lipschultz/live-tweets-journalism-mi_b_3779940.html

Luckie, M. S. (2011). *The Digital Journalist's Handbook*. Lexington, KY: Mark S. Luckie.

Maras, S. (2013). *Objectivity in Journalism*. Cambridge, UK: Polity Press.

Matheson, D. (2004). Weblogs and the Epistemology of the News: Some Trends in Online Journalism. *New Media & Society 6*(4), 443–468.

McCombs, M., Holbert, R. L., Kiousis, S., & Wanta, W. (2011). *The News and Public Opinion, Media Effects on Civic Life*. Cambridge, UK: Polity Press.

McCombs, M., & Shaw, D. (1972). The Agenda-Setting Function of Mass Media. *Public Opinion Quarterly 36*(2), 176–187.

Mitchell, A., Kiley, J., Gottfried, J., & Guskin, E. (2013, October 24). The Role of News on Facebook, Common Yet Incidental. Pew Research Center. www.journalism.org/2013/10/24/the-role-of-news-on-facebook/

Newspaper Association of America (2013). Across Platforms, 7 in 10 Adults Access Content from Newspaper Media Each Week. www.naa.org/Topics-and-Tools/SenseMakerReports/Multiplatform-Newspaper-Media-Access.aspx

Nunnelley, C. (2006). *Building Trust in the News, 101+ Good Ideas for Editors from Editors*. New York, NY: Associated Press Managing Editors.

Paulussen, S., & Ugille, P. (2008). User Generated Content in the Newsroom: Professional and Organisational Constraints on Participatory Journalism. *Westminster Papers in Communication and Culture, 5*(2), 24–41.

Pew (2012). *In Social Media and Opinion Pages, Newtown Sparks Calls for Gun Reform*. Washington, DC: Pew Research Center's Project for Journalism Excellence.

Pew (2013). *The State of the News Media, An Annual Report on American Journalism*. Washington, DC: Pew Research Center's Project for Journalism Excellence. http://StateOfTheMedia.org

Pew Research Center's Journalism Staff (2012). *YouTube & News*. Pew Research Journalism Project. www.journalism.org/analysis_report/youtube_news

Pogue, D. (2013, October 21). Goodbye—and Hello. *Tumblr*. http://pogueman.tumblr.com/post/64682813641/goodbye-and-hello

Rettberg, J. W. (2008). *Blogging*. Cambridge, UK: Polity Press.

Reuters (2013). Study Shows Average Twitter Account Has Only 1 Follower. Circa. http://cir.ca/news/average-followers-on-twitter

Roston, M. (2014, January 6). If a Tweet Worked Once, Send It Again—and Other Lessons from *The New York Times'* Social Media Desk. Nieman Journalism Lab. www.niemanlab.org/2014/01/if-a-tweet-worked-once-send-it-again-and-other-lessons-from-the-new-york-times-social-media-desk/

Schmierbach, M., & Oeldorf-Hirsch, A. (2012). A Little Bird Told Me, So I Didn't Believe It: Twitter, Credibility, and Issue Perceptions. *Communication Quarterly, 60*(3), 317–337.

Singer, J. B., et al. (2011). *Participatory Journalism, Guarding Open Gates at Online Newspapers*. Malden, MA: Wiley-Blackwell.

Terms and Conditions. (2014). *The Huffington Post*. www.huffingtonpost.com/terms.html

Tewksbury, D., & Rittenberg, J. (2012). *News on the Internet: Information and Citizenship in the 21st Century*. New York, NY: Oxford University Press.

Thornburg, R. M. (2011). *Producing Online News: Digital Skills, Stronger Stories*. Washington, DC: CQ Press, p. 405.

Tian, D., & Chao, C.-C. (2012). Testing News Trustworthiness in an Online Public Sphere: A Case Study of *The Economist*'s News Report Covering the Riots in Xinjiang, China. *Chinese Journal of Communication* 5(4), 455–474.

Wardle, C., & Williams, A. (2010). Beyond User-Generated Content: A Production Study Examining the Ways in WHICH UGC Is Used at the BBCMedia. *Culture & Society 32*(5), 781–799.   http://mediaeducation.org.mt/wp-content/uploads/2013/05/User_gnerated_content_journalism_BBC1.pdf

Westlund, O. (2008). From Mobile Phone to Mobile Device: News Consumption on the Go. *Canadian Journal of Communication* 33(3), 443–463.

Williams, A. E. (2012). Trust or Bust? Questioning the Relationship between Media Trust and News Attention. *Journal of Broadcasting & Electronic Media 56*(1), 116–131.

4   SOCIAL MEDIA IN PUBLIC RELATIONS

"We try to amass followers and likes as if it's a 'thing.' We try to get views because that's how we justify and substantiate our work. But why? What's it all for? What does it mean? What does it matter?"

—*Brian Solis (@briansolis, 2013)*

When Brian Solis, principal analyst at the Altimeter Group, took the stage at the PRSA 2013 International Conference in Philadelphia, he challenged public relations professionals to re-focus PR on relationships and influence:

> We go through this journey and that journey is a mess. Why? Because the people who own mobile don't talk to people who own the website. The people who own the website don't talk to the people who are running Facebook . . . It's the same problem over and over again. So you see multiple brands, multiple voices instead of one company. That is PR's opportunity—redefine the whole journey, the entire experience (PRSA, 2013, para. 10).

Solis' social media PR formula centers on ART—actions, reactions and transactions—that can impact outcomes, behaviors and actions (paras. 11–12).

The flood of daily emails announcing public relations (PR) webinars, white papers and other resources suggests that the field is experiencing a fundamental transformation. This book is about how social media are shifting the work in many fields, including PR. The emphasis is moving from press releases and traditional media relations to "shareable online content" with a relatively new interest in the direct reach of a message.

Traditional print and broadcast media, from *The New York Times* and CBS News to your local radio stations and newspaper, once were *the* leaders of most public discussion.

Within PR, there has been a developing interest in influencing the **C-suite**, which refers to top senior-level executives at a corporation. The terminology is used to identify chief executive officers (CEO), chief operating officers (COO), chief information officers (CIO) and, most recently, chief digital officers (CDO). From a business perspective, PR seeks to influence the influencers who make key decisions and have the power to spend money hiring outside the company for social media services. Often, large corporations have a vice president of corporate communications with responsibilities to develop in-house PR offices, as well as outside services. Depending upon corporate structure, the C-suite may or may not be interested in social media decision-making. PR firms wanting to land new clients or grow existing businesses must keep an eye on the C-suite, which has the power to hire and fire agencies representing them as clients.

PR Management

PR stakeholders are no longer impressed with simply including social media within a campaign. Increasingly, clients want a return on investment (ROI) for dollars spent on advertising, public relations and marketing efforts. In the **eCommerce** environment, use of Google Analytics and other social media data dashboards allow businesses to link social media efforts to results that go beyond Facebook likes and shares. A company may be trying to increase website traffic, generate sales leads, increase conversions to online purchases, reduce company expenses and improve customer awareness and relations.

So-called **key performance indicators (KPIs)** focus on continuous monitoring of social media and sales activity data. In other words, businesses want social media to be connected to their larger goals and strategies for maintaining and growing business. This is what some thought leaders have termed "social business." It places social media within the more traditional context of word of mouth activity related to brands. Social media conversation can assist with ongoing branding activities, which are crucial to developing, maintaining and generating customer brand loyalty.

In social media, influence is important. While data suggest that actual friends are most influential, PR seeks to tap into the influence of social networks. By creating content within social networks and mobile social platforms, such as Instagram or Vine, it may be possible to increase measured influence. Klout, for example, has hundreds of millions of users. Each is measured using the Klout algorithm. By identifying influencers, even in a rough sense, a brand may seek to engage with people or brands that can move toward a larger set of strategic goals. Whether or not you place much trust in the specific scores, Klout (despite its non-transparent methodology) is useful for tracking broad engagement across a large number of social media platforms. Most importantly, it allows a user to identify influencers connecting with previous social media content and perceived brand influence. By doing this, the strategy might be to reach out to specific influencers with targeted content that would drive an increase in future influence. Tracking data over time allows the user to observe whether the influence tactics have any measureable effect.

While mainstream or traditional media continue to be opinion leaders, they now share the spotlight with three other overlapping media environments, as depicted in the Edelman PR cloverleaf.

Edelman President Richard Edelman, shown here speaking to media professors at a 2012 Academic Summit in Palo Alto, California, urged that PR embrace the shift to integrating tradition and social media into campaigns. The development of the Internet and Web in the 1990s led companies, organizations and individuals to create websites. These **owned media**, along with apps, turned all of those with online identities essentially into media companies. In this century, **hybrid media** (also called "new media" or "tra-digital"), emerged from blogging. *The Huffington Post* was one of the earliest hybrid media to take advantage of the shift by commercializing it. Edelman Digital in Chicago, owned by Edelman PR in New York (the largest global firm) developed a cloverleaf that classified these types of media. Technology sites, such as Mashable, political sites like Politico, and other specialized niche markets flourished in this new space. Finally, social media, through early popular sites, such as Facebook, Twitter and YouTube, empowered individuals to interact as media producers. The rapidly growing mobile media market driven by smartphones and tablets created a need for new apps and new platforms, such as Vine and Tout for video, Instagram for photographs and video, and FourSquare and Yelp for geo-location services.

Figure 4.1 Edelman President Richard Edelman frequently uses the Cloverleaf to place social media within the context of other media forms.

The blending of PR functions with "paid amplification" through social media has led to a degree of chaos in the field. Edelman PR (@EdelmanPR) gathered top leaders in Hamburg, Germany, in 2013 to develop company strategy for responding to rapid industry change (Sudhaman, 2013). Edelman's $750 million in annual revenues and 12.5% growth rate were not enough to keep President Richard Edelman (@RichardEdelman) from worrying about challengers, such as GolinHarris (@GolinHarris), which earlier had restructured account teams (para. 8). Edelman's "Hamburg Principles," which urged a public relations focus that utilizes digital media and research and partners with advertising agencies when working with large clients. In an era of convergence of PR with advertising and marketing functions, Edelman defines PR work as being a "reference point for how smart marketers are playing the game (para. 46). The brand-building function leads Richard Edelman to say that "PR is actually an attitude"—one that enters the business conversation amid dramatic social media shifts (para. 47).

Edelman's David Armano (@armano) has classified five content archetypes that offer examples of how PR advice now flows to large clients. Armano (2013) describes curated, co-created, original, consumer-generated and sponsored content amid the new mobile publishing environment:

1. *Curated content* is managed by brands determining "highest value to consumers" (para. 1).
2. *Co-created content* "is co-produced either peer to peer or brand to participant" (para. 2).

3. *Original content* is exclusive brand messages (para. 3).
4. *Consumer-generated content* happens "without the brand's involvement" (para. 4).
5. *Sponsored content* is "paid" promotion (para. 5).

From this framework, Armano (2013) sees a digital world that is mobile, social and responsive to changes in online search. He sees social media as defined by mobile "newsfeeds" (para. 6). From Facebook's feed to other mobile platforms, such as Instagram, "dominated by content and sharing" that "is only a button tap or click away" (para. 7). Perhaps the most volatile area for PR is sponsored content. A brand may purchase **promoted posts** on Facebook, which function similar to **paid search** by appearing atop a feed. At the same time, though, sponsored content refers to paid content that mimics online editorial content through native advertising that is seen along side a publication's traditional media.

From small stores to global brands, social media triggered a shift in resources toward communicating directly with potential and existing customers through the use of online content. At the same time, valued content was created to raise awareness, inform consumers, strengthen brand loyalty, build trust and manage reputation. This has resulted in a focus on branded content, content marketing, strategy and planning. What started as text-based information quickly shifted to rich media campaigns complete with photographs, info-graphics, memes, viral videos, new media channels and a push toward precise measurement of results through web analytics. The purpose of online content marketing often is to drive traffic to a commercial website, which may be a link for rapid sharing of content. Platforms, such as Twitter, Facebook or Pinterest, allow users to gain earned media without the high cost of national advertising. At the beginning and end of online PR is evaluation in the general sense, as opposed to the specific formula, of return on investment (ROI). In other words, was the effort worth our valuable resources and time?

PR History and Tactics

PR was not always the way we see it now. Message management began with church and political propaganda centuries ago, and it was fueled by 20th-century technological and social change. From P. T. Barnum's circus to early practitioner Edward Bernays, PR began to shift from wild and false claims to "professionals as comparable to attorneys, counseling clients" (Smith, Kaufman, & Martinez, 2012, p. 20). In the 1940s, PR featured traditional tactics, such as traveling publicity tours. A company selling home hair permanents in a radio and print advertising campaign that featured store visits across the country, for example, used the Toni Twins. The 75-city media tour was the idea of Dan Edelman, who went on to found what is today the largest global PR firm:

> Politicians and celebrities had long toured America, going from one speaking engagement to the next. What if, Dan thought, a company organized a tour geared not toward events, but aimed at local media? A media tour would ignite conversation everywhere it touched down. They could easily cobble together a reason to be in town, but the real purpose would be to generate coverage in the local newspapers, magazines, and on local radio. (Wisner, 2012, p. 13)

Amid lobbying by beauticians against home hair treatments, the Toni Twins were arrested in Tulsa, Oklahoma for "practicing salon procedures without a license" (p. 10). Crisis communication was born. Edelman turned the arrest into a photo opportunity and national press coverage by the AP and other news organizations. The events spawned Edelman's first 60-page PR plan, a large corporate budget, and eventually the launching of his own firm based upon a simple philosophy: "Do good. Tell other people about it" (p. 18).

The timing was perfect. Harry Truman in 1948 had conducted a nationwide "whistle stop" train tour designed to obtain live local radio coverage (Carroll, 1987). It would be called the last radio campaign. Between 1949 and 1952, when Edelman launched his small PR firm, post-war America had quickly adopted the new technology of television with millions watching *I Love Lucy* and other popular shows. News and politics also drew large audiences. Early television did not have clear separation between programming and advertising, and celebrity scandals generated a need for reputation management.

PR today is managed within social media as planned and interactive communication. Practitioners focus on reputation management and crisis communication. It may function as internal communication within organizations, but it also serves external communication needs for publicity, government and community relations, and even fundraising.

Published academic public relations studies fall into three general categories— "introspective" articles about PR as a profession, "practice/application" of PR, and development of theory (Fussell Sisco, Pressgrove, & Collins, 2013, p. 286). Among these studies, important areas of theory (p. 290) include:

- PR/excellence theory
- Organization-public relationship
- Framing
- Dialogic communication
- Situational theory
- Role theory
- Diffusion of innovation

Within this context, it appears that both the industry and academic researchers identify the growing importance of non-profit public relations. This sector typically works with small budgets, and social media are seen as a way to generate awareness and interest through direct communication and engagement with the public.

PR Theories

The field of public relations tends to have a focus on communication strategies and tactics, organizational practices and management. For example, common PR tactics include use of news releases, press conferences, events and publications. All of these may be connected to a social media campaign, which pushes content to media and the public. As with the broader communication industry, there is debate about the value of theory versus practice. Key theories may enhance critical thinking abilities of students, interns and professionals (Latchaw, Allen, & Ogden, 2009). Among the most commonly mentioned theoretical perspectives are agenda-setting, cultivation, ethics, issues management, organizational communication and persuasion (Miller & Kernisky, 1999). These theories may be applied to communication message strategies (Toth, 2006). Social media are closely related to mediated communication, which is built upon interpersonal communication theories. Tactics alone, without strategies, are not enough to manage complex issues (Elliott & Koper, 2002).

Grunig (1989) contended that PR "practice is dominated by the presupposition that the purpose of public relations is to manipulate the behavior of publics for the assumed, if not actual, benefit of the manipulated publics as well as the organization" (p. 29). He identified four models (Grunig, 1989, p. 29):

- Press agentry/publicity—"propagandistic" PR seeking "media attention in almost any way possible"
- Public information—"journalists-in-residence" disseminating "generally accurate information," but "do not volunteer negative information"
- Two-way asymmetrical—the Bernays approach uses research and sophisticated manipulation methods "to identify the messages most likely to produce support of publics without having to change the behavior of the organization"
- Two-way symmetrical—has "effects that a neutral observer would describe as benefitting both organization and publics" through "bargaining, negotiating, and strategies of conflict resolution to bring about symbiotic changes"

Grunig found through research that "the models function as situational strategies that organizations use for different publics and public relations problems," and "presuppositions of the models function as part of an organization's ideology" (p. 31). Grunig also articulated the importance of organizational "orientation," which described such characteristics as closed-mindedness, elitism and traditionalism (pp. 32–33). There is no reason to believe that social media participation would change fundamental organizational viewpoints, but these should impact the manner of communication and degree of engagement with the public. If old PR rules apply in social media spaces, organizations may be overestimating the value of message distribution in raising awareness, as opposed to employing Grunig's symmetrical approach. On the other hand, public social media communication may also create opportunities to discuss, engage and even negotiate social change. It also could be that social media communication reflects traditional persuasion constraints of behavior reinforcement, cognitive beliefs and evaluation intention of future behavior, and involvement (Hamilton, 1989).

An early study of Twitter references to "public relations" and "PR" by Xifra & Grau found eight specific categories (2010, p. 171–172):

Labour introspective 15.2% (N = 99): All direct references to the vacancies and applications for positions in public relations.
Academic introspective 2.3% (N = 15): Both references clearly issued by students and lecturers, as well as information in the university public relations universe.
Practice 10.9% (N = 71): All information sent out by public relations practitioners, either as members of a company or the press agent of an organization . . . It also comprises tweets that refer to work by firms.

Press release references 4.3% (N = 28): Announcements of the issue of press releases and links to read and/or download the press release.

General information on the public relations sector 14.4% (N = 94): General information on the public relations sector. It comprises the group of tweets that deal with the industry, on the state of the art or references to public relations as a concept, economic sector or important part of organisations' communication strategies.

The sender of the tweet and their dialogue with the community 18.7% (N = 122): It groups opinions and thoughts on the sector, heavily marked by the sender's viewpoint. Also @replies (answers) to other users involving the existence of a dialogue with them on public relations.

Research 5.6% (N = 37): It includes all requests and invitations to answer or to involve all users that read or capture a question or questionnaire issued to the community.

Announcements, reviews, agenda, followfriday, and retweets 28.6% (N = 187): This group includes all tweets that facilitate acceleration, transmission and expansion of communication between the members of the community.

The study confirmed that Twitter was seen as an alternative channel for presenting a positive company image. Twitter often was used as a tool for professional information, including listings for jobs.

Curtis et al. (2010) found gender and other differences in perception of Twitter. While Twitter use was ubiquitous, practitioners with "defined public relations departments are more likely to adopt social media technologies and use them to achieve . . . organizational goals" (p. 92). Social media use was related to perceived credibility, strategic message targeting, client relationships and an ability to reach the public.

Credibility

The potential for attitude and behavior change through social media communication requires an understanding of credibility. It has been related to believability, leadership, warmth, salience, trustworthiness, expertise, attractiveness, skills, accuracy and sincerity (Hwang, 2013). In a study of Twitter use by Korean politicians, attitudes about Twitter use influenced perceived credibility of the politicians using Twitter. Politicians were perceived as "attractive and classy" by "challenging themselves" to use the new tool (p. 254):

> Social media makes it possible for organizations to fully engage in dialogic communication with stakeholders . . . the word *dialogue* indicates open-minded, specific message content and a sincere listening attitude . . . When politicians actively share their candid opinions through the open public sphere of Twitter, this can cultivate an open-minded image that leads members of the public to perceive politician users as sincere and reliable. (p. 254)

At the same time, however, there are numerous examples of U.S. politicians speaking their minds on Twitter, only later having to retract or apologize for saying something that was perceived by media and the public as beyond normative boundaries.

Social Capital, Conflict and Collaboration

Social capital is a popular idea within the social sciences and has been related to social interaction, trust, shared value and social media use (Lin & Lu, 2011). It refers to the ability of individuals and organizations to benefit from communication behavior. In the context of social media, "Gaining social capital really means becoming a strong, consistent member of the online community" (Solomon, 2013, p. 35). A Save Ohio Libraries 2009 campaign on Twitter was unable to leverage social capital because it was primarily one-way, outbound communication. Librarians have since learned the importance of regularly engaging with their communities by providing helpful information and links. Solomon (2013) urges libraries to make social capital deposits within their social media sites:

> Every time your library promotes something or asks for a favor, it is making a withdrawal. If your withdrawals exceed your deposits, your library effectively becomes a community leech—and in some cases, a pariah. Spend social capital wisely. (p. 37)

Conceptually, Robert Putnum popularized social capital in the mid-1990s, as he argued for declining American social relationships. "This is a shorthand way of saying learning, motivation, best practice, problem solving and access to resources, among other factors, can often be better facilitated through networks—the social contacts made with professional colleagues—than individually" (Taylor, 2013, p. 34). Individual and organizational social capital may have value in economic terms, and it also may offer benefits for professional development and working culture. Across a wide variety of fields, social capital is seen as a way to understand intangibles that are important within prospering communities. Taylor (2013, p. 35) lists important benefits:

- Trust—"information, knowledge and skills" sharing, as well as "support."
- Shared norms and values—"understanding" of others' "perspectives," and "shared language and common goals" with "a particular context."
- Shared resources and knowledge—"wider access to resources and knowledge" for "taking forward good practice."
- Reciprocity—"it is likely that others in the network will reciprocate and give to that relationship."
- Resilience within relationships—"Strong networks are resilient in the face of challenges," and are accepting of "constructive conversations around difficult areas."
- Co-ordination and co-operation for the achievement of common goals—as "best professional practice extends beyond traditional organisational boundaries."

In other words, using social networking and media to cultivate social capital should generate opportunities to collaborate beyond organizational boundaries. Twitter, for example, can be seen as valuable individual career support through sustained relationship building while serving in "complex roles" (Taylor, 2013, p. 37). Beyond the obvious value to individual workers, collaboration may grow into "strategic business alliances" that cut costs by sharing the need to keep pace with rapid industry change (Harper & Norelli, 2007, p. 15). In PR, there are potentially a large number of opportunities within most communities to utilize virtual collaboration through social media.

Social Media Tactics

Historically, PR people had a heavy reliance on the simple press release or news release. The idea was that, if the writing and ideas were attention getting to news gatekeepers, a story about an event, product or service would follow. Enter the digital era and the Internet. Every release of information today should be designed for online consumption by news media and the general public. PR people are in search of "traction" amid the noisy and cluttered world of social media. One way to break through the clutter is to use SEO keywords and structure them in order to move the information toward the top of a Google search. At the same time, social media demand more.

Edelman's Phil Gomes examined buzz in the early days of Twitter and researched how online chatter could be monitored through social media measurement techniques, which are much more sophisticated now. There is a need to share rich media content— photographs, audio, video, info-graphics and links—across social platforms, such as Facebook, Twitter and Pinterest. Developing tactics can create buzz, if the content is engaging and truly employs media storytelling techniques.

The PR professional in search of earned media and social sharing, even viral distribution, must be strategic by offering timely information. Increasingly, PR content is integrated within the news cycle, which is very fast. As news breaks, Twitter content may light up the social network with activity. Real-time PR professionals, often working from "war rooms" ready to respond, link the strategic goals of their clients with relatable **organic** content. Still, there are so many people now trying to take advantage of the moment in social media spaces that it has become increasingly difficult to be clever enough to break through the noise with valuable content.

📡 BOX 4.1 THOUGHT LEADER PHIL GOMES

Suddenly, PR people became part of the story, which was always a kind of "fourth wall" that was never to be breached. This is both good *and* bad. It's good in that PR is a largely distrusted profession and I'm a big proponent of earning that trust by "open sourcing" PR's "operating system" to some degree. Social media is one way to do that.

However, it's bad because there are an awful lot of PR people who want to insert themselves into the conversation to such a degree that it 1) actually adds to the distrust, and 2) produces further confusion as to what PR is.

Figure 4.2 @philgomes.

A recent survey of CMOs showed that "data explosion" and "social media" were the top two—perhaps linked—concerns that they have. People

(continued)

talk a lot about "Big Data" but I think this is a distraction, as if insights spontaneously appear when you're sitting on enough exabytes. It actually doesn't take a whole lot to accumulate a ton of data. At a certain level of play, it's quite possible that Company A's data warehouse might not be markedly different in size or content from Company B's. What companies need to talk about is "Big Math." In other words, how do you approach, manipulate, and present that data to achieve competitive business value?

I am looking forward to—and am actively working toward—a day when such a distinction will be as meaningless as asking "What is the largest opportunity your field has because of the fax machine?" All media is social and, despite what many legislators might say, all social is media. "Digital" departments will be a firm's core group of innovators and trendspotters while basic social media and digital skills will be just as much a part of communications strategy client service as, say, media relations. The distinctions will evaporate over time.

Phil Gomes is senior vice president (SVP) at Edelman Chicago, where he has worked since 2005. He holds a B.A. from St. Mary's College of California and an MBA from Purdue University. He began as account service and media/analyst relations for SRI International, Hitachi Semiconductor, J. D. Edwards and others. Gomes is a strategist applying his Silicon Valley background to current PR industry best practices.

Social media tend to blur the lines between PR, advertising and marketing. Vaynerchuk (2013), for example, instructs brands to do storytelling with the context of a particular social media platform. He calls this type of social media marketing "native," in that it understands a platform and is fluent within it (p. 16). This rule also applies to PR. The difference is that while PR may emphasize brand awareness, influence or positive sentiment, marketing ultimately seeks conversion from interaction to sales: ". . . successful social media marketing requires throwing many jabs before converting the sale with a right hook" (pp. 17–18). Vaynerchuk narrows social media to the nine most important platforms: Twitter, Facebook, Google+, Instagram, LinkedIn, Tumblr, Pinterest, Vine and Snapchat. While marketers jab, PR professionals seek new ways to engage in timely and relevant exchanges.

PR Newsrooms and Message Targeting

Edelman PR developed its Creative Newsroom idea to address the need for real-time social media monitoring, response and strategy. The firm hired former journalists to staff the newsroom:

> Edelman built the Creative Newsroom, to provide clients with an agile and integrated platform for storytelling, for both planned and real-time marketing. We partner with clients to produce relevant content and real-time creative assets that support traditional, hybrid, social and owned strategies and align with longer-term brand and corporate narratives. (Edelman, 2014)

Edelman PR focuses on client media storytelling for engaging audiences. Edelman's plan focuses on client partnerships with five U.S. newsrooms and one in the U.K. Edelman newsroom "trend spotters" identify trends and events, collaborate with account leaders and design creative concepts. Ideas are shared with clients, and then decisions are made about posting or not.

Real-time social media are transforming marketing and public relations. GolinHarris created The Bridge two years earlier than Edelman. GolinHarris hired professional journalists, but also created "a holistic engagement network" to offer businesses "a front-row seat to the most important conversations, broadcast and news headlines tied to your industry" (GolinHarris, 2014). The firm has had journalists in Chicago and Dallas running The Bridge since 2012. GolinHarris constructed 13 global "command centers" for this new form of industry collaboration, and The Bridge:

> . . . pairs mainstream and digital experts with creative specialists like copywriters, digital designers and video producers to uncover storytelling opportunities in real time, deliver critical business insights, engage influencers and customers and create the content that shapes news and conversations. (Ibid., para. 4)

The Bridge won a *PR Week* award for innovative design of "holistic engagement." The basic idea is to provide 24/7 conversation monitoring for clients and offer rapid response within social media. When Al Roker overslept his *Today Show* shift for the first time ever, for example, the McDonald's account tweeted at him:

> @McDonalds: Stick with us @AlRoker, we'll help you wake up for the next 39 years #McCafe. (August 6, 2013)

Figure 4.3 The Bridge in Chicago utilizes real-time social media monitoring, strategy and response.

The tweet was read on the air, which is earned media from social media engagement with traditional media. Traditional media—television, radio, newspapers and magazines—are blending with real-time PR and marketing content. News organizations are now in the business of conversation monitoring and engaging. In this sense, the news model shares with PR the goal of creating viral videos, flashy graphics, photographs, memes and other popular social media content. Everyone is competing for measurable engagement that may translate into new revenue.

The integration of digital requires that PR newsrooms "keep brands' names alive on the **trending** charts as well as the daily zeitgeist" (*PR News*, 2013b, para. 3). Ogilvy, which came to social media from an advertising agency perspective, strategizes about real-time events but urges their clients to create their own newsrooms through what Edelman PR would call earned media. Golin Harris's head of The Bridge at its New York office told *PR News* that public relations newsrooms should encourage participation by: 1) being at the center of a PR office, 2) monitoring traditional and social media and 3) developing a mindset of constantly generating ideas for clients.

PR Blogging and Case Studies

Public relations blogging has been used to give personal and company brands voice within new social media spaces. More generally, bloggers may be social media influencers. While companies pay some bloggers, the vast majority is unpaid and fairly independent. In some cases, bloggers seek to build their personal brand and promote products, such as books.

📱 **BOX 4.2 THE CHICAGO CUBS AND A WRIGLEY FIELD
               PEARL JAM CONCERT**

The Chicago Cubs used social media to help promote a summer Pearl Jam concert at Wrigley Field. The summer concerts have become a new way to generate revenue while the baseball team is on the road. Cubs Manager of Communications Kevin Saghy (@CredibleKev) utilized existing relationships. Pearl Jam musician Edder Vedder (@PearlJam) is a huge Cubs fan, and Cubs President of Baseball Operations Theo Epstein (@Cubs) is a Pearl Jam fan. Saghy told a Cision (@Cision) marketing webinar (Denten & Saghy, 2013), "We executed a social media leak strategy." It began one morning with cryptic Facebook and Twitter posts using #StayTuned to heighten interest. "Over the course of the day, people following both accounts started to pick up on this, and the buzz just built throughout the day."

Because of the mysterious posts, traditional media eventually called the Cubs and Pearl Jam publicists. Late in the day, a media alert was distributed, posted on the Cubs' marquee, and posted online. The announcement of the forthcoming concert attracted traditional local media coverage and morning television the next day. The Cubs also attracted attention in music industry publications, such as *Rolling Stone*. Saghy told PRSA that the Cubs "rely on traditional PR tactics to attract attention to our social

Figure 4.4 The Chicago Cubs used social and mass media to promote a Pearl Jam concert at Wrigley Field.

media outlets" by securing "quite a bit of coverage" for the Pearl Jam concert and a Social Media Night at Wrigley Field (Jacques, 2013, para. 18):

> We're active on nearly every major social media platform—Facebook, Twitter, Pinterest, Instagram, Vine, Google Plus, Tumblr—and we keep an eye on other emerging outlets to see where we should focus our efforts. We cover every game, home or away, and constantly monitor for breaking news (para. 16).

The Cubs use content, contests, polls and fan engagement during games at Wrigley Field. Saghy's work is split between traditional PR outreach and social media. "I usually check my email and our Twitter feed to see if there are pressing issues to address" (para. 6). The PR function aligns with baseball operations on release of personnel information, roster moves and updates during games. The Cubs connect "memorable" offline experiences to social media; "fans remember these interactions for life, and the positive stories spread organically" (para. 10).

Social media have become PR tools that offer many unique ways to be creative and generate customer brand interest. There are many examples frequently mentioned by PR professionals, including:

- The Old Spice Guy, a brand representative, created more than 150 personalized videos for fans.
- Microsoft and Bing announced a partnership during a Twitter chat.
- Hershey's launched its Simple Pleasures candy with a Sweet Independence Facebook page that encouraged follower posts and generated more than 200 million media impressions.

PR people can reward loyal customers by making simultaneous Facebook page and media release announcements. Using social media to cover press conferences and national launch tours can help coordinate the integration of traditional and social media. By inventing new hashtags or hijacking an existing trending topic, a brand can connect with new potential customers.

During NBC's live "Sound of Music" broadcast with singer Carrie Underwood, pizza brand DiGiorno capitalized on the highest TV ratings since the E.R. finale to live tweet using the official tag:

> @DiGiorno: #TheSoundOfMusicLive Can't believe pizza isn't one of her favorite things smh. (December 5, 2013)

"Now of course DiGiorno got a ton of pizza references in there by seamlessly incorporating their brand with the conversation, but they were not pushing products" (Quintana, 2013, para. 6). The increase in this type of live tweet, however, runs a risk of turning off fans who see this as too opportunistic.

The connection of PR events and social media may produce numerous positive outcomes. PR influence now extends to blogger and VIP influencers by creating experiences that lend themselves to social media content creation. Traditional news media increasingly are active on social media, and social media engagement may cut across traditional and new media. Many brands have incorporated prize packages and scavenger hunts into their social media plans.

Companies also need to consider the role that employees play within social media. Their employees may be connected to very active social networks, and they are brand ambassadors. Employees also may be able to help a social media brand manager by taking photographs and having their posts featured on a blog or social media site. Employees increasingly are seen as stakeholders with a voice inside and outside the company. The integrated approach to PR and digital marketing may be positive for brand visibility, customer loyalty and even sales. Social media may generate new business through use of new platforms and engagement with fans and followers—ideally within a responsible business framework.

Corporate Social Responsibility (CSR)

With so much attention being paid to seemingly self-serving company and brand efforts within social media, there has been renewed interest in looking beyond sales and profits. Perhaps driven by an era of government deregulation that began in the late 1970s in the United States, CSR asks companies to consider the effects of their businesses on social and environmental conditions. Corporate citizens operating within a CSR model would consider long-term social interests, not just quarterly profits. Clearly, social media engagement can be related to CSR by emphasizing social responsibility for individuals, groups and companies. CSR also can be seen as a way to develop legal, ethical and global best practices within a large corporation. Freeman (1984/2010) influenced thinking about the need for multinational corporations to move beyond the narrow interests of stockholders to the broader interests of stakeholders. Freeman's book was published at a time when U.S. manufacturing, particularly the automobile industry, was being overtaken by imports from Japan. As such, CSR was framed within a strategic management perspective that considered suppliers, owners, employees and customers as stakeholders within an environment of "internal and external change" (p. 12). Most notably, companies were receiving media scrutiny based upon the emergence of consumer protection and employee rights and responsibilities. If a company moved away from top-down management practices, then it should involve employees at all levels in decision-making and listen to customer wants and needs. In other words, CSR emphasized self-regulation within companies as a more effective way to achieve social good over previous efforts of "big government" regulation. The CSR message resonated in the 1980s U.S. political environment, which saw President Ronald Reagan pushing for aggressive deregulation of "bureaucracy" in all sectors (p. 15).

> Let us consider the customer of a firm, and suppose that for whatever reason, the customer is unhappy with the product. He or she can exit, simply take the business elsewhere and buy from another producer, given that there is a reasonable number of competing firms. Exit is the paradigm of the "economic" strategy. When enough customers exit, the firm gets the message that the product is no longer viable, that it is not producing at the "efficient frontier." (pp. 18–19)

An alternative approach is the use of customer "voice." Freeman (1984/2010) saw customer feedback to management as "more immediate" (p. 19). Brand loyalty in the marketplace, then, is a combination of consumer decisions and voice. Traditional, mainstream media might identify a particular consumer complaint or problem, but social media allow consumers to voice immediate dissatisfaction and engage with others having similar issues. Yelp, for example, is driven by consumer reviews. If a number of people report a similar problem at a restaurant, the social media content may affect business. Social media amplify and accelerate consumer voice, not only forcing company response, but also nudging interest in CSR.

The CSR approach suggests that responsible behavior may also be good for business, but it is not clear that social good always has a positive economic impact (McWilliams & Siegel, 2001). As early as 1970, it had been argued (via "agency theory") that "managers who use" shareholder and "corporate resources to further some social good are doing so only to advance a personal agenda such as promoting their self image" (McWilliams, Siegel, & Wright, 2006, p. 4). Corporate Social Performance (CSP) instead emphasized the need to test CSR against traditional financial outcomes (Carroll, 1979). One view of CSR emphasizes stakeholders, ethical behavior, "trust and cooperation," (McWilliams, Siegel, & Wright, 2006b, p. 3). This approach has been shown to "demonstrate that the returns to socially responsible behavior are captured through the reputation of the firm" (McWilliams, Siegel, & Wright, 2006a, p. 6). Particularly on the international stage, communicating CSR may result in positive effects, such as increased brand loyalty for those customers in search of socially responsible products and company behavior. Communicating brand differentiation through CSR may be part of a broader engagement strategy.

Non-profits

Non-profits have perhaps the most to gain from the social media communication PR shift. They typically are faced with low or non-existent media budgets and hope to benefit through earned media. While it is still possible to place stories in the local newspaper or on radio and television stations to gain community awareness, there are greater possibilities within social media. Non-profits may cultivate social friends and fans, drive traffic to fundraising campaign sites, and generate interest in community events.

Successes

Chief executive officers (CEO) may play an important role in developing social media PR success stories. *PR News* reported that CEO sociability may have a positive impact on company reputation, and CEO blogging magnifies effect. When a CEO becomes a thought leader, she or he has the potential to influence conversation and followers. As blog posts spread across social media spaces, the CEO and company brands should grow. Among benefits listed in an Intel chart are those shown in Table 4.1.

CEO social media use has the potential to increase perceptions of credibility, when strategic and careful. By establishing a presence within social media, a CEO should be more ready to handle media and public backlashes during times of crises. There are, however, no guarantees. Participating within social media also opens brands to potential criticism and attack.

Failures

The most common problem for individuals and companies is the distribution of a social media message without thinking it through and filtering it in terms of PR strategic planning and goals. The online site *Mental Floss* reported 16 cases in which people had been fired from their jobs because of a tweet (Conradt, 2013). Among the examples, an employee tweeting for Chrysler thought he was on his own private account:

> @ChryslerAutos: I find it ironic that Detroit is known as #motorcity and yet no one here knows how to fucking drive. (March 9, 2011)

While this firing was immediate, sometimes an old tweet comes back to haunt an employee. This 2011 tweet was discovered and reported by the *Milwaukee Journal Sentinel* after Taylor Palmisano was hired as deputy finance director for Wisconsin Governor Scott Walker's campaign.

> @itstaytime: This bus is the worst fucking nightmare Nobody speaks English & these ppl don't know how 2 control their kids #only3morehours #illegalaliens. (January 2, 2011)

Table 4.1 Top Five Benefits of CEO Blogging and Social Media Use

Benefits	Social Media Use	CEO Blogging
1. Shows innovation	76%	85%
2. Build media relations	75	84
3. Human face/personality	75	80
4. Business results	70	76
5. Workplace perception	69	76

Source: PR News (2013a, June 7). Benefits of CEO Participation in Social Media. PR News. www.prnews online.com/topics/research/2013/06/10/social-media-and-mobile-video-equal-more-web-sharing-death-of-newspapers-greatly-exaggerated-for-a-change/attachment/chart2-2/

Most employers clearly will not tolerate racist rants. Another problem is disclosure of confidential information. *Glee* extra Nicole Crowther "tweeted a spoiler of a pivotal scene" (para. 4) of the popular primetime television show. She was banned from future work through her casting agency (Conradt, 2013).

Lessons

PR practitioners can use social media communication content in the promotion of client products and services. Ogilvy's director of media influence calls this "the age of content" (Risi, 2013):

> Media relations has undergone a sea change in recent times with the proliferation of platforms, fusion of formats, and blurring of lines between traditional and social media. What has persisted is the potency of media exposure—it can make or break your PR campaign and thereby, your client's brand. It can establish newbies, transform dogged perceptions, and restore tarnished brands. Companies are increasingly turning to PR agencies for brand building and reputation management, and agencies must navigate their clients through an increasingly muddled media landscape. (para. 1)

Risi (2013, paras. 4–6) talks about traditional, social and earned media focused on business results.

1. **Measure what matters** . . . Impressions and ad equivalency are moot points if your media efforts aren't impacting the company's bottom line.
2. **Re-think media placements** . . . social sharing, online pieces are often driving conversation better than print coverage.
3. **Adopt a channel-agnostic approach** . . . by connecting content across earned, owned, and paid media, brands can tell a cohesive story that resonates with discerning consumers today.

The emphasis is away from traditional press releases and media relations tactics and toward engaging content that is timely and contextual. By producing the right content at the right time, and on the right social media platform, it is possible to meet ROI business objectives that can be measured. PR is converging and blending with advertising and marketing. Social media engagement calls for customer focus and clear content strategy (Edelman, 2013). In the next chapter, the attention turns to social media for advertising and marketing purposes.

■ DISCUSSION QUESTIONS: STRATEGIES AND TACTICS

1. How is PR changing because of social media use? What are the positives and negatives of the shift?
2. How is it possible to integrate the different media forms described by the Edelman cloverleaf? What are the most important limitations to integrated PR?
3. What do you see as the most important corporate social responsibility issues related to social media? How might these change in the future?

References

Armano, D. (2013, October 28). The Five Content Archetypes. *Edelman.* http://darmano.type pad.com/logic_emotion/2013/10/content.html

Carroll, A. (1979). A Three Dimensional Model of Corporate Performance. *Academy of Management Review 4*, 497–505.

Carroll, R. L. (1987, Spring). Harry S. Truman's 1948 Election: The Inadvertent Broadcast Campaign. *Journal of Broadcasting & Electronic Media 31*(2), 119–132.

Conradt, S. (2013, December). 16 People Who Tweeted Themselves into Unemployment. *Mental Floss.* http://mentalfloss.com/article/54068/16-people-who-tweeted-themselves-unemployment

Curtis, L., Edwards, C., Fraser, K. L., Gudelsky, S., Holmquist, J., Thornton, K., & Sweetser, K. D. (2010). Adoption of Social Media for Public Relations by Nonprofit Organizations. *Public Relations Review 36*, 90–92.

Denten, L. L., & Saghy, K. (2013, October 24). Bridging Social to Traditional PR. *Cision.* http://us.cision.com/events/on-demand-webinars/Bridging-the-Gap-to-Traditional-PR.asp

Edelman, D. (2013, October 30). Say Hi to the Social Media Elephant in the Room. *LinkedIn.* www.linkedin.com/today/post/article/20131030130324–1816165-say-hi-to-the-social-media-elephant-in-the-room

Edelman PR (2014). Creative Newsroom. www.edelman.com/expertise/creative-newsroom/

Elliott, G., & Koper, E. (2002). Public Relations Education from an Editor's Perspective. *Journal of Communication Management 7*, 21–23.

Freeman, R. E. (1984/2010). *Strategic Management: A Stakeholder Approach.* Cambridge, UK: Cambridge University Press.

Fussell Sisco, H., Pressgrove, G., & Collins, E. L. (2013). Paralleling the Practice: An Analysis of the Scholarly Literature in Nonprofit Public Relations. *Journal of Public Relations Research 25*(4), 282–306.

GolinHarris (2014). The Bridge: Holistic Engagement Centers. http://golinharris.com/#!/approach/the-bridge/

Grunig, J. E. (1989). Symmetrical Presuppositions as a Framework for Public Relations Theory. In C. H. Botan & V. Hazleton, Jr. (Eds.), *Public Relations Theory*, pp. 17–44. Hillsdale, NJ: Lawrence Erlbaum.

Hamilton, P. K. (1989). Application of a Generalized Persuasion Model to Public Relations Research. In C. H. Botan & V. Hazleton, Jr. (Eds.), *Public Relations Theory*, pp. 323–334. Hillsdale, NJ: Lawrence Erlbaum.

Harper, T., & Norelli, B. P. (2007). The Business of Collaboration and Electronic Collection Development. *Collection Building 26*(1), 15–19.

Hwang, S. (2013). The Effect of Twitter Use on Policians' Credibility and Attitudes toward Politicians. *Journal of Public Relations Research 25*(3), 246–258.

Jacques, A. (2013, August 1). Take Me Out to the Ball Game: Kevin Saghy on Managing Communications for the Chicago Cubs. *PRSA Tactics.* www.prsa.org/Intelligence/Tactics/Articles/view/10277/1081/Take_me_out_to_the_ball_game_Kevin_Saghy_on_managi#.UqE5LWRDuvk

Latchaw, J., Allen, C., & Ogden, D. (2009). Public Relations Professionals as Shapers of Public Information: The Role of Theory in Their Education. *Simile 9*(1).

Lin, K.-Y., & Lu, H.-P. (2011). Intention to Continue Using Facebook Fan Pages from the Perspective of Social Capital Theory. *Cyberpsychology, Behavior, and Social Networking 14*(10), 565–570.

McWilliams, A., & Siegel, D. (2001). Corporate Social Responsibility: A Theory of the Firm Perspective. *Academy of Management Review 26*, 117–127.

McWilliams, A., Siegel, D. S., & Wright, P. M. (2006a). Corporate Social Responsibility: International Perspectives. *Rensselaer Working Papers in Economics*. Troy, NY: Rensselaer Polytechnic Institute Press.

McWilliams, A., Siegel, D. S., & Wright, P. M. (2006b). Corporate Social Responsibility: Strategic Implications. *Journal of management Studies 43*(1), 1–18.

Miller, D. P., & Kernisky, D. A. (1999). Opportunities Realized: Undergraduate Education Within Departments of Communication. *Public Relations Review 25*(1), 87–100.

PR News (2013a, June 7). Benefits of CEO Participation in Social Media. *PR News*. www.prnewsonline.com/topics/research/2013/06/10/social-media-and-mobile-video-equal-more-web-sharing-death-of-newspapers-greatly-exaggerated-for-a-change/attachment/chart2-2/

PR News (2013b, October 21). PR Teams Build Internal Newsrooms as Communications Strategies Shift. *PR News*. www.prnewsonline.com/topics/media-relations/2013/10/21/pr-teams-build-internal-newsrooms-as-communications-strategies-shift/

PRSA (2013, October 27). Conference Recap: Brian Solis on the Future of Public Relations. *PRSA Tactics*. www.prsa.org/SearchResults/view/10397/105/Conference_Recap_Brian_Solis_On_the_Future_of_Publ#.UqTXWWRDuvk

Quintana, J. (2013, December 5). Real-Time Marketing Lessons from DiGiorno. *Lonelybrand*. http://lonelybrand.com/blog/real-time-marketing-digiorno/

Risi, J. (2013, November 4). Three Ways to Maximize PR in the Age of Content. *PR Week*. www.prweekus.com/three-ways-to-maximize-pr-in-the-age-of-content/article/319180/

Smith, B. L., Kaufman, C. O., & Martinez, G. D. (2012). *Engaging Public Relations: A Creative Approach, third edition*. Dubuque, IA: Kendall Hunt.

Solomon, L. (2013, May). Understanding Social Capital. *American Librarian Magazine 44*(5), 34–37.

Sudhaman, A. (2013, December 1). The 'Organized Chaos' of the World's Largest PR Agency. *The Holmes Report*. www.holmesreport.com/featurestories-info/14285/The-Organized-Chaos-Of-The-Worlds-Largest-PR-Agency.aspx

Taylor, R. (2013). Networking in Primary Health Care: How Connections Can Increase Social Capital. *Primary Health Care 23*(10), 34–40.

Toth, E. L. (2006). On the Challenge of Practice Informed by Theory. *Journal of Communication Management 10*(1), 110–111.

Vaynerchuk, G. (2013). *Jab, Jab, Jab, Right Hook: How to Tell Your Story in a Noisy Social World*. New York, NY: HarperCollins.

Wisner, F. (2012). *Edelman and the Rise of Public Relations*. Chicago, IL: Daniel J. Edelman.

Xifra, J., & Grau, F. (2010). Nanoblogging PR: The discourse on public relations in Twitter. *Public Relations Review 36*, 171–174.

5   SOCIAL MEDIA IN ADVERTISING
AND MARKETING

"Fifty-five percent of social network users reported they typically keep in touch by visiting brands' websites—the top method of staying connected to a brand."
—*@eMarketer (2013)*

The online publication eMarketer, which covers digital marketing, marketing and commerce, tracks social media impact on traditional advertising and marketing. "Advertising is commonly defined as paid, one-way promotional communication in any mass media" (Tuten, 2008, p. 2). Social media, however, are interactive two-way consumer and brand communication. "Online, advertising becomes more about conversations, connections, and shared control and less about passive consumption of packaged content" (p. 3). Online advertising also blurs the traditional line between it and marketing functions, and it offers key advantages. "Because of the networked nature of online computers, the Internet has proven to be highly measurable" (Kelley, Jugenheimer, & Sheehan, 2012, p. 253).

Context, including the level of consumer involvement with media, has become increasingly important:

> . . . media should be thought of more from the consumers' viewpoint, and it is no longer enough to know basic media usage figures . . . Rather consumers' relationships with the media can be critical to they way they respond to the brand message. (Katz, 2007, p. 29)

Social media are maturing into an industry that aligns with traditional media advertising and marketing plans designed to reach large audiences (Miller, 2013). Beyond offering additional marketing channels, social media are unique because of relationship building. **Earned exposure** is defined as when customers "relay their positive experiences" to others "via social media sites for reviews and ratings" (p. 89). In fact, early research found that three-fourths of comments to retailer sites were positive. Still, potential customers "want to see negative reviews to be able to accurately assess the degree of product risk they face when purchasing" (Tuten, 2008, p. 121). The ultimate goal in most advertising and marketing campaigns is to convert people, through a **conversion** process, from having initial interest into completing a sale of products or services:

> The basis of social media is informal conversation. Prospects want to be involved in a dialogue, not subjected to a stream of sales pitches. Even when no back-and-forth conversation is taking place, a company's posts need to sound like human speech. (P. Miller, 2013, p. 92)

McKinsey Partner David Edelman (2013) writes that social media began as unstructured, spontaneous activity, but organic development generates little strategy and may inflate company fears and sometimes lead to denial of importance. His Boston marketing firm identified four foundations:

1. *Customer care* must address complaints: "Having a formal social care team that peels off those posts and handles them in a structured way, with real case management tools to resolve problems is essential" (para. 3). Cost per case is a fraction of telephone customer service.
2. *Risk management* involves careful use of filters and disclaimers: "Few have a formal triage system laid out for which types of posts can simply adhere to some basic guidelines and go out, which ones need legal review, and what just cannot be sent" (para. 4).
3. *Content maximization* relates to leveraging conversation monitoring and content repurposing: "Stepping back and rethinking how to unlock more vectors of content and then funneling access to it to those on the front line of posting can amortize the value of content investments, and open up more ways to get engagement" (para. 5)
4. *Analytics* are important "to get ahead of the sentiment of the market" and amplify content in it: "[W]e have seen enormous value from social analytics that enable spotting new innovation ideas, building social lead flows, and testing marketing messages before going big" (para. 6).

Because of the nature of the more subtle social media conversion process, advertising and marketing content are being adapted to blend with editorial content.

Digital native advertising, which looks like online journalism, is projected to increase 30% in 2014 at Forbes' BrandVoice (Mickey, 2013). The BrandVoice 10% annual increase pushed beyond 20% of all ad revenue in 2013, which means that online advertising is beginning to pay the bills. One of more than two dozen advertisers, Zurich Insurance, created a newsroom link from the ad. This drives traffic to news releases, newsletters and other media content. BrandVoice allows advertisers to attach their brands to the trusted Forbes business brand. The idea is to present sponsored and branded content within an editorial context of Forbes content, and to move the content based upon trending topics and popularity. It is easy to see why advertisers would be pleased to be associated with business news content and the Forbes online brand. At the same time, the rapidly growing revenue stream is good news for traditional print publishers, as magazines struggle to survive in an era of print declining circulation and advertising revenues. The idea that online advertising can be larger than print advertising is seen as a life jacket for print journalism. The key to successful native advertising campaigns is linkage to audience measurement of social network activity, as the content is shared.

David Carr, media reporter at *The New York Times*, worried that native advertising might diminish the credibility of journalism because of its proximity to news content:

> Now the new rage is "native advertising," which is to say advertising wearing the uniform of journalism, mimicking the storytelling aesthetic of the host site. Buzzfeed, Forbes, The Atlantic and, more recently, *The New Yorker*, have all

developed a version of native advertising, also known as sponsored content; if you are on Buzzfeed, World of Warcraft might have a sponsored post on, say, 10 reasons your virtual friends are better than your real ones. (Carr, 2013, para. 3)

Carr wrote that Wonderfactory founder Joe McCambley, one of the pioneers of banner advertising in 1994, is among those raising issues about native ads. Among the questions about sponsored content is clear disclosure through labeling for the reader. McCambley told Carr that it is a mistake for publishers to offer PR and advertising firms direct access to content management systems. *The Atlantic* made one of the earliest mistakes when it allowed the Church of Scientology to publish a sponsored story within the site's content stream. The publication quickly issued a simple apology: "We screwed up" (Stelter & Haughney, 2013, para. 1).

Online publications, anxious to grow revenue, are tempted to allow sponsored posts that may look much like editorial content—even using similar design and art standards. Forbes' online site features a mixture of content types, which may add to the confusion by diminishing traditional advertising separation from news. Forbes was "incubating this whole notion of giving marketers a seat at the table" beginning in 2010, and the native advertising idea spread to other online publications desperate to grow new revenue streams (Sebastian, 2013, para. 4). In this sense, current trends return us to the early issues faced with media advertising.

Advertising and Marketing Theories

The advertising and marketing industries experienced explosive growth, as products were marketed through commercial mass media, such as radio and television. We are now experiencing an important online shift. As the book *Youtility* describes it, consumers now expect trustworthy online information and answers: "Success flows to organizations that inform, not organizations that promote" (Baer, 2013, p. xi):

> Youtility is marketing upside down. Instead of marketing that's needed by companies, Youtility is marketing that's wanted by customers. Youtility is massively useful information, provided for free, that creates long-term trust and kinship between your company and your customers. (p. 3)

Baer (2013) relates this fundamental shift to traditional marketing ideas:

- Top-of-Mind Awareness—branding through "a sustained level of marketing and messaging" (p. 7) that influences customers at the time of purchase.
- Frame-of-Mind Awareness—"reaching potential customers when they are in an active shopping and buying mode" (p. 17).
- Friend-of-Mine Awareness—"your prospective customers must consider you a friend" (p. 26) to compete for their time, attention and loyalty.

This type of "smart marketing" uses data to determine what customers want, and then it offers planning and social media strategy that attempts to account for ROI. A solid social marketing plan must account for labor and technology costs related to social media operation, and then determine if the effort produces satisfactory results.

📱 **BOX 5.1   4 P'S—PRODUCT, PRICE, PLACE AND PROMOTION
           MARKETING MIX**

E. Jerome McCarthy, a marketing professor at Michigan State and Notre Dame, developed the often-mentioned marketing decisions first known as the 4 P's in his book *Basic Marketing: A Managerial Approach* (1960/1981). Product refers to goods, services and support. Price is about the cost of something, including money and time. Place refers to either a point-of-sale or other contexts, such as online, geography, demographic target or sales experience. Promotion is about advertising, publicity and branding. The model helps companies ask the right marketing questions in development of a plan. For example, marketers want to know how a product satisfies consumer wants and needs, which features are unique to the competition, and who wants it. Pricing is a function of perceived value, profit margins and price points. Place focuses on where consumers can find the product or service. Promotion is the P that we are interested in most when examining social media. Online conversation may be very important in terms of friends functioning as opinion leaders. Traditional marketing media may diffuse to individual influencers within social media spaces. For example, Pinterest is considered a good platform for sharing product photographs and descriptions. This may trigger sharing, questions and even website clicks that could be converted to sales.

McCarthy (1960/1981) explored what he called a "marketing mix" within a "dynamic social and political environment" (pp. v–vi). By the seventh edition of the popular book, he viewed "social responsibility" and "consumerism" as "hot" marketing topics (p. vi). Yet, in advance of what later was called the corporate responsibility movement, McCarthy's marketing focus was on individual cognitive steps in the process: motivation, investigation, organization and utilization (p. viii). The idea that "selling" and "advertising" were "negative" words (p. 3) cultivated an idea that we produce and consume: "Consumers and producers must continually interact" (pp. 11, 13). If the four P's happen within "controllable" spaces that are "cultural" and within a "social environment" (p. 52), then marketing would need to be focused on how to "manage channels" (p. 338). The match between "target customers and media" (p. 495) was somewhat uncertain because of challenges in tracking media exposure. Marketing, then, was a promotion challenge of "informing, persuading, reminding" within a "frantically competitive" environment (p. 600). The traditional marketing view in 1981, however, could barely see the coming impact of the personal computer and electronics industry. New products were about to be introduced in very new places.

By 2013, a *Harvard Business Journal* posting urged that it was time to update the marketing mix. The **business-to-business (B2B)** model is less focused on products and more related to "the imperative to deliver solutions" (Ettenson, Conrado, & Knowles, 2013, para. 1). Research suggested that the four P's approach has three shortcomings: it leads to technology and quality, which do not differentiate; it does not emphasize enough the value of solutions; and it "distracts them from leveraging their advantage as a trusted source of diagnostics, advice, and problem solving" (para. 2). Their SAVE model shifts each of the four P's:

- Products → Solutions
- Place → Access
- Price → Value
- Promotion → Education

The SAVE marketing approach fits nicely into the social media context of talking to favorite brands for informational purposes.

Sources:

Ettenson, R., Conrado, E., & Knowles, J. (2013, January-February). Rethinking the 4 P's. *Harvard Business Review.* http://hbr.org/2013/01/rethinking-the-4-ps/

McCarthy, E. J. (1960/1981). *Basic Marketing: A Managerial Approach, seventh edition.* Homewood, IL: Richard D. Irwin.

Mind Tools (n.d.). The Marketing Mix and 4 Ps, Understanding How to Position Your Market Offering. www.mindtools.com/pages/article/newSTR_94.htm

Critical perspectives see what is happening across screens as feeding consumption:

> Media marketing narratives engage in materially oriented hegemonic address to consumer citizens, seeking to align and reconcile the interests of all . . . Our immersing in brandscapes from Coffee Bean culture to Starbucks connoisseurship may be imagined . . . Consumption across these familiar forms of life does not so much require our engaging in the diversified "work of culture." (Wilson, 2011, pp. 29–30)

Product branding is seen as immersing individuals in physical and virtual spaces that help define meaning for consumers. "They are not only public but private (e.g., the personal branding of the self as a subject to trust on Facebook)" (p. 117).

Consumers

The selling process typically has been structured on generating leads for sales people, who qualify a prospect and make a pitch or proposal. This also may involve a selling process that ends with closing or losing a sale. Paige Miller (2013), however, proposes that consumers follow a social media marketing customer-driven path of *finding* sites and content, *learning* through engagement and listening, *validating* information through reviews and community conversation, *using* via demonstrations or a trial, *buying* through a sales process, and *advocacy* after the purchase (p. 95). The last step is perhaps most unique to social media. Companies may announce through social media that they have a new client, or the new customer may endorse the product. A company may reward brand loyalty through a special program that has a linkage to their social media marketing communication plan. Throughout the process, social media conversation plays an important role in strengthening public perceptions of the brand.

Branding

Corporate brand management may be seen as a PR function of "promoting and protecting the reputation of the corporation" (Morley, 2009, p. 4). At the same time, advertising agencies see that their work is to "build a strong, distinctive, memorable brand" (Williams, 2005, p. 3). Branding is closely related to a company's purpose, or "reason for being" (p. 9). This may drive a desire to position the brand as being distinct from all others. "It means not only deciding what you are, but what you are not" (p. 10). Leaders of a "focused, engaged business" (p. 181) must determine how to execute branding through communication. In an age of social media, branding involves both purposeful online communication and also recognition of critical moments when the best choice is silence.

Branding involves a "bond," which has been described as "a powerful emotional connection" (Morley, 2009, p. 7). Social media engagement creates real-time opportunities for brand representatives to connect with the public and establish or reinforce relationships. Advertisers showed a lot of early interest in buying space on Facebook. Edwards (2013) notes that $1.8 of Facebook's $2 billion in quarterly revenue is generated by advertising (para. 1). *Business Insider* used a variety of data and sources to estimate top Facebook advertisers over a 12-month period. Samsung, with about $100 million in advertising, appeared to top all other brands, and it spent about $10 million per week during the launch of its Galaxy S III smartphone. Edwards (2013) listed the top 12 advertisers:

1. Samsung
2. Procter & Gamble
3. Microsoft
4. AT&T
5. Amazon
6. Verizon
7. Nestlé
8. Unilever
9. American Express
10. Walmart
11. Coca-Cola
12. Starbucks

Coca-Cola, with more than 82 million Facebook fans, has more than any other brand. The complete list of advertisers represents many of the top global brands and advertisers.

Promotions, Market Research and Segmentation

Customers use social network sites to create and distribute "brand-centric" content and media (Tuten, 2008, p. 101). Within this broad concept are several types of potential relationships with companies (pp. 102–103):

- Simple consumer-generated media is created without prior request.
- Consumer-solicited media, or participatory advertising, occurs when brands ask consumers to create, for example, their own advertisement.
- Incentivized consumer-generated media offers prizes for submissions.

- Consumer-fortified media result occurs when a professional advertisement sparks trusted consumer conversation.
- Compensated consumer-generated media is a term used to describe paid bloggers and other arrangements.

The various arrangements may create a more democratic form of advertising, may encourage crowdsourcing, may develop engagement, and may offer opportunities for long-term relationships.

Integrated Marketing Communication (IMC)

The IMC concept addresses a need to integrate brand-marketing communication across previously separate industries of PR, advertising and marketing. IMC is designed to take a step back from specific messaging and employ integration of approaches to achieve strategic goals. Clow & Baack (2011) see IMC as involving coordination of all marketing—including promotions and social media. An IMC plan, for example, might address shifting funding from traditional advertising to non-traditional media, including social media platforms.

This involves more than simply having a presence on a social media site. Vaynerchuk (2013), an early promoter of social marketing, identifies his rules of engagement:

> Brands and small businesses want to look relevant, engaged, and authentic, but when their content is banal and unimaginative, it only makes them look lame. Content for the sake of content is pointless. Tone deaf posts, especially in the form of come-ons and promos, just take up space, and are justifiably ignored by the public. Only outstanding content can cut through the noise. (p. 16)

Vaynerchuk defines outstanding content as that which: 1) is native to platform; 2) does not interrupt the social media flow; 3) rarely makes demands; 4) leverages pop culture; 5) contains micro-nuggets of "information, humor, commentary, or inspiration;" and 6) stays consistent and self-aware (pp. 16–28). Within this framework, social media storytelling may resonate with viewers and spread sometimes at a viral rate. The "native to platform" idea is an extremely important social media consideration. A photograph posted on Facebook may not fit the context and moment within Instagram, which is stylized. A tweet with a Twitter handle, shortened words and a hashtag will appear out of place on Pinterest. Likewise, Twitter feeds are a good example of flow that changes by the moment. While it may be useful for a content manager to use Tweetdeck or Hootsuite to organize social media conversations, it is crucial to recognize what is being said within a particular platform at a given time. Online engagement translates to conversation that is aware of what is happening within the culture—from Super Bowl chatter to a storm response. A social media brand manager understands her or his personal brand, company brands and those of others. Consistent and sensitive messages help build online trust over time, which may be leveraged in the future.

Social Media Strategic Planning

One important distinction between social networking site activity and social media is the role of social business models. Cha (2013) identified value creation, sources of competency, target market and revenue as four business considerations. Value is theoretically created through successful brand positioning within the market, but branding also is considered a specific competency (p. 63). Social media engagement is created through positive interaction within a specific social media online space. For example, Twitter's real-time information positioning is different from LinkedIn's professional and job seeker target market, which typically is not as connected to a moment in time (p. 76). It is important within advertising and marketing perspectives for a team to develop social media plans that guide responses during a crisis, but also direct the general purposes and goals of ongoing engagement. Increasingly, teams employ an integrated media approach that weds PR, advertising, marketing and general business plans.

Awareness and Engagement

Awareness begins with online **impressions**. An advertising buyer may bid on a sponsored search keyword that matches a user search and produces a high page ranking. This creates a consumer point of entry (Jansen, 2011, p. 77). A click-through rate (CTR) may be measured as the number of clicks divided by impressions (p. 77). In other words, advertisers are interested in how a sponsored search was observed by consumers and served as a catalyst to drive a percentage of these users to a website for possible conversion. Social media conversation is important as a means to either spark the initial search or generate traffic through use of a direct link. CTRs appear to be in decline from the height of an era of searching for online content. This is being replaced by content that is pushed out across social media sites. Awareness is a cognitive processing of initial information about a product or service. Through engagement with other consumers, paid brand managers or other representatives may increase motivation to learn more.

Google (2013) studied rapidly growing mobile media usage. In a Nielsen study, Google explored the purchase path when consumers use mobile devices, such as smartphones and tablets. The research team studied 950 people, as well as a panel of mobile users over two weeks, and found the following points to be true:

1. **Consumers spend time researching in mobile.** Consumers spend 15+ hours per week researching on their smartphone and, on average, visit mobile websites 6 times.
2. **Mobile research starts with search.** More smartphone users start researching about products or services on a search engine vs. a branded mobile site or app.
3. **Location proximity matters to mobile consumers.** 69% of consumers expect businesses to be within 5 miles or less of their location.
4. **Purchase immediacy is key.** Over half of consumers want to make a purchase within an hour of conducting research on their smartphone.
5. **Mobile influences purchases across channels.** 93% of people who use mobile to research go on to purchase of a product or service. Most purchases happen in physical stores (p. 3).

The proliferation of smartphones and inexpensive tablets is leading marketers to focus on the mobile path to purchase in order to strategically develop campaigns that start with a search trigger and end with purchasing at a local store. A website visit is part of the process, but not all of it. In areas such as health and nutrition (41%), automotive (38%) and home and garden (42%), more than one-third of consumers begin the shopping process with a mobile search (p. 8). Branded apps are also important in beginning the purchase process in finance (36%), electronics (22%), and apparel and beauty (21%) (p. 9). For some areas, such as restaurants, a nearby location is very important to a majority of mobile consumers (61%) (p. 12). The desire for purchase immediacy means that the brick and mortar retail world remains important—83% of mobile consumers want to buy within a day, although about half of those now make an online purchase (pp. 14, 17). The social media component of the mobile path to purchase is the important role that consumer reviews play in the process. Google talks about consumer research, with 93% of the people in their study using mobile devices to help them decide. This is consistent with Stanford University research findings: "As you might suspect, the research shows that a wealth of online product information and user reviews is causing a fundamental shift in how consumers make decisions" (Richtel, 2013, para. 2). Traditionally, consumers would pick a mid-priced option between three choices, but reviews now allow consumers to dig deeper in determining value. This finding has important social media implications. It means every consumer has the power to be an influencer through his or her reviews on sites such as Amazon and Yelp. Advertisers and marketers that engage with consumers likely to be reviewers have an opportunity to create positive experiences, brand loyalty and future purchasing persuasion.

Search Engine Optimization (SEO)

Online searches remain one of the most important methods for finding information on the Internet. While information pushed out through social media is increasingly a factor, SEO literacy skills help practitioners achieve successful reach with their messages. More people, for example, will see bloggers' content, if headlines and tags are SEO-friendly. Likewise, an online press release should be optimized with the SEO words that people associate with when thinking about the ideas. A Google search begins with a person thinking about what they are looking for and then entering a word or phrase. Quickly, Google begins to suggest keywords (also identified within computer coding of a site) that are popular, and continuously changing computer algorithms, also driving Yahoo! and Bing, benefit some Web pages over others. Website and content operators can control **search engine result placements (SERP)** (Fleischner, 2013, p. 24). "Off-page optimization" is a function of links to a page from other popular and similar pages (p. 61). Social media may positively impact SEO through profile links and rankings:

> If you have a Facebook account it likely includes links of various kinds—links to books you're reading, products and websites you recommend, and hopefully links back to your websites and blogs. By the very nature of Facebook, it carries tremendous authority. If you are linking to your own website, it passes that authority back to you. (p. 120)

Beyond links, social media activity—likes, favorites, comments, etc.—may be influential. Google property YouTube, for example, is an important social media site for practicing great SEO. Through keywords and links, video offers access to "one of the largest sources of traffic on the planet" (Fleischner, 2013, p. 123).

Kaushik (2010) offers a comprehensive model for understanding SEO. He uses clickstream data, multiple outcomes analysis, and experimentation and testing to focus massive consumer data into usable customer information (p. 7). Customer voice, competitive intelligence and insights help businesses understand why products are purchased or not:

> The degree of positive or negative engagement lies on a continuum that ranges from low involvement, namely, the psychological state of apathy, to high. An engaged person is someone with an above-average involvement . . . Customers can be positively or negatively engaged with a company or product. (p. 57)

Kaushik (2010) views this involvement as connected to "emotional states and rational beliefs" (p. 57). One can easily see how social media conversation, with its use of trust, may elevate or lower involvement. For example, a company post might express pride of winning an award, and this may be connected to an increase in trust levels. Likewise, a company representative engaging with a complaining customer might express sympathy and offer to correct the problem.

Google has an approved set of strategies to improve a page rank, and this is referred to as "white hat SEO" (Williams, 2013, p. 7). There also are "black hat" SEO strategies, such as "on-page keyword stuffing to backlinking blasts using software" (p. 7). Google and other search engines seek to point users to trusted sites, whether or not high search rankings are a function of payment. An historically trusted site has a lot of positive SEO, and search engine algorithms allow for some negative SEO that would label a new site as spam. Social media interaction is an important way to generate positive conversation: ". . . if they ask a question, make sure you answer it as this starts a dialogue with your target audience and builds trust and authority" (p. 87).

Return on Investment (ROI)

Most of what we call advertising and marketing is predicated on the goal of converting consumers into customers of products or services. The consumer process may begin with an online search that leads to social media engagement. The use of a search engine, such as Google, involves entry of a "term" that may be linked to a "keyword," an advertisement or a "sponsored-search result" (Jansen, 2011, p. xviii). For businesses, ROI measurement is related to the use of online platforms for generated leads and conversions to sales:

> The objective of the advertiser is to find the "sweet spot" of terms that will generate significant volumes of convertible traffic. This set of keywords is advertiser-dependent. This selection can generally be done through concentration of a few keywords in the head, a lot of terms in the tail, or a combination of both. (p. 55)

ROI can be achieved through alignment of social media terms used with advertising and marketing website keywords. In order to be effective, these keywords must surface in specific screen locations identified through "eye-tracking patterns" research (p. 72). In general, paid search is most effective when it appears at the top of a page or on the left side of it. These are hot areas of screen viewers for those using languages that read left to right, such as in the United States.

There is ongoing debate about whether or not ROI can or should be computed for social media activities. Initially, there was an interest in justifying social media to the C-suite managers who did not understand it by making an ROI argument. ROI social media measures, though, tended to be secondary and indirect. Current thinking focuses on clear social media benefits: "the new metrics evaluate social media strategies in terms of audience-building, brand awareness and customer relations" (Heggestuen, 2013, para. 3). Marketers moved away from revenue per customer metrics, at the same time as they increased social media budgets. From this perspective, "audience reach, engagement, and sentiment" are most important (para. 9). A Facebook friend's share, for example, is more likely to be seen in news feeds (29–35%) than brand pages (para. 10). According to *Business Insider*, "Post reach is the most fundamental indicator of reach on Facebook, but it's important to track it relative to the number of page fans and enrich it with complimentary indicators" (para. 12). Fans and likes alone are seen as "feel good" or "vanity measures" that do not reflect meaningful marketing context (para. 16). Social media probably have more in common with traditional personal influence than advertising or marketing impact. Still, advertising media buyers now seek to develop integrated marketing campaigns in which social media components reinforce other messages.

At the same time, social media have the potential to spark negative sentiment within social network conversations. Brand managers must tune in on regular and systematic conversation monitoring and engagement in order to avoid missing important moments of influence.

Cost of Ignoring (COI)

MacLean (2013) identified the cost of ignoring (COI) as a measurement of "social shyness" (para. 2). Companies need to respond to those consumers and customers using social media to communicate. Therefore, social listening and engagement is a very important strategy for customer service, reputation management, crowdsourcing, collaboration and recruitment (para. 5–9). Engagement may drive customer loyalty and help manage any negative sentiment being expressed by consumers. By being a part of social media communities while not in an advertising or marketing mode, it is possible to build credibility that may be important to use later.

Advertising and Marketing Case Studies

The University of Chicago, in the south side neighborhood of Hyde Park, is in a bit of a food desert with few stores and restaurants. Beyond the campus, there is a nearby, small business district with only a few places to eat lunch. Food truck vendors have seen the opportunities for driving onto campus and offering students, faculty and staff a variety of selections from convenient locations. These change from day to day, so the food trucks use Twitter and other social media to identify daily locations and cuisines.

> @BridgeportPasty1m: UofC, you get to see us again for our scheduled day, you lucky dogs! Try the new Gobbler AND Broccoli and Cheese soup while they last. Yum! (November 13, 2013)
>
> @taquerofusion54m: #HydePark (58th & Ellis) . . . We'll be in your area by 11 am!! Come and get your #HumpDay Taco on! @UChicago @uchiNOMgo. (January 30, 2013)

Figure 5.1 University of Chicago food trucks tweet in the morning before they serve lunch customers. Photo courtesy Holly Lipschultz, October, 2013.

Real-time Social Marketing

Social media marketing frequently happens in real-time without much of a delay between the time of an initial conversation and commercial response. Mobile smartphones position a consumer at a specific location within a specific amount of time. Applications such as FourSquare encourage users to check in at a business for access to specials and coupons. Customer loyalty programs can take advantage of communication tools by literally reaching out to nearby customers with new offers. Macy and Thompson (2011) connect real-time social marketing to a system of **customer relationship management (CRM)** that includes customer satisfaction, loyalty and retention (pp. 40–41). "When marketers approach social media as a viable business intelligence platform, they often get unexpected insights into consumer opinions and shared experiences" (p. 58).

Successes

Wendy's turned fast food marketing on its head with a campaign designed to shift the focus away from issues often associated with consuming unhealthy food. The pretzel pub chicken sandwich was promoted using overly dramatic soap opera YouTube videos that were produced based on tweets that used the #PretzelLoveStories hashtag, such as:

> @Cborbzz3: You caught my eye, your scent made me float, you make my mouth salivate. I miss you. #PretzelLoveStories. (July 8, 2013)

The user-generated content features humor that engages the audience and potential customers. Wendy's initiated the campaign with two videos—one about a love triangle and the other with a woman behind bars. The result was positive social media across platforms. On Facebook, for example, a video was shared more than 2,000 times and liked more than 12,000 times. The use of crowdsourcing for video content development was a unique way to utilize engagement. At the same time, though, some complained about not knowing that the hashtag was related to a Wendy's sandwich promotion. The successful social media campaign also opened the door to brand confusion, as some users tweeted about other pretzel brands.

((•)) BOX 5.2 THOUGHT LEADER ROBERT MOORE

Before the advent of social media, institutions had the opportunity to be more considered and/or deliberate in how they addressed their stakeholders or the public-at-large. While there might have been rumors or word-of-mouth concern about certain actions of the institution, these were circulated relatively "locally" among existing communities, alumni groups, or other interested observers. With Twitter, in particular, that has entirely changed. News now breaks on Twitter (supported by Facebook, Instagram, Tumblr, etc.) and can spread like wildfire—whether or not the news is actually based in fact. As a result, the institution has to balance on a knife-edge of conflicting

Figure 5.2 @LipmanHearne.
Courtesy LipmanHearne.

responsibilities: the need for transparency and engagement with its concerned stakeholders, and the need to actually be sure of what's going on before responding—which isn't always easy. This also brings up the issue of "who speaks for the institution" and whether or not a staff member tweeting on his/her feed is authorized to be the transmitter of official information (which can bring up a whole can of worms in terms of the conflict noted above), or if the tweets are strictly personal.

Institutions must stay current and integrate traditional (print, earned media, print and out-of-home advertising, etc.) and emerging media in strong, effective programs that build upon each other in order to capitalize on the strength and potential of each medium or channel—rather than cannibalizing one to feed the other or having it all run amok. And, as is often the case in higher education, having to manage and fill all these emerging media without significant additional staff, new training investments, new technology, and other resources remains and will remain a real problem.

I believe that "engagement management" is going to be a big issue moving forward: the training and deployment of communications professionals who can understand, integrate, and utilize the complex opportunities that traditional and emerging media offer in terms of outreach, behavior tracking, analytics, program design and refinement for timely and effective response, budget allocation, and the like. Professionals trained or experienced in more traditional media will have to learn the new realities, and digital communicators will have to understand and deploy the "tried and true" methods that still work with many stakeholder audiences. To date, training and professional development tend to go down these two separate paths; in the future, integration will be absolutely necessary.

(continued)

Robert Moore, Ph.D. is President & CEO at Lipman Hearne—a firm that helps market higher education, non-profit and other organizations. He is a nationally recognized authority on non-profit branding and marketing practices in higher education. Moore has more than 30 years of experience providing marketing counsel and creative services for non-profit organizations. Outside of academe, his clients have included the Ford Foundation, Mayo Clinic and others. He is founding member of the CASE Industry Advisory Council. His doctorate is in English from the University of Illinois at Chicago.

Failures

During the first years of the social media communication era, numerous companies have struggled to use the new form of branding. Miranda Miller (2013) reported on KFC's use of #IatetheBones—a Twitter campaign that continued to produce negative sentiment. In attempting to raise awareness about its new boneless chicken brand, KFC's hashtag led to "sharing memes of people choking on chicken bones, or Hannibal Lecter" (para. 7). Apparently, neither KFC nor its agency predicted that the brand would be associated with the cannibalistic killer featured in the film *The Silence of the Lambs*.

At about the same time, social media erupted over automaker's Hyundai's use of a failed suicide attempt in a video designed to say its emissions are clean (Brockwell, 2013). It sparked an open letter from a woman whose father had died in a similar suicide:

> Surprisingly, when I reached the conclusion of your video, where we see that the man has in fact *not* died thanks to Hyundai's clean emissions, I did not stop crying. I did not suddenly feel that my tears were justified by your amusing message. I just felt empty. And sick. And I wanted my dad. (para. 7)

The competition for attention within social media in some cases has led advertisers and marketers to ignore the risks associated with edgy content. In a digital world in which everyone has a platform to respond, more than ever creative teams must be able to predict all possible responses. In 2012 alone, a long list of social media failures resulted from a lack of anticipation to how people would use content:

- The McDonald's #mcdstories hashtag was used by people telling about bad experiences, resulting in unexpected negative publicity.
- Celeb Boutique tweeted following the Aurora, Colorado movie theatre shootings: "#Aurora is trending, clearly about our Kim K inspired #Aurora dress; Shop" (July 20, 2012).
- @KitchenAidUSA tweeted, "Obamas gma even knew it was going 2 b bad! She died 3 days b4 he became president. #nbcpolitics" and then had to apologize (October 3, 2013).
- @Gap tweeted, following Hurricane Sandy, "All impacted by #Sandy stay safe! We'll be doing lots of Gap.com shopping today. How about you?" The company removed the tweet following a negative reaction (Fiegerman, 2012).

Clearly, some of the largest brands ran into trouble for a variety of reasons—poor advertising content, unsupervised content managers, weak editing for real-time processes and even hacked accounts. It appeared that brands were learning through trial and error to be careful in social media.

Lessons

A case can be made that all digital marketing departs from traditional forms, and social media magnify the differences. Greg Satell (@Digitaltonto, 2013) contrasts the traditional purchase funnel (Awareness -> Opinion -> Consideration -> Preference -> Purchase) with a triangular visualization of Awareness, Advocacy and Sales (para. 8). Within it, consideration and loyalty flow. The non-linear continuum should lead marketers to "shift from grabbing attention to holding attention" (para. 10). The idea is to create a valuable exchange between the brand and the consumer. For example, the Nike+ community page told users which Facebook friends have joined, and shares competitive training data across social networks.

Richards and Yakob (2007) were among the first to recognize that consumers began to see traditional advertising as an interruption:

> Today, in response to an aversion to advertising, some of the world's leading brands have begun to craft an entirely new model for communications to help them earn the right to talk to consumers. They're doing this by making their marketing valuable, developing brand communications that deliver a genuine service value to consumers, free and with no strings attached. (para. 4)

Social media fit nicely into the marketing shift toward creating valuable consumer services—so valuable that people want to share positive experiences with connections on their social networks. At the same time, there is skepticism about the effectiveness of social media marketing. An IBM report on Black Friday sales in 2013 suggested that "only 1% of orders on shopping sites came from people who visited a social network immediately before" (Fiegerman, 2013, para. 2). IBM Smarter Commerce Strategy Director Jay Henderson told *Mashable* that "social networks have a 'huge indirect influence' on shopping decisions by building brand and product awareness" (para. 3). Social marketers have not developed precise measurement of what happens when a future customer is exposed to social media, leaves these sites but then is later motivated to visit a website to purchase products. While retailers, such as Amazon and Walmart, have hundreds of thousands of brand interactions during the holiday season kickoff period, only some lead to sales. Pinterest and Facebook appear to be influential generating consumer interest.

The bottom line in social media marketing is developing a program with an eye toward generating new leads and sales, whether or not there is an immediate ROI (Baer, 2013). Social interaction requires patience. "That doesn't mean it will, or should, take you multiple years to start seeing return on your useful marketing, but recognize that you are planting seeds that will bloom in time, not necessarily overnight" (p. 184). Development of blog content as a marketing vehicle, for example, may have some links back to a commercial website, but not too many. "These blogs should add value and be high quality . . . and post unique information" (Williams, 2013, p. 64). Authenticity of branding is built upon the role of quality content in developing reputation and relationships (Morley, 2009, p. 204). All industries interact with audiences through content presented within media networks (Ognyanova & Monge, 2013). "In a new media landscape characterized by networked production, networked distribution and networked consumption, relational thinking should be an essential aspect" (p. 85). Contextual social media should yield positive outcomes for advertisers and marketers.

■ DISCUSSION QUESTIONS: STRATEGIES AND TACTICS

1. How can we better understand relationships consumers have with brands through social media sites? What are the most important benefits and constraints within these interactions?
2. What risks may exist for brands using native advertising and sponsored content to drive media exposure within contexts that appear similar to traditional news stories?
3. How can brands leverage the importance of social media interaction with consumers to grow product sales through indirect effects from ongoing online communication?

References

Baer, J. (2013). *Youtility, Why Smart Marketing is About Hype Not Help*. New York, NY: Penguin Group.

Brockwell, H. (2013, April 25). An Open Letter to Hyundai. *Slate*. www.slate.com/blogs/browbeat/2013/04/25/hyundai_suicide_ad_an_ad_exec_responds_with_memories_of_her_father.html

Carr, D. (2013, September 15). The Media Equation: Storytelling Ads May Be Journalism's New Peril. *The New York Times, B1* (September 16). www.nytimes.com/2013/09/16/business/media/storytelling-ads-may-be-journalisms-new-peril.html?pagewanted=1&_r=1&smid=tw-share&&pagewanted=all

Cha, J. (2013). Business Models of Most-visited U.S. Social Networking Sites. In A. B. Albarran (Ed.), *The Social Media Industries*, pp. 60–85. New York, NY: Routledge.

Clow, K. E., & Baack, D. (2011). *Integrated Advertising, Promotion and Marketing Communications, fifth edition*. Boston, MA: Prentice Hall.

Edelman, D. (2013, October 30). Say Hi to the Social Media Elephant in the Room. *LinkedIn*. www.linkedin.com/today/post/article/20131030130324-1816165-say-hi-to-the-social-media-elephant-in-the-room

Edwards, J. (2013, November 28). These Are the 35 Biggest Advertisers on Facebook. *Business Insider*. www.businessinsider.com/top-advertisers-on-facebook-2013-11#ixzz2mKOsoSGf

Ettenson, R., Conrado, E., & Knowles, J. (2013, January-February). Rethinking the 4 P's. *Harvard Business Review*. http://hbr.org/2013/01/rethinking-the-4-ps/

Fiegerman, S. (2013, November 30). Social Media Drove Just 1% of Black Friday Online Sales. *Mashable*. http://mashable.com/2013/11/30/black-friday-statistics/

Fiegerman, S. (2012, November 25). 11 Biggest Social Media Disasters of 2012. *Mashable*. http://mashable.com/2012/11/25/social-media-business-disasters-2012/

Fleischner, M. H. (2013). *SEO Made Simple, Strategies for Dominating the World's Largest Search Engine, third edition*. Lexington, KY: Michael H. Fleischner.

Google (2013, November). *Mobile Path to Purchase, Five Key Findings*. Google Insights. www.google.com/think/research-studies/mobile-path-to-purchase-5-key-findings.html

Heggestuen, J. (2013, October 22). The Death of Social ROI—Companies Are Starting to Drop the Idea That They Can Track Social Media's Dollar Value. www.businessinsider.com/the-myth-of-social-roi-2013-10

Jansen, J. (2011). *Understanding Sponsored Search, Core Elements of Keyword Advertising*. New York, NY: Cambridge University Press.

Katz, H. (2007). *The Media Handbook, third edition*. Mahwah, NJ: Lawrence Erlbaum.

Kaushik, A. (2010). *Web Analytics 2.0, The Art of Online Accountability & Science of Customer Centricity*. Indianpolis, IN: Wiley.

Kelley, L. D., Jugenheimer, D. W., & Sheehan, K. B. (2012). *Advertising Media Workbook and Sourcebook, third edition*. Armonk, NY: M. E. Sharpe.

MacLean, H. (2013, May 28). The Cost of Ignoring Social Media. Salesforce Marketing Cloud Blog. www.salesforcemarketingcloud.com/blog/2013/05/cost-of-ignoring-social-media/

Macy, B., & Thompson, T. (2011). *The Power of Real-Time Social Media Marketing*. New York, NY: McGraw-Hill.

McCarthy, E. J. (1960/1981). *Basic Marketing: A Managerial Approach, seventh edition*. Homewood, IL: Richard D. Irwin.

Mickey, B. (2013, October 10). Forbes BrandVoice Accounts for 20 Percent of Total Revenue. www.foliomag.com/2013/forbes-brandvoice-accounts-20-percent-total-advertising-revenue#.UmE4cJTwKeu

Miller, M. (2013, April). Brands Gone Wild: Social Media Marketing Fails & Lessons Learned. Online Marketing Blog. www.toprankblog.com/2013/04/social-fails-lessons/

Miller, P. (2013). Social Media Marketing. In A. B. Albarran (Ed.), *The Social Media Industries*, pp. 86–104. New York, NY: Routledge.

Mind Tools (n.d.). The Marketing Mix and 4 Ps, Understanding How to Position Your Market Offering. www.mindtools.com/pages/article/newSTR_94.htm

Morley, M. (2009). *The Global Corporate Brand Book*. New York, NY: Palgrave Macmillan.

Ognyanova, K., & Monge, P. (2013). A Multitheoretical, Multilevel, Multidimensional Network Model of the Media System. In E. L. Cohen (Ed.), *Communication Yearbook 37*, pp. 67–93. New York, NY: Routledge.

Richards, B., & Yakob, F. (2007, March 19). The New Quid Pro Quo. *Adweek*. www.adweek.com/news/advertising/new-quid-pro-quo-88322

Richtel, M. (2013, December 7). There's Power in All Those User Reviews. *The New York Times*. www.nytimes.com/2013/12/08/business/theres-power-in-all-those-user-reviews.html

Satell, G. (2013, February 1). What Makes Digital Marketing Fundamentally Different? *Forbes*. www.forbes.com/sites/gregsatell/2013/02/01/what-makes-digital-marketing-fundamentally-different/

Sebastian, M. (2013, December 2). Need a Native-Ad Rock Star? Find a Former Forbes Exec. *Ad Age*. http://adage.com/article/media/forbes-breeding-ground-native-ad-experts/245475/

Stelter, B., & Haughney, C. (2013, January 15). Media Decoder: The Atlantic Apologizes for Scientology Ad. *The New York Times*. http://mediadecoder.blogs.nytimes.com/2013/01/15/the-atlantic-apologizes-for-scientology-ad/?_r=0

Tuten, T. L. (2008). *Advertising 2.0, Social Media Marketing in a Web 2.0 World*. Westport, CT: Praeger.

Vaynerchuk, G. (2013). *Jab, Jab, Jab, Right Hook*. New York, NY: HarperCollins.

Williams, A. (2013). *SEO 2013 & Beyond, Search Engine Optimization Will Never Be the Same Again!* Lexington, KY: Andy Williams.

Williams, T. (2005). *Take a Stand for Your Brand, Building a Great Agency Brand from the Inside Out*. Chicago, IL: The Copy Workshop.

Wilson, T. (2011). *Global Advertising, Attitudes and Audiences*. New York, NY: Routledge.

6   SOCIAL MEDIA METRICS AND ANALYTICS

"Prove your point with numbers, but make sure you attempt to do so with numbers that matter."

—Jay Baer (@jaybaer, 2013)

Social media offer a unique opportunity to measure human nature and communication behavior. With every online click, we leave a digital trail. Experts in measurement metrics and analytics are discovering how to collect, analyze and present data. Social media measurement serves basic business goals, which include raising revenue, lowering costs and increasing satisfaction among customers. In other words, measurement helps make the ROI case for social media tactics to sometimes-skeptical C-suite managers.

Traditional communication research methods emphasize rigorous and transparent methodologies. Researchers seek to ground studies in social theory, conceptualize measurement and operationalize definitions. Scientific research offers **reliability** or consistency of measurement from one time to the next (Wimmer & Dominick, 2013). This is important when using sampling to generalize about larger populations, as is the case in survey research. We hope to be able to reproduce results of our systematic observation. "Mass media researchers have a great deal to see, and virtually everyone is exposed to this information everyday" (p. 5). The research process can be divided into "phases"— the medium, its uses, medium effects and improvement (p. 6). Academic researchers also have concerns about the **validity** of measures because we cannot assume to know what social phenomena are being measured. Data points may or may not measure what we think is a valid observation. Only through repeated measures and replication of data can we build concepts around predictive theory and analytics. While social science involves statistical tests or rigorous qualitative frameworks, these requirements have not always been applied in the new field of social media measurement. Academic rigor is beginning to come to social media research through **transparency** of methods, but "cool" new online tools, more than scientific method, have, thus far, driven proprietary social media measurement.

Social media is still a young field that tends to be grounded in the business of social media marketing. As we become interested in social media, we naturally seek to measure online behavior. Unlike traditional experimental research, survey research, focus groups or content analyses, measurement of social media involves tracking online behavior and responding to it in real time. Savage (2011) explains that Twitter, for example, is "a surprising window" into "moods, thoughts, and activities of society" that may not be discovered by traditional research data: "Researchers are finding they can measure public sentiment, follow political activity, even spot earthquakes and flu outbreaks, just by running the chatter through algorithms that search for particular words and pinpoint message origins" (p. 18). We conceptualize social media measurement around awareness, engagement, persuasion, conversion and retention (Sterne, 2010, p. 15). We are interested in those users visiting sites, as well as their behavior while there.

Social Media Measures

Sterne (2010) was one of the first to understand the power of social media data and catalog dozens of possible measures. Some of the earliest important measurements of social media marketing consumers were (pp. xx–xxv):

- Buzz based upon number of impressions at a given time, on a specific date, time of year, channel, etc.
- Popularity
- Mainstream media mentions
- Number of fans, followers, friends, etc.
- Reach, or second-degree impressions
- Likes or favorites
- Sentiment
- Number of interactions or engagement rate
- Conversions to purchases

Behind these sometimes-crude measures was a desire to demonstrate social media ROI, which may be measured also as a business cost. Just as companies typically do not attach ROI to a receptionist's work, Edelman's Phil Gomes has asked, so why measure social media ROI? Further, a Cost of Ignoring (COI) was introduced as a way to say that social media offer both opportunities and risks (Radian6, 2013): "The COI of social media comes down to missed opportunities . . . you need to question your opportunity costs" (para. 4).

Miller (2013) sees social media marketing as part of the larger marketing task for businesses. This includes "relationship building" with prospects and customers, "earned exposure" through "unrequested endorsement" and customer sharing, "authentic insight" from comments, "search engine visibility" from posts, "cost savings" and tractable "results" (pp. 89–90). The marketing process involves ongoing engagement with customers. Much of what happens within social sites may be seen through the lens of earned media, or content the user spends time creating. In other words, ROI exchanges the cost of staffing brand community managers against measurable results that translate to new clients, potential new business and increased revenue opportunities.

See, Say, Feel, Do

One group has conceptualized social media measures as involving breaking down behavior into four fundamental types linked to ROI:

> The greatest obstacle to determining ROI doesn't happen on the back end once you've collected mounds of user engagement data like RTs, bounce rates, and the

number of "Likes." The main obstacle to determining ROI comes from a failure to define the "R" on the front end. What is the return you are trying to create? Without knowing what you are trying to accomplish, it's impossible to measure your success. (Gordon, 2012, p. 2)

KPI,

Gordon finds that social media are frequently related to "see" measures. Reach, for example, is a function of the number of eyeballs seeing a Facebook post. Impressions are this type of measure. Gordon (p. 5) lists the following "see" metrics:

- Facebook Page Like totals
- Twitter Follower totals
- Website traffic
- Email sign-ups
- RSS subscriptions
- Advertising impressions
- Earned media impressions

As social media content activate users through engagement Gordon's "say" measures—content likes, shares, re-tweets, email forwards, and Google +'s—all are data that can be measured. Beyond the quantitative measures, we can examine the qualitative comments and sentiment. It is easier to measure online comments than to track those offline statements activated by the original content. Social media users may have emotional responses to what they see or comment about, and the reaction, or the sentiment, may be important. Totaling the number of likes or +'s also provides a quantitative measure for "feel." At the end of the social media measurement process, "do" metrics allow us to track behavioral outcomes, such as making a product purchase. Conversion to sales is the most obvious behavioral objective. Organizations, such as non-profits, may be more interested in increasing the number of members and donations. Public radio stations, for example, need to raise money during annual fund drives, and social media tactics have become an important way to grow the numbers. Likewise, a campaign may be designed to increase attendance at a sponsored event, activate advocacy for a political position or candidate, or identify a new crop of volunteers to replace those leaving. Social media campaigns usually are connected to organization or company websites, which also offer opportunities to measure activity. Even if direct ROI cannot be shown, nearly every personal brand, organization or company benefits from raising awareness through maintaining a strong and consistent presence within social media.

Google Analytics

On websites, individuals, organizations or companies may interest users in what Edelman PR has called owned media, or content residing on sites that are maintained by owners. A strategic campaign may use techniques, such as banner advertising on other sites, email marketing or social media to attempt to drive traffic back to a homepage. By incorporating Google Analytics tracking code on a page, owners are provided with data on the sources of web traffic, such as search engines, referrals from other sites, direct traffic and social media linkages. While a majority of site visitors typically still arrive via searching, a campaign can produce a spike in traffic of more than 10%.

The importance of searching to find online content means that the keywords need to be carefully selected and tracked. Google Adwords has maintained a tool for analyzing data on keywords and phrases. For example, the term "social media" produces data on this search.

The search produces other keywords that may be relevant to a particular business website, such as one selling consulting. Keywords allow us to strive for Search Engine Optimization (SEO). By identifying popular searches, content creators can focus on some words and avoid others. The top words should generate more clicks at the owned website. Words such as "sale," for example, may generate new traffic and interest. Web coders need to incorporate the tags that align with the words used by customers or brand fans.

Referrals—online traffic that comes from a link on another page—are an important way to generate interest. An analysis of referrals on a site, for example, might reveal that visitors clicked on a link while spending time on Twitter, Facebook or a blog site. This could be the result of owned or earned media. By checking the source of referrals, users learn more about what works. A check of similar or competitor sites should reveal web traffic secrets. At some level, referrals could be the result of a social relationship

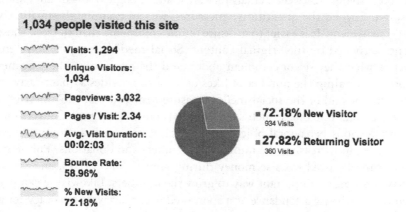

Figure 6.1 Keywords are very useful in social media searches, and this helps explain why search engine optimization remains important.

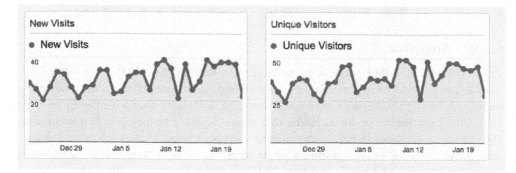

Figure 6.2 Page views include data on the number of visitors returning to a page.

that may be built over time, maintained or even reinforced through a strategic social media plan and tactics.

Once users land at a website, we are interested in learning more about the type of content and its placement that generates clicks, time spent or other results. Analytics allow a site manager to examine page bounce rates, which measure how quickly a user exits an individual page. Engaging content keeps users on a page, or it moves them to another page that meets the goals for the site. For example, a news or sports site may be selling a cap or t-shirt. The goal would be to display the product on a main page and persuade users to click on a "buy now" link.

For social media sites, such as Facebook pages, we are interested in increasing the number of page views, unique visitors and likes (which are similar to fans, followers and members on other social sites). While we want visitors to respond to each post, we also seek higher levels of engagement through liking comments of others and making comments of our own. Within the comments section, we are interested in sentiment analysis of those opinions as positive, neutral or negative. Frequently, there is a lack of neutral commenting within most social media sites. Long-term analyses tend to find a preponderance of either very negative criticism or glowing praise. Obviously, the goal typically is to maximize positive sentiment and minimize the negative feelings that may exist toward a personal or organizational brand. At a minimum, measuring sentiment offers a benchmark starting point for moving the needle away from negativism and toward positive outcomes.

Strong bonds between social media users and media content should produce these benchmark data. By identifying a standard for measuring success, we can set goals for tracking growth in unique visitors and their levels of engagement through time spent, as well as satisfaction. For products, sales create customers—some of whom require additional support. In fact, a lot of brands see the ROI of social media as found within the customer service business function. Social media have become important online spaces for responding to complaints, engaging customer problems, solving issues, converting unhappy customers to loyal fans, and promoting brands. A good customer experience will generate likes, positive comments and shares of information.

Facebook Insights

Facebook, arguably one of the most important social media sites this decade with more than one billion users worldwide, has developed a useful set of free insight data. For each Facebook page created, a site manager can download and analyze real-time data compared each week.

Ideally, a site sees continuous growth in the number of likes, increases in the **reach** of posts beyond those users liking the page and following it on their feeds. By creating engaging content, a manager can spark comments, shares and post clicks. Some managers export insight data to an Excel spreadsheet and track long-term data for seasonal shifts or effectiveness of post attributes. Beyond the quantitative measures of engagement, a page manager should drill down and examine the most engaging content.

In the above example, the weekly reach spiked higher because of a newly posted YouTube video. In this example, the post had a small number of likes, but there were clicks through to watch the video. Reach can be used to identify promising potential

Week of 3rd February, 2014

	LAST WEEK	PREVIOUS WEEK	TREND
Total Page Likes	750	750	0.0%
New Likes	1	0	0.0%
Weekly Total Reach	2,295	523	338.8%
People Engaged	206	126	63.5%

Figure 6.3 Analysts examine individual Facebook page posts for clues about fan engagement.

for future content. Although the content generated only two likes, so far, the clicks through to the video and relatively high reach offer promising potential. It is also possible to link a Facebook page to a Twitter account. By posting on the page, an automatic tweet generates a headline and link for Twitter followers. This, in turn, may also increase the reach for content. On a news-sharing page, for example, Twitter can be used to boost the number of clicks for an item of high interest. Following Miley Cyrus' sexually charged *MTV Video Music Awards* 2013 performance, for example, there was considerable buzz in terms of reach and engagement. The linkage of Facebook and Twitter profiles can be useful in strengthening overall brand awareness and activity.

Twitter Analytics

The open environment of Twitter, as compared to the gated online communities of Facebook and LinkedIn, presents a unique opportunity to access and analyze open and accessible data. On Twitter, there are obvious measures, such as number of followers, number of re-tweets and replies. Twitter includes the activity of human users and automated robot "bots," which are computer-generated scheduled tweets. On Twitter, we can measure following to followers as a ratio, we can study content, and we can explore social networks. One raw measure is number of tweets per day.

Until early 2014, Edelman Digital generated a TweetLevel.com score based upon four dimensions: influence, popularity, engagement and trust. These are important measures from a PR perspective, as they offer opportunities to score and improve online behavior of influencers. Trust is viewed by Edelman PR as an association, such as through a retweet. Engaging content generates new connections and may increase influence. The "permanent beta" model attempted to develop measurement variables important within social media, as seen in Figure 6.4.

AMEC's Barcelona Declaration of Measurement Principles (2010) serves as useful guidance to practitioners. The seven principles are:

1. Importance of Goal Setting and Measurement
2. Measuring the Effect of Outcomes is Preferred to Measuring Outputs
3. The Effect on Business Results Can and Should Be Measured Where Possible

📱 BOX 6.1 TWEETLEVEL METHODOLOGY

Beyond followers (Fo) and follower to following ratio (Fo:Fg), the model focused on updates (UP), retweets (Rt), broadcast to engagement ratio (B:E), the Topsy.com influence score (To), as well as engagement (e) and trust (t). Edelman TweetLevel (2013) was removed in early 2014: "We are currently assessing new methods and technologies to measure influence on Twitter. We appreciate your patience as we explore the realm of possibility. Please reach out to tweetlevel@edelman.com for more information." http://TweetLevel.Edelman.com Trust is a proprietary measure that is not disclosed. TweetLevel also includes in the Edelman formula number of name pointing (@U) and recent replies (@R). It also is important to appear on follower lists and exhibit measures of influence (i). Overall popularity (p) tends to be an obvious measure, although it is vital to filter raw numbers of followers for the presence of bots and spammers using Twitter for direct marketing. While the overall model is transparent, some of the actual data fall under proprietary company information. So, we cannot fully evaluate reliability of measures for trust and influence. Likewise, without clear evidence of data consistency, it is impossible to be sure about validity of the measurement.

$$\text{TweetLevel} = \text{Rg} \left| \frac{\text{Fo+Fg+Fo:Fg+Up+Up}^{30}\text{+L}^{Q}\text{+Up}^{v}\text{+@U+[Rt Q/Ed]+@R}^{30}\text{+B:E+Is+To+li+Vi}}{Z} \right| \text{xw (i\p\e\t)}$$

Variables

Fo	= Number of followers	Fg	= Number users following
Fo:Fg	= Follower to Following ratio	Up	= Number of updates all time
UP^{30}	= Updates over the past 30 days	L^{Q}Fo	= Number of lists following you related to the number people following that list
Up^{v}	= Number of updates over specific time period	@U	= Number of name pointing
(Rt Q/Ed)	= Retweets related to quoted and edited proportioned to all	@ R^{30}	= Replies sent related to all time and previous 30 days
B:E	= Broadcast to engagement ratio	Is	= Idea Starter score
To	= Topsy influence score	li	= Involvement index score
Vi	= Velocity index score	w	= Weight assigned each attribute
Z	= Standardized score	p	= Popularity
e	= Engagement	i	= Influence
t	= Trust	Rg	= Range assigned to score

Figure 6.4 Tweetlevel aggregates many measures in generating a standardized score.

Source: http://tweetlevel.edelman.com/ (Accessed January 2014; as of February 2014, the site had been discontinued for updates to the model, as Edelman PR assessed "new methods to measure influence on Twitter.")

4. Media Measurement Requires Quantity and Quality
5. AVEs [Averages] are Not the Value of Public Relations
6. Social Media Can and Should be Measured
7. Transparence and Replicability are Paramount to Sound Measurement

Social media measurement is considered "a discipline" rather than "a tool" under the principles. Principle 6 calls for "clearly defined goals and outcomes," multi-method analysis, quantity and quality evaluation, of "no 'single metric'" for conversation and communities, and precision of data: "Understanding reach and influence is important, but existing sources are not accessible, transparent or consistent enough to be reliable; experimentation and testing are key to success" (Principle 6, bullet 6). Public relations professionals have concluded that transparency is central to credible and trusted social media measurement: "PR measurement should be done in a manner that is transparent and replicable for all steps in the process" (Principle 7). The content source and method of analysis ("whether human or automated, tone scale, reach to target, content analysis parameters") should be transparently reported to clients and the public (Principle 7, bullet 2).

The exploratory efforts to measure social media behavior are important in identifying general strengths and weaknesses, as long as one understands that current data may reflect a fairly large amount of **measurement error**. No social measure is exact and without various sources of error, but we would like to look at individual scores and be able to *estimate error*. Currently, this is not a standard for social media measurement.

In the TweetLevel conceptualization, the tool places active Twitter users within five possible roles: viewer, commentator, curator, idea starter and amplifier. The author of this book is measured as an idea starter (78.7). A score in this model is the sum of four sub-scores: influence (78.7), popularity (67.8), engagement (62.2) and trust (63.3)—each on a 100-point scale. Larger media personalities @GaryVee (88.4) and @LadyGaga (93.3) are classified as amplifiers to a much larger, more popular Twitter following.

Edelman developer Jonny Bentwood (@jonnybentwood) says idea starters are "creative brains" behind talked about thoughts. They connect with other idea starters, curators and amplifiers—those with very large followings. The processes of curating and commenting may be influential, while viewers observe but do not "leave a foot print" on Twitter.

Once we can measure a Twitter user type, it is also valuable to be able to examine **word clouds** to see key words frequently used by and about an influencer. Lady Gaga, with more than 41 million global followers, is an interesting example of a brand using social media to reinforce fan relationships.

From a PR and branding perspective, the words of the influencer should mirror personal and professional branding of a consistent message to the Twitter audience. The most important branded words should appear in a word cloud as the largest words shown. All of the important brands should at least appear within the cloud. If not, the speaker should adjust message over time and re-examine the data.

Other Twitter measurement tools include We Follow, which generates an aggregate "prominence" score. In the example in Table 6.1, we see the top four on Twitter for social media. The Mashable.com site, represented by Pete Cashmore, has a perfect 100 for social media and also a near-perfect 98 for tech and news. Users may add themselves to the database and compare word scores with word cloud emphases. By using multiple tools to connect a brand with words, we can look for rough patterns in the data.

Figure 6.5 Reporters and fans gather outside Lady Gaga's hotel in Bucharest prior to a performance in 2012. Courtesy of Shutterstock, Inc.

Table 6.1 Top Social Media Influencers as Measured by We Follow

Name	Twitter Handle	Identity	We Follow Score
Pete Cashmore	@mashable	News and Commentary	100
TechCrunch	@techcrunch	News and Commentary	99
Kevin Rose	@kevinrose	Google Ventures partner	98
Ashton Kutcher	@aplusk	Actor and Entrepreneur	97

Source: WeFollow (http://wefollow.com)

Other top Twitter tools have included:

- ReTweetRank (http://retweetrank.com)—Track re-tweets and the number of influential followers.
- TweetReach (http://tweetreach.com)—Measure reach (accounts reached), exposure (impressions) and activity.
- Topsy (http://topsy.com)—compare recent Twitter activity of brands and link to specific tweets.

The potential to measure Twitter influence is an exciting development, even if it cannot capture offline influence. Still, popularity on Twitter also cannot be directly associated with measurement of other social media activity. The centrality of engagement is important across all social media. Hootsuite, Tweetdeck and other platforms have attempted to integrate and aggregate social media data across sites with varying degrees of access and success. Twitter, for example, controls the technology for limiting access to data retrieval. Likewise, news sites now behind paywalls require paid licensing to access their social media data.

Many companies now offer to clients what is called a **social media dashboard**. The idea is to synthesize key insights on a screen to offer the user key data without needing to jump from screen to screen. Universal Information Services (@Universal_Info) is an international media tracking and news monitoring company that offers a dashboard product. President Todd Murphy (@Todder4News) says Universal examines keywords, performs indexing, and uses human coding of content instead of computerized, online coding with poor accuracy. Other companies, such as Cision (@cision), Vocus (@Vocus) and Burell (@BurrellPR) also combine computer tools with human coding. A Universal dashboard tracks top hashtags, total word counts, top tweeters, top mentions, influence via social **network visualization**, top websites, impressions, top journalists, key topics, impressions by state and other measures. The goal is to measure impact and publicity value for influencers.

A dashboard provides the client with the aggregate amount of social media conversation, but it goes further in breaking down types of content across key platforms. Facebook and Twitter in this example are stronger social media spaces for an organic packaging of the message, but Facebook is much more active in a debate over mustard versus ketchup. At the same time, charity engagement appears stronger on blogs and YouTube. A user would need to drill down deeper into the data to examine specific content and posts to better understand how the results align or fail to measure up to strategic goals.

📡 BOX 6.2 THOUGHT LEADER TIMOTHY AKIMOFF

The changing landscape for storytelling is the biggest change. When Twitter first came out, it allowed us to expand our marketing of stories. With developments like video capabilities and longer-form display

Figure 6.6 @timakimoff. Photograph by Jeff Rivet, courtesy of Tim Akimoff, WBEZ.

areas in Facebook, social media has taken much of the gusto from front page newspaper exclusives and even specialized web storytelling templates. As social media become the common CMS for our lives, our storytelling will shift more and more to the social realms as opposed to specialized, monetized platforms.

Social media grow exponentially because of changes in technology. The more iPhones and Androids sold, the more people use Twitter, Facebook, Instagram and other various social media services. The biggest challenge will be to keep ahead of the massive changes taking place on the social media landscape due to technology improvements. Mobile-only applications like Path could be true disruptions, because of how much they divorce us from websites.

Looking ahead, there will be more brand-exposure for individual reporters. By developing brand-making skills in college, young journalists can build their expertise in whatever direction their interests lie. With a newsroom full of branded, social-media driven reporters, that news organization will excel in its coverage and spread of information.

Live coverage and breaking news remain the biggest hurdles and opportunities with social media. In all the big-scale news events since the advent of social media, not one single news organization has risen above the rest in terms of accurate and innovative social media usage. The first news organization to figure this out will gain a significant advantage over others.

Timothy Akimoff is Director of Digital Content at Chicago Public Media, which includes WBEZ Radio. He previously held positions at KTUU-TV in Anchorage, Alaska, and at Lee Enterprise and the *Missoulian/Ravalli Republic* in Missoula, Montana. He studied journalism at the University of Oregon and has reported in Oregon and in Kiev, Ukraine.

Network Analyses

Academic researchers have begun to explore online behavior and measurement through application of social network theory. The systematic study of how individuals interact in social settings has been the focus of research for more than 50 years. Tubbs and Moss (1983), for example, traced investigations in the nature of "popular" or "overchosen" and "unpopular" or isolated people (pp. 108–109). In describing social interaction between popular and unpopular people, they diagrammed through the "sociogram" how positive traits, such as enthusiasm and maturity, may be related to judgments about "sincerity" of another's conversation (p. 110). In the current era of social networks and social media, these connections are important to journalism and public relations (PR). Social networking generates measures of branding, influence, trust and dispersion of ideas through Twitter and Facebook, and offers an opportunity to be seen as an opinion leader.

Information theory and models emphasize flow of messages through channels. The perception of communication depends upon situations and context (Severin & Tankard,

2001). Much of this work was grounded in Heider's balance theory and Festinger's cognitive dissonance theory from the 1950s, which may be related to social judgment (Milburn, 1991). Burnett and Marshall (2003) link communication models to Internet discussion:

> At the very core of the meaning of the Web is linkage and connection: it is fundamentally about modes of communication and presenting possibilities about how those modes might intersect. Thus the Web is simultaneously a mass-mediated *and* one-to-one form of communication. It is a site of incredible cultural consumption *and* cultural production and makes it harder to establish the boundary between these two activities. (p. 59)

Twitter users (sometimes called "tweeps") may be analyzed to identify "visual patterns found within linked entities" (Hansen, Shneiderman, & Smith, 2011, p. 32). Researchers have proposed and developed methods for analysis of structure and grouping of categories and clusters in a social network. One model is called Group-In-A-Box (GIB):

> One particularly important aspect of social network analysis is the detection of *communities*, i.e., sub-groups of individuals or entities that exhibit tight interconnectivity among the other wider population. For example, Twitter users who regularly re-tweet each other's messages *may form cohesive groups* within the Twitter social network. In a network visualization they would appear as clusters or sub-graphs, often colored distinctly or represented by a different vertex shape in order to convey their group identity. (Rodrigues, Milic-Frayling, Smith, Shneiderman, & Hansen, 2011, para. 2; emphasis added)

Some researchers call the network graph that is produced by analysis software a "sociogram," which has "vertices (also called nodes or agents) and edges (also called ties or connections)" (Hansen, Shneiderman, & Smith, 2011, p. 33). In social network analyses, Twitter users are connected by a series of lines in social space. The maps represent a center of people at the core of a network, as well as "isolates" at the periphery.

Network analyses are grounded in nearly 300 years of study in graph theory. In modern terms, "It is often useful to consider social networks from an individual member's point of view" (Hansen, Shneiderman, & Smith, 2011, p. 36). Information from journalists and PR practitioners, either to one another or spreading to the general public, may be visually displayed through computer-generated mapping. As early as the 1930s, researchers were developing hand-drawn "pictures of patterns of people and their partners" (p. 38). This theoretical perspective has influenced the modern study of relationships. For example, Heaney and McClurg (2009) applied social networks to the study of American politics. They found social networks useful in understanding information flow, as well as collaboration within political organizations. Garton, Haythornthwaite, and Wellman (1997) describe social network analysts as examining relations:

> They treat the description of relational patterns as interesting in its own right—e.g., is there a core and periphery?—and examine how involvement in such *social networks* helps to explain the behavior and attitudes of *network members* . . . They use a variety of techniques to discover a network's densely-knit clusters and to look for similar role relations. (para. 3)

Communication theory also has been concerned with how networks relate to personal influence. Cooley (1909/1966) identified four factors: expressiveness, permanence, swiftness and diffusion of communication—he viewed the extension of messages as "enlargement" and "animation" (pp. 149–159).

> Social contacts are extended in space and quickened in time, and in the same degree the mental unity they imply becomes wider and more alert. The individual is broadened by coming into relation with a larger and more various life, and he is kept stirred up, sometimes to express, by the multitude of changing suggestions which this life brings to him. (p. 150)

Baran and Davis (2006) suggest that influence of opinion leaders may be understood through similar interests and social stratification of leaders and their followers. At one time, the shift from interpersonal to mediated communication reduced feedback (Westley & MacLean, 1957), but the lines between interpersonal and media communication have now blurred. Even so, Gumpert and Cathcart (1986) concluded that, "Every type of communication, from face-to-face to mass communication, is still basically an interpersonal communicative act" (p. 19). Influence may disperse from the center of a social network. This influence often accelerates when a leader is "stimulating" what has been called "virtual communities" (Koh, Kim, Butler, & Bock, 2007, p. 70). In order to be sustainable, the researchers contend that four principles must exist: clear purpose/vision, clear member role definition, moderator leadership, and *online/offline events* (p. 70–71; emphasis added). Events, in fact, play a key role in strengthening member identification within a social network. It is for this reason that the present research focuses on a specific international event that receives widespread media coverage.

Data analyses can be performed using NodeXL software. A white-listed company on Twitter may collect 20,000 queries per hour, but a regular user is limited to 150 queries per hour. Researchers use NodeXL, which is a social network analysis tool built into Microsoft Excel in current versions and is specifically designed for non-programmers, to collect, analyze and visualize network data from social media sites, such as Twitter. In a Twitter network, there are times when researchers are less concerned about importance of a specific account and more concerned about position in the network. A position in the network may have something to do with having access to information or the flow of information. For example, a PR practitioner may appear near the center, if she or he is disseminating new information to be used by electronic news media. Thus, it is important to examine the betweenness centrality measurement. Utilizing the NodeXL filter, tweeps with a low betweenness measurement can be removed. NodeXL has the capability to identify clusters or cliques of tweeps based upon the network structure. The software uses an algorithm that looks for groups of densely clustered tweeps that are only loosely connected to other tweeps in another cluster.

Russo and Koesten (2005) address the concepts of centrality and prestige. Within a network, an individual can be placed within a social space occupied by others:

> An actor's *centrality* (out-degree) represents his or her ability to touch others in the network. In particular, centrality is a measure of potential influence and popularity based on who an actor seeks to interact with within the social network . . . An actor's *prestige* (in-degree) represents the degree to which others seek out a particular actor in a social network. (p. 256)

It is possible to examine centrality of network positioning, as contrasted with being on the periphery, to determine importance in the flow of information. A person at the center of a network has a lot of information flowing through them. Prestige is another way to say that influence happens when others seek out an individual in the network. For example, a financial journalist may be sought out by a PR person with a goal of gaining media attention for her or his event. Centrality and prestige may place an individual in the role of being "the object of communication," (p. 256) without necessarily being the original source.

Consider the example of an annual and very popular stockholders' meeting. Billionaire Warren Buffett attracts more than 30,000 each May to Omaha, Nebraska. In 2013, 665 users actively tweeted using #BRK2013, which was the official hashtag designated by the corporation's Borsheims jewelry store.

📱 **BOX 6.3 OVERALL SOCIAL NETWORK VISUALIZATION OF #BRK2013**

The #BRK2013 hashtag demonstrated a large amount of activity. There were a total of 1,517 mentions and re-tweets using the hashtag between May 4 and May 10. The top 10 influencers included key business websites and media. According to their Twitter bios (and June, 2013, N of followers), they are:

1. @andrewrsorkin—"New York Times Columnist & CNBC Squawk Box (@SquawkCNBC) Co-Anchor. Author Too Big To Fail. Founder, @DealBook." (442,413)
2. @themotleyfool—"Helping the world invest . . . Fool on! Alexandria, VA—fool.com." (423,175)
3. @QSAYTHAT—"Everyone follow me on #Instagram QSAVAGE & go like my page www.facebook.com/qsavagepromotions . . . Baton Rouge, La." (127,474)
4. @dealbook—"News from The New York Times about deals and those who make and break them. New York, NY—nytimes.com/dealbook." (66,377)
5. @TheStreet—"Stock market coverage with an edge. Valuable information. Unique insight. Strong opinions . . . From the Heart of Wall Street—thestreet.com." (64,045)
6. @xiaolai—Individual's site in "Beijing—lixiaolai.com." (56,004)
7. @DirectorsTalk—"the most followed in the UK providing London Stock Exchange AIM news and interviews with Directors of leading PLC's. DirectorsTalk.com." (54,813)
8. @TrendsSthAfrica—"Real-time South Africa Twitter trends South Africa—trendsmap.com/south+Africa." (54,036)
9. @beckyquickcnbc—"Co-host of CNBC's Squawk Box from 6–9 am Eastern with Joe Kernen and Andrew Ross Sorkin. Fortune Columnist. Former WSJ reporter. Rutgers grad."(52,919)

(continued)

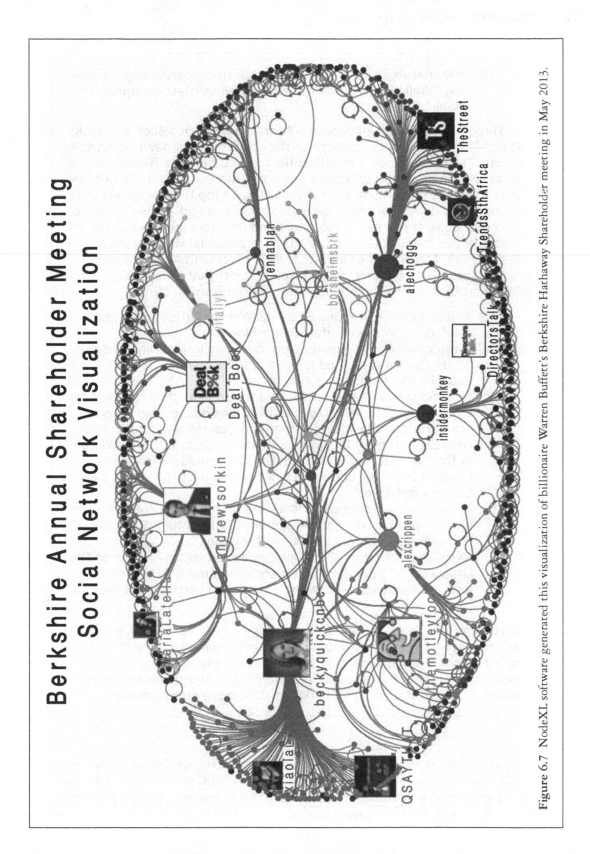

Figure 6.7 NodeXL software generated this visualization of billionaire Warren Buffett's Berkshire Hathaway Shareholder meeting in May 2013.

10.   @MariaLatella—SKY TG24 Italian television personality following "Wall Street—www.facebook.com/marialatellapaginauffi ciale." (47,263)

Three of the top ten influencers—Andrew Sorkin, DealBook and Becky Quick—all had direct connections to the CNBC business news channel. A fourth, The Motley Fool, is an influential business blog site. These were all found within the center of the complex social network, which did not feature any Berkshire companies. The remaining six top ten influencers were found along a well-defined edge of the social network within three distinct sub-areas. The Street, Trends Africa and Directors Talk were distanced from the top four influencers. QSAYTHAT and xiaolai were connected to Becky Quick. Maria Latella's main connection was with Andrew Sorkin.

The social network map showed six accounts that had fewer Twitter followers than the top ten, but generated significant re-tweets:

1.   @alexcrippen—"Tracking all things Warren Buffett for http:// CNBC.com's Warren Buffett Watch blog."
2.   @insidermonkey—"Finance blog following insiders and hedge funds. Our small-cap hedge fund strategy beat the S&P 500 index by 18 percentage points per year."
3.   @alechogg—"Writer, broadcaster, entrepreneur, thinker, striver for an open mind; founder Moneyweb . . . tweets breaking news and links to interesting info. Johannesburg, Gauteng—alechogg.com."
4.   @borsheimsbrk—"The ultimate guide for updates about Warren Buffett's annual Berkshire Hathaway shareholder's meeting— brought to you by Borsheims Fine Jewelry & Gifts. Omaha, NE— borsheimbrk.com."
5.   @jennablan—"Editor of US Investment Strategy at Reuters. Sharing my world in covering biggest, most influential US investors. Barron's alum (wrote Current Yield column)."
6.   @vitaliyk—"Investor—CIO at IMA, educator, writer—author of The Little Book of Sideways Markets and writes monthly column for Institutional Investor Magazine. Denver, CO—activevalueinvesting. com."

Borsheims was the only Berkshire company to appear in the graph as an influencer. The Borsheims Twitter account began using the #BRK2013 days before the annual meeting, and their placement among media as a main re-tweeter of content was important. The @borsheimsbrk account was the main official voice for Berkshire during the annual meeting.

By analyzing the visual appearance of the network we can see that most of the users ringed an oval shaped social network dominated by CNBC affiliated and other business opinion leaders. Most of the audience for tweets was not tightly connected to the media sources. Users are paying attention to each other, and there is a symmetric exchange of attention and information in this social network (Hansen, Shneiderman, & Smith, 2011). The top-ten influencers clustered around four major starbursts and triads between users with strong social ties (Hansen et al., 2011). The users with the highest between-ness centrality revealed the bridging users. These users are vitally important to the structure of the network and are important for three reasons: 1) these users are in a better position than others in terms of having access to information; 2) these users are a bridge to *different people in other networks,* which have the potential to carry the message further and thus increase the reach; and 3) these users are connected to *different people,* and they have greater chances of having access to *different information.*

The measurement of social networks opens the possibility to develop greater sophistication in social media analyses. By understanding communication patterns of influence, as well as the content of the communication, we should be able to understand impact of Twitter and other social tools. This is important for social networks and media, as well as social marketing efforts.

At the same time, social networks offer an opportunity to understand political communication. Himelboim, McCreery, and Smith (2013) integrated network and content analyses to study political views on Twitter. By mapping conversation on ten controversial subjects, the team discovered subgroups of "highly connected users—clusters—that were loosely connected to users outside their clusters" (p. 167). Conservative and liberal clusters were common, as younger users tended to move away from neutral news sites. Academic research will continue to develop and help us better understand the nature of communication on Twitter and other social media sites.

Other Social Network Measurement

As Miller (2013) observes, social media marketing involves a lot of variables and media channels and opportunities:

> Social media are exciting new marketing channels deserving serious experimentation and analysis for integration into marketing programs. They provide hundreds of channels for networking and building relationships . . . The conversation must be unfettered . . . The company must respond honestly to complaints or criticism and trust its customers to distinguish unfair comments from fact. (p. 102)

Social media can be a powerful force to reach large audiences with important messages. Audience size and "connectedness" matter in "online word of mouth" campaigns, as well as general conversation (Sterne, 2010, pp. 51, 57).

Social media measurement returns us to central issues of computer-mediated communication (CMC). These spaces allow us to develop online relations, explore interaction with new people, create identities and grow communities of interest. Tools such as Klout.com attempt to measure influence across social media platforms. Conversation monitoring of relevant quantitative and qualitative data offers opportunities to learn from social networking and social media. Sentiment analysis techniques continue to be developed that will take us beyond broad measures of influence and trust toward understanding the quality of engagement and the nature of impact.

Mobile media provide a relatively new glimpse into the future of social media measurement. *Advertising Age* (2013) summarized important trends data:

- 50% of the U.S. population and 24% of the world population were projected to have a smartphone by the end of 2014.
- Growth in U.S. mobile advertising spending was 75% in 2013 at about $8 billion.
- 110 million unique visitors to Facebook place its revenues only behind Google.
- Mobile media are growing among all of the top five social networking platforms: Facebook, Twitter, LinkedIn, Tumblr and Pinterest.
- Facebook has the fourth largest overall multiplatform audience behind Google, Yahoo and Microsoft.

These changes have opened the world of big data in which marketers have access to large amounts of consumer data. The measurement industry offers "deliverables" to clients, and social media metrics and analytics have become big business. The ongoing development of best practices for measuring communication tone, for example, should yield greater precision in the future. Whether or not social media engagement increases or decreases on specific sites over time, scientifically reliable and valid data will be needed.

In the United States, there are few government regulations of the Internet. Smartphone and tablet access now includes high quality video, which is extending the average amount of time users spend online. Video sites are integrating social chats and other functions, and new tools are likely to emerge to measure user behavior. Social media platforms are viewed as branding opportunities for media industries (Greer & Ferguson, 2011). This will push marketers to develop more complex social media measurement tools and techniques.

■ DISCUSSION QUESTIONS: STRATEGIES AND TACTICS

1. If you were advising a CEO who had never been on Twitter to create a profile, which key concepts would you discuss with her or him?
2. Consider ways to use social media to improve trust and influence. Which Twitter measures would you want to track?
3. Is there ever a case for disengagement from social media? Which circumstances would provide reasons to lower levels of engagement?
4. How could you integrate the findings from data on Facebook and Twitter to use best practices at other social media sites? Which other data points are of interest to you?
5. Explore your social network. What do the data tell you about your use of Twitter? What is missing from the data? How could you improve measurement and your use of Twitter?

References

Advertising Age (2013, Aug. 18). Mobile Fact Pack. Chicago, IL: Crain Communication.

AMEC (2010, July 19). *Barcelona Declaration of Measurement Principles*. http://amecorg. com/2012/06/barcelona-declaration-of-measurement-principles

Baran, S. J., & Davis, D. (2006). *Mass Communication Theory, fourth edition*. Belmont, CA: Thomson Wadsworth.

Burnett, R., & Marshall, P. D. (2003). *Web Theory*. London, UK: Routledge.

Cooley, C. H. (1909/1966). The Significance of Communication. In B. Berelson & M. Janowitz (Eds.), *Reader in Public Opinion and Communication, second edition*, pp. 147–155. New York: Free Press.

Garton, L., Haythornthwaite, C., & Wellman, B. (1997, June). Studying Online Social Networks. *Journal of Computer-Mediated Communication, 3*(1). http://jcmc.indiana.edu/vol3/issue1/garton.html

Gordon, J. (2012). See, Say, Feel, Do: Social Media Metrics That Matter. Fenton. www.fenton.com/see-say-feel-do/

Greer, C. F., & Ferguson, D. A. (2011). Using Twitter for Promotion and Branding: A Content Analysis of Local Television Twitter Sites. *Journal of Broadcasting & Electronic Media 55*(2), 198–214.

Gumpert, G., & Cathcart, R. (Eds.) (1986). *INTER/MEDIA, Interpersonal Communication in a Media World, third edition*. New York: Oxford University Press.

Hansen, D. L., Shneiderman, B., & Smith, M. A. (2011). *Analyzing Social Media Networks with NodeXL*. Burlington, MA: Elsevier.

Heaney, M. T., & McClurg, S. D. (2009, September). Social Networks and American Politics. *American Politics Research, 37*(5), 727–741.

Himelboim, I., McCreery, S., & Smith, M. (2013). Birds of a Feather Tweet Together: Integrating Network and Content Analyses to Examine Cross-Ideology Exposure on Twitter. *Journal of Computer-Mediated Communication 18*, 154–174.

Koh, J., Kim, Y.-G., Butler, B., & Bock, G.-W. (2007, February). Encouraging Participation in Virtual Communities. *Communications of the ACM, 50*(2), 69–73.

Milburn, M. A. (1991). *Persuasion and Politics*. Belmont, CA: Wadsworth.

Miller, P. (2013). Social Media Marketing. In Alan B. Albarran (Ed.), *The Social Media Industries*, pp. 86–10. New York, NY: Routledge.

Radian6 (2013). The Cost of Ignoring Social Media. Sales Force Marketing Cloud. www.salesforcemarketingcloud.com/blog/2013/05/cost-of-ignoring-social-media/

Rodrigues, E. M., Milic-Frayling, N., Smith, M., Shneiderman, B., & Hansen, D. (2011). *Group-in-a-Box Layout for Multi-faceted Analysis of Communities*. http://hcil.cs.umd.edu/trs/2011–24/2011–24.pdf

Russo, T. C., & Koesten, J. (2005, July). Prestige, Centrality, and Learning: A Social Network Analysis of an Online Class. *Communication Education, 54*(3), 254–261.

Savage, N. (2011, March). Twitter as Medium and Message. *Communicators of the ACM 54*(3), 18–20.

Severin, W. J., & Tankard, Jr., J. W. (2001). *Communication Theories, fifth edition*. New York, NY: Longman.

Sterne, J. (2010). *Social Media Metrics*. Hoboken, NJ: Wiley.

Tubbs, S. T., & Moss, S. (1983). *Human Communication, fourth edition*. New York, NY: Random House.

Westley, B. H., & MacLean, Jr., M. S. (1957). A Conceptual Model for Communications Research. *Journalism Quarterly, 34*(1): 31–28.

Wimmer, R. D., & Dominick, J. R. (2013). *Mass Media Research: An Introduction, tenth edition*. Boston, MA: Wadsworth.

7 NEW AND MOBILE MEDIA TECHNOLOGIES, INNOVATION AND INVESTMENT

"Twitter is the socialization of our inner lives."

—@UncleDynamite (2013)

Digital media ushered in an era of continuous innovation. Beginning with multimedia software programs and the early Web in the 1990s, the United States became a global hotbed for an innovation culture that spread to many parts of the world. The investment in new technologies increasingly has a connection to social media communication. Some large corporations created the title of Chief Digital Officer (CDO) to incorporate the need for internal thought leaders who attempt to keep pace with the changing landscape of social and mobile media, as well as to focus the previous work of Chief Information Officer (CIO).

Social networking sites that employ social media must transform innovation into a business model. Social business is complex, involving at least four key sources: value creation, competencies, target markets and revenue (Cha, 2013). A successful social media platform must provide a needed product or service, it must function within user expectations, it must serve a particular market, and it must ultimately generate revenue in order to survive and prosper: "The inherent nature of social networking sites keeps users coming back on a regular basis, which also likely increases the exposure of these returnees to the goods and services marketed on these sites" (p. 78). Amazon.com, for example, offers Today's Deals as a way to motivate customers to return and engage. Each product is rated by a five-star average, and consumers may also read customer reviews. The social media communication of customer engagement provides important texture and context for site visitors. Social media observers have connected customer engagement to sharing, altruism, value creation, influence and other important marketing concepts.

📱 BOX 7.1 VIEWPOINTS CURATED PRODUCT AND SERVICE REVIEW SYSTEM

Amazon and other sites have shown that shoppers consider product reviews an accurate way to gauge consumer experiences, and a site known for independent and trusted reviews in 2014 reached out to marketers. In an age of social media, brands cannot ignore the voice of the people. The challenge, however, is building consumer engagement that

(continued)

---

does not game the system. Viewpoints.com, a consumer reviews platform, launched Pulse for brands to listen to and engage more directly with consumers.

"For the first time we're giving the brands, the owners of the products, the ability to now claim those products and collect reviews . . . manage those reviews and promote them," founder and CEO Matt Moog said. Viewpoints collected nearly 600,000 reviews of more than 37,000 products and 450 categories in seven years. The site attempts to verify reviewers, and uses an editorial process before publishing reviews.

Viewpoints reviewers complete a proactive disclosure form, including required Federal Trade Commission (FTC) disclosure of any payments or products received. Beyond this, every review is screened "at multiple points," Moog said. "We also have a number of fraud detection signals . . . that are automated . . . We then human moderate every review that comes on the site." Each review is scored, and about 25% are rejected—20% for poor quality and 5% spam, Moog said.

Viewpoints seeks to know its reviewers and build "a rich social profile of them" by collecting reviews "as an independent third party," Moog said, and organizing and curating them to "validate their authenticity" as a "trusted intermediary." Unlike typical retailer sites designed to sell products, Moog says Viewpoints tells consumers products *not* to buy, highlights those with low ratings and offers access to negative reviews. By identifying reviewers and their review history and offering reviewer badges (trusted, verified trusted and VIP), Viewpoints is different from retailers.

By having a large number of reviews and active community of millions of users, Moog says Viewpoints limits the impact of an illegitimate review that might initially sneak through. Viewpoints has questioned reviewers, and Moog says "if we're not satisfied that it's a legitimate review, we'll remove it."

"I would never tell you or anyone else that it's a perfect system," Moog said, "but you can certainly over time be able to trust more people who contribute regularly, whose opinions are spread across many different products and categories, who have many interlocking relationships."

Online shoppers are not the only ones checking reviews. A growing number of in-store shoppers also read product reviews, survey data suggest. Nearly half of all shoppers check for reviews prior to making a buying decision.

While Viewpoints will allow brands to engage with consumers, marketers will pay to add information—not delete or re-order existing reviews. By creating a corporate account, Pulse offers review collection tools, product description publishing and reply management, analytics and promotion tools through a partnership with Google Shopping and Google Search, Moog said.

The collection, management and promotion of reviews also features social media tools that connect with Facebook and Twitter.

Moog sees the model as having an "opportunity to bring greater transparency and accountability to the market" by shining a light on good *and* bad products. "When you think about the environment and sustainability and peoples' need to spend money in places where it matters," Moog says, "I'd rather get something that lasted for a long time, that didn't fill a landfill and go spend my money on health care or education rather than disposable consumer goods."

Source: Lipschultz, J.H. (2014, January 23). Consumer Review Credibility, Brand Marketing and Social Media. The Huffington Post, Media. www.huffingtonpost. com/jeremy-harris-lipschultz/consumer-review-credibili_b_4634447.html

When Foursquare Co-founder Dennis Crowley launched the location-based app, he saw it as social media communication. The concept of "checking-in" somewhere quickly became connected to the Facebook **social graph**, which Crowley described as "anyone you've ever shaken hands with" (Crowley, 2010, at 0:21). Twitter, Crowley concluded, was more about entertaining people. Foursquare, in its initial concept, was "people you actually overlap with in real life." Crowley began his work in graduate school with "a lot of creative freedom" to follow what he was passionate about (at 2:12): "Creativity is people trying interesting things without the fear of failure or ridicule" (at 2:28). The focus is on "rapid iteration"—building something that probably will not work, and then fixing it and improving the product each week (at 2:46). This is the nature of start-up culture and thinking. It begins with learning what has been done in the social media space and then trying to improve it. In a few short years, social media moved from innovation to important function within small and large established companies.

((•)) BOX 7.2 THOUGHT LEADER ZENA WEIST

My career took a complete shift in 2006 because of social media. I was Group Manager of Online Branding for a telecom and was responsible for all corporate digital marketing and our online voice. It became very apparent that our customers were talking about us on discussion boards and blogs – Facebook was still gated for universities, and Twitter hadn't been launched yet. We began working with our customer service team to create an online response team that listened and responded to customer inquiries. We launched a YouTube "How To" video channel and by 2007 we were active on

Figure 7.1 @zenaweist.
Courtesy Zena Weist.

(continued)

Facebook and Twitter, as well. Our mantra was listen, respond, resolve and engage. I was recruited to become the first Social Media Director at H&R Block in 2010, and I have been focused on integrated marketing, including social media, ever since.

Social media has been "siloed" into Marketing or Communications. It really flows across all business functions and needs to be part of change management and operations. The shift in thinking that needs to occur to move social media programs from tactical to more strategic and company-wide will be the biggest challenge for organizations. I bumped into this narrow line of thinking while brand-side and agency-side and see it has the largest pain point for current clients.

The opportunity is largest with social media in customer experience and product innovation. We will have our customer service, marketing and communication foundation solid within social media, and organizations will focus more attention on utilizing social media to enhance customer experience and product innovation through predictive analytics from social media listening.

Zena (Monsour) Weist is Strategy Director at Level Five Solutions in Kansas City. She has more than 18 years experience, including at Edelman Digital and H&R Block, leading online marketing and interactive agency branding. In 2011, TopRank named Weist "One of the 25 Women Who Rock Social Media." She is a founding member of the Kansas City Chapter of The Social Media Club.

Entrepreneurs

Social media innovation captured the imagination of those energized by an entrepreneurial spirit. The same open approach to development that was seen during the personal computer and Internet revolution seems present with social and mobile media. The development of smartphone apps almost immediately helped define social media as mobile. Rapid diffusion of smartphones and dropping prices for tablets created a ready market for new social media platforms, such as Vine and Snapchat. Initially, entrepreneurs may start projects with little or no money, but eventually it requires investment to launch, grow and sustain a company as a profitable business.

Angel Investors and Start-ups

A social media start-up, once beyond initial development and testing, would be expected to make a "pitch" to an investor or investment group. These are people who have large amounts of money. They are willing to participate in a risky investment because of the potential to earn huge gains. An angel investor brings capital to the business and buys into the start-up. Some investors have organized into groups that share debt and evaluate new ideas within a competitive environment. An investor must weigh **opportunity** costs of what else could be done with the money, if not invested in the concept. It is common for start-ups to be developed with a goal of either selling to a large corporation or issuing public stock.

Many start-ups attempt to take advantage of the fact that we rarely go anywhere without our smartphones. HearHere Radio, a Chicago-based start-up for example, launched the Rivet News Radio app (Glenn, 2013). Users may "hear news on their own schedules—starting, stopping, skipping and selecting stories as they wish" (para. 2). Founder John MacLeod planned to expand to other major markets in 2014. It is a crowded market for smartphone apps, as developers compete for our limited attention.

Big Ideas and Business

Social media reach billions of people, so it should not be a surprise that this is now about big business. Facebook was one of the earliest social media sites to generate large amounts of revenue by selling advertising. Once Facebook sold stock, it offered small and large investors the opportunity to participate in its growth in exchange for risking money on it. Estimates of active social media users are rough but offer some idea of the size of these businesses, as shown in Table 7.1.

"Crush It" and the Thank You Economy

Gary Vaynerchuk (2009) was an early adopter of social media platforms as a way to build brand identity. His book and eBook *Crush It, Cash in on Your Passion* reflected the entrepreneurial spirit embodied in the social media shift. The Internet "lowered the entry barriers to monetizing," (p. 5) and he argued that personal branding was a key to success through storytelling—writing, podcasts or videos. Vaynerchuk linked social media content, such as blogs, to marketing principles of making "the extra effort" to "show genuine appreciation" (p. 28). Social media communication ushered in an era in which entrepreneurs comfortable in social media spaces may be able to skyrocket in popularity and become a rock star within the innovation culture. This, in turn, generates interest and potential funding of new ideas.

Table 7.1 Estimates of Active Users on Top Social Network Sites

SNS	Launch Year	Estimated Active Users
1. Facebook	2004	1.19 billion
2. Google+	2011	540 million
3. LinkedIn	2003	259 million
4. Twitter	2006	232 million
5. Instagram	2010	150 million
6. Pinterest	2010	70 million

Source: Dustin.tv (2013, December 9). Social Network Active Users 2013. *Google+*. https://plus.google.com/+ChristopherRizzo1/posts

Crowdfunding

A relatively new way to fund a start-up is by going to the public and using Internet interest rather than angel investment. A social media start-up can capture the interest of thousands of small investors through viral media rather than risking the idea on an investment group that may want to control it. Kickstarter.com pioneered the idea.

📱 BOX 7.3 KICKSTARTER

Kickstarter (2013) describes itself as "a new way to fund creative projects" using "direct support of people" (para. 1). It was launched in 2009, and the numbers are impressive: 53,000 projects, more than 5 million pledges, and nearly one billion dollars in support.

Projects are independent of Kickstarter, which protects the creative process. "Anyone can launch a project on Kickstarter as long as it meets our guidelines" (para. 2). Funding on Kickstarter is all-or-nothing—projects must reach their funding goals to receive any money" (para. 3). Kickstarter reports that 44% of projects have reached funding goals. Under the model, creators retain all ownership of their ideas. Creators decide what those who pledge obtain. Sometimes it is the product or service. Kickstarter views this as an extension of the patron or subscriber model of funding: "Kickstarter is an extension of this model, turbocharged by the web" (para. 5). There is a clear connection between this and the social media Web:

> It's supporting their dream to create something that they want to see exist in the world. People rally around their friends' projects, fans support people they admire, and others simply come to Kickstarter to be inspired by new ideas. Some projects take longer than anticipated, but creators who are transparent about issues and delays usually find their backers to be understanding. (para. 6)

Kickstarter makes its money by charging a 5% fee to successfully funded projects.

Emergence of New and Mobile Media

Much of what we call in this book *social media* is happening as users of mobile devices connect with their social networks worldwide. Researchers are beginning to take on the task of understanding mobile access and use. In South Korea, for example, it is possible to predict mobile divides by measuring demographic and skill variables (Jung, Chan-Olmsted, & Kim, 2013). While South Korea has "one of the highest smartphone penetration rates," the "younger, more innovative" users downloaded more apps:

> Specifically, male respondents used news/information applications more frequently, whereas female respondents used communication, utility, and commerce applications more frequently . . . the observed gender differences in

technology might be attributed more to differences in functional preferences . . . women prefer online person-to-person communication more than men, and women use social media for relational purposes more frequently than their male counterparts. (pp. 728–729)

The research team suggested that a gender difference in news and information applica-tion use may magnify social and human capital differences.

Social media are beginning to also drive mobile video viewing. Harris Interactive (2012) reported that about 67% in their study found videos to watch through social sharing. A declining number of survey respondents (41%) use search engines to find videos, but platforms such as YouTube and Hulu internally drive much of the viewing (64%). The U.S. study found about one third (35%) were watching on mobile devices, with about 35 of the 50 million mobile viewers discovering videos through social media. Similar to the South Korean gender difference findings, men in the U.S. were slightly more likely to watch mobile video, and users 18–44 were three times more likely. During the annual March Madness college basketball tournament, for example, about one third watch games on mobile devices, and two-thirds check scores (Harris Interactive, 2012).

📱 BOX 7.4 BRICKFLOW

Marketers and branding gurus frequently promote social media storytell-ing and content curating. Tom Grasty, co-founder of Stroome (a collabor-ative video editing site), interviewed Peter Langmar, CEO and founder of Brickflow, a site tracking social media conversation hashtags to generate "cinematic slideshows" (para. 8). The goal is to be able to work with the mass of content while staying within an online environment:

> These can be Tweets, photos, or videos, and they disappear just as instantly as they came. It's very hard to handle content when it comes from multiple platforms and disappears in seconds. Journalists often want to collect the best quotes and videos on a topic, and embed them into their stories. Doing it one by one can take a whole day. Marketers and brands are trying to conduct campaigns around social media con-tent and often end up having to develop their own solution for engage-ment campaigns. This is expensive and time consuming. (para. 11)

Brickflow, then, replaces scrolling with a video presentation. Once gen-erated, the summary can be edited and shared back within social media platforms. The B2B business model for the company is targeted at mar-keters and journalists trying to effectively tell social media stories. The start-up seeks to improve the user experience created with Storify, which requires users to manually curate content within a stream.

As a start-up, Langmar said the biggest challenge was finding their product market, listening and responding to early adopters, and

(continued)

understanding the risk of failure from lack of platform traction. In this environment, start-up team members may decide to move on to another project that looks more promising before success can be achieved.

The social media market continues to grow at a rapid rate (34% per year), but there are no guarantees that Brickflow will be the next Instagram. Still, a lot of people are willing to take risks with new ventures because of the potentially huge rewards from an app that becomes popular.

Source: Grasty, T. (2013, October 25). Brickflow Founder Tells His Tale Behind 'Social Media Storytelling.' *The Huffington Post.* www.huffingtonpost.com/tom-grasty/brickflow-founder-tells-his-tale_b_4138962.html

Implications of Revolutionary Mobile and Social Media

Social media behavior tends to favor a crowdsourcing desire because mobile technologies create flexibility to briefly bring people together physically or virtually and "plug in valuable information" (Greengard, 2011, p. 20). At the heart of social and mobile media are relationships, social ties, social capital and motivation (Brown, 2011). Social capital theory has been applied to research on Facebook fan pages. Social interaction, shared values and trust are important predictors of future use (Lin & Lu, 2011). The researchers suggest that there is a complex process involving structure, cognition and relational aspects. As expected, "shared values are an important factor influencing trust" of social media content (p. 568).

Barack Obama was one of the first politicians to harness the power of social and mobile with an innovative campaign app in 2008 (Kenski, Hardy, & Jamieson, 2010). For example, young voters allowed the presidential campaign app to access their contact lists, and then sorted these with a focus on key swing states.

The app tracked calls in which users were urged to encourage their friends in swing states to remember to vote on election day. The app also was a mobile portal for

Figure 7.2 Candidate Barack Obama's 2008 presidential election iPhone app changed modern political campaign strategy by incorporating social media communication.

campaign information, upcoming events, Obama videos and positions on key issues. The technology opened the door to mobile and social media campaigning. By 2012 in the key swing state of Ohio, PBS reported that President Obama's campaign utilized an extensive ground network of volunteers, an iPad app for door-to-door campaigning and a big data approach to filtering and targeting messages at different types of voters.

Facebook also became a battleground for social media sharing in the 2012 presidential election. Facebook's Randi Zuckerberg identified social networking as social space for activism and change:

> Through social media, people not only donate money, but even more importantly, their reputation and identity. Each time someone clicks "like" or joins a cause on Facebook, they are broadcasting that message to hundreds of their friends, and aligning themselves with a particular issue . . . the awareness generated from that simple action has a ripple effect and has the potential to recruit some extremely engaged volunteers and donors in the future. (Vericat, 2010, p. 177)

Zuckerberg suggests that Facebook may fill a void in face-to-face conversation lost for social or political reasons: "I believe that Facebook's ability to occupy the space of a free and unmoderated media and civil space will bring many more opportunities for meaningful democratic change" (p. 178). Online social networks may allow us to visualize "clear patterns" of affiliation and communication (Langlois, Elmer, McKelvey, & Devereaux, 2009, p. 425)—even among weak "acquaintances and other people with shallower connections" (Brown, 2011, p. 31).

Mobile and social media developed new media channels created and maintained by new players (Mathison, 2009). The Twitter space, for example, lends itself to mobile use at large events (Pogue, 2009). In a stadium crowd, the 140-character text format functions with low bandwidth availability when other platforms, such as Facebook, bog down.

Many residents of large cities commute on trains and busses, and this leaves a lot of time to access mobile devices. In the same way that commuters once read newspapers, magazines and books while riding, mobile apps offer access to information and entertainment. The difference is that smartphones and tablets offer more options and extremely current content. Bloggers have capitalized on the desire for more and diverse content (Rettberg, 2008). Access to new points of view may influence social change and acceptance of new political positions and adoption of ever-newer technologies (Rogers, 2003; Genachowski, 2010). In countries where democracy is struggling to flourish, there have been numerous attempts to use social and mobile media as tools of mobilization, revolution and international awareness (Motadel, 2011).

While political discussion may account for relatively small proportions of social media on Facebook—especially outside of a presidential election—it is more common among those using Twitter (Pew, 2009). One can envision a social network as a place where opinions are activated by distribution of news, information, data and opinion. At the same time, salience of a particular social issue reflects the rise and fall of news cycles and various social contexts.

Twitter Impact

Time (2013) listed 140 Twitter moments, and this serves as a way to understand how social media buzz may translate into a business success. Twitter has been a social media space for #fails—including the many failed attempts by brand managers to take advantage of events in real time. For example, baked goods brand Entenmann's tweeted immediately following the Casey Anthony case verdict (and then quickly apologized):

> @Entenmanns: Who's #notguilty about eating all the tasty treats they want?!
> (July 5, 2011)

Naturally, the failed attempt to hijack a popular hashtag—**hashjacking**—backfired, as Twitter users responded with criticism. Keenan (2013) explains that brands need to research whether or not a hashtag is promoted by another brand or linked to a tragic event. In either case, it is a good idea to avoid using the tag. The key is relevance: "With #RoyalBaby, brands like Pampers and Johnson & Johnson had a perfect opportunity to throw some fun, branded images into the mix" (para. 5). Twitter is a mobile platform that favors smart social media communication. In real time, mistakes happen, but apologies can work. An American Red Cross social media manager, for example, accidentally tweeted from the official account about getting "slizzered," and a well-timed correction diffused the crisis:

> @RedCross: We've deleted the rogue tweet but rest assured the Red Cross is
> sober and we've confiscated the keys. (February 15, 2011)

By responding with a designated driver reference, the Red Cross appropriately used the context of Twitter to apologize and move on. Twitter is one of many popular mobile social media apps that take advantage of real-time communication, as well as other characteristics of mobile devices.

((•)) BOX 7.5 THOUGHT LEADER BRIAN ZUERCHER

The company called Seen, a Columbus, Ohio, start-up that uses visual marketing to drive customer engagement, encouraged Indy 500 fan sharing on race day. Twitter and Instagram photographs were tagged by fans with #Indy500orBust. The photos were incorporated into race marketing through an interactive map and geo-tagging. The Indy 500 gained new followers to their social media accounts, and greater reach

Figure 7.3 @bzuerche.
Courtesy Brian Zuercher.

across the social media landscape. CEO and Co-Founder Brian Zuercher identifies a continuous environment:

> The most significant change for marketing professionals is the concept of "always on." Additionally, it's managing industry information flow, personal identity (i.e. public persona and perception) and channel awareness.
>
> - Industry information flow: We now have access to a fire hose of data and understanding how to manage and synthesize the massive amount of incoming information can be a challenge. At the same time, with the right tools the data can be turned into actionable insights.
> - Personal identity: It's essential to keep your brand's personal voice authentic and in line with your company's positioning. Because of social media, marketing professionals need to be aware of the various networks, apps and services available and then decide on the places to focus their time and effort. For example, instead of road tours and speaking engagements, it's possible to develop an expert view by creating and sharing valuable content to social networks.
> - Channel awareness: Marketing professionals must have a true understanding of this and it should not be delegated.
>
> The largest challenge will be having a healthy balance between your time spent participating online and offline. You still need to be aware of the conversation surrounding your industry, but at the same time, as information spreads faster and new platforms pop up, it's easy to get lost in all the information available online. The best way to strike a balance between the two is to understand the mediums and be strategic about which platform makes the most sense for your business's audience.
>
> Our business is focused on consumer visual media. The confluence of data will enable major opportunities to provide marketers critical insights to make smart, quick decisions. As transactional, social and customer data evolve, it also becomes a major opportunity for marketers to drive growth.

Brian Zuercher has a graduate degree in management and technology from Rensselaer Polytechnic Institute, and an undergraduate degree from Butler University. He has worked for GE, Honeywell, ABM, Clearwish, The Ohio State University Technology Commercialization, Seen and others. He was an advisor for UQ Marketing. He has been an account manager, product manager, consultant, advisor, reviewer and company founder.

Mobile Geotagging

Location-based services (LBS) leverage mobile and social media by linking "people, places and things to enhance interactions" (Humphreys & Liao, 2011, p. 407). Armed with smartphones, users interact with two-way data interaction that may facilitate real-time social media behaviors. Conceptually, a sense of place may be meaningful to people: "Space is considered a more abstract term. Whereas place is considered more concrete" (p. 408). Researchers do not fully understand how users' mobile geotagging—placing digital tags on people, places or objects—develops within a social context, but there appears to be "place-based storytelling and self-presentation through place" (p. 415). At the heart of these social networking and social media activities, "people make meaning" (p. 418).

Google Glass

There has been a lot of interest in the Google Glass technology. Wearable mobile technologies appear to be the next wave by allowing users to have hands free for activities instead of holding a smartphone. Basically, Glass allows you to see a screen via a pair of glasses.

Google released the technology, and developers have begun to build apps for it. Among the ideas: hands-free information for bike riding, cooking, golf and travel (Google, 2013). Wearable technologies may either enhance social interaction or inhibit it as a distraction. It will take some time for social media platforms to incorporate data from wearable technologies, but it is easy to see how they may improve the quality of crowdsourcing. Mobile technologies allow for new relationships between people and technologically mediated social communication, and they raise issues about personal privacy, law, ethics and media literacy.

■ DISCUSSION QUESTIONS: STRATEGIES AND TACTICS

1. How is the push toward technological innovation changing your life? How do you think it may impact work during your career?
2. What are the challenges of connecting mobile technologies to social media communication? What are the new opportunities to benefit from this connection?
3. What are the privacy concerns about geo-location and tagging mobile social media services? How do you think these services and concerns will evolve in the future?

References

Brown, A. (2011, March–April). Relationships, Community, and Identity in the New Virtual Society. *The Futurist 29–31*, 34.

Cha, J. (2013). Business Models of Most-Visited U.S. Social Networking Sites. In A.B. Albarran (Ed.), *The Social Media Industries* (pp. 60–85). New York, NY: Routledge.

Crowley, D. (2010, May 16). Foursquare Co-Founder Dennis Crowley. *YouTube.* www.youtube.com/watch?v=UjEc85wosw4

Genachowski, J. (2010, October 15). U.S. Senate Committee on Small Business and Entrepreneurship, FCC chair's response, http://fjallfoss.fcc.gov/edocs_public/attachmatch/DOC-302374A1.pdf

Glenn, L.R. (2013, December 5). Press Release. Chicago-based Startup Launches App to Reinvent Radio News for Smartphone Era. http://rivetnewsradio.com/about/

Google (2013). Glass. www.google.com/glass/start/

Grasty, T. (2013, October 25). Brickflow Founder Tells His Tale Behind "Social Media Storytelling." *The Huffington Post.* www.huffingtonpost.com/tom-grasty/brickflow-founder-tells-his-tale_b_4138962.html

Greengard, S. (2011). Following the Crowd. *Communications of the ACM 54*(2), 20–22.

Harris Interactive (2012, March 15). *One in Five Adults With Mobile Devices Will Use Social Media to Follow March Madness in 2012.* www.harrisinteractive.com/vault/IMRE%20Sports%20 Research%20Release-3-15–12.pdf

Humphreys, L., & Liao, T. (2011). Mobile Geotagging: Reexamining Our Interactions with Urban Space. *Journal of Computer-Mediated Communication 16*(3), 407–423.

Jung, J., Chan-Olmsted, S., & Kim, Y. (2013). From Access to Utilization: Factors Affecting Smartphone Application Use and Its Impacts on Social and Human Capital Acquisition in South Korea. *Journalism & Mass Communication Quarterly 90*(4), 715–735.

Keenan, C. (2013, July 25). *Hashjacking: Hot or Not? Social Solutions Collective.* http://socialsolu tionscollective.com/hashjacking-hashtag-hot-or-not/

Kenski, K., Hardy, B. W., & Jamieson, K. H. (2010). *The Obama Victory: How Media, Money, and Message Shaped the 2008 Election.* New York, NY: Oxford University Press.

Kickstarter (2013). Seven Things to Know About Kickstarter. www.kickstarter.com/hello? ref=nav

Langlois, G., Elmer, G., McKelvey, F., & Devereaux, Z. (2009). Networked publics: The Double Articulation of Code and Politics on Facebook. *Canadian Journal of Communication 34*(3), 415–434.

Lin, K.-Y., & Lu, H.-P. (2011). Intention to Continue Using Facebook Fan Pages from the Perspective of Social Capital Theory. *Cyberpsychology, Behavior, and Social Networking 14*(10), 565–570.

Lipschultz, J. H. (2014, January 23). Consumer Review Credibility, Brand Marketing and Social Media. *The Huffington Post*, Media. www.huffingtonpost.com/jeremy-harris-lipschultz/ consumer-review-credibili_b_4634447.html

Mathison, D. (2009). *Be the Media.* New Hyde Park, NY: Natural E Creative Group.

Motadel, D. (2011). Waves of Revolution. *History Today 61*(4), 3–4.

Pew Research Center. (2009, June 24). Strong Public Interest in Iranian Election Protests: Many Know Iranians Using Internet to Get Message Out. Pew Research Center. http://people-press.org/report/525/strong-public-interest-in-iranian-election-protests

Pogue, D. (2009). *The World According to Twitter.* New York, NY: Blackdog & Levanthal.

Rettberg, J. W. (2008). *Blogging.* Cambridge, UK: Polity.

Rogers, E. (2003). *Diffusion of Innovations, fifth edition.* New York, NY: Free Press.

Time (2013, November 4). Twitter: The 140 Moments That Made Twitter Matter. Tech. *Time.* http://techland.time.com/2013/11/04/the-140-moments-that-made-twitter-matter/slide/all/

Vaynerchuk, G. (2009). *Crush It, Cash in on Your Passion.* New York, NY: Gary Vaynerchuk. http://crushitbook.com/wp-content/themes/CrushIt/images/crush_it_ebook.pdf

Vericat, J. (2010). Accidental Activists: Using Facebook to Drive Change. *Journal of International Affairs 64*(1), 177–180.

8   BIG DATA AND PRIVACY

"Funny how technerds are all suspicious about Google and privacy, unless Google wants to run a big data pipe right into their house."
—*Brad Daily (@bradleyboy, 2014)*

Social media and the ability to track and collect behavioral data have created "issues at the center of a polarized debate" (Lee, 2013, p. 146). By providing personal information in exchange for the use of social media sites, there are risks:

> Information on social media sites may not only be searched without permission or knowledge but may be permanently stored, meaning some material intended to be private may never enjoy a cloak of privacy. Photos, rants, relationship statuses, and people's whereabouts, for example, may always be "out there" for future employers, dates, neighbors, police investigators, and commercial businesses to mine, share, and utilize. (p. 147)

Privacy protection depends upon a patchwork of state and national laws, and these provide little in the way of consistency across the large global social network. The collection, organization, analysis, distribution and use of big data—huge online datasets tracking user action and interaction—is very relevant for those concerned about social media communication privacy.

Privacy Development

The concept of privacy was conceived by Cooley (1888), theorized by Warren and Brandeis (1890), and later developed in law by Brandeis as a right "to be let alone" (*Olmstead v. United States*, 1928, p. 478). Cooley viewed privacy as an absolute protection, while Warren and Brandeis sought to challenge a right of newspapers to invade domestic life through words and new flash photography. Many years later, Prosser (1960) and Bloustein (1964) debated a framework, but Prosser's categories were widely accepted: "intrusion upon seclusion or solitude; public disclosure of private facts; false light; and appropriation of persona for commercial exploitation" (Lipschultz, 1988, p. 509). Growing from British common law, the tort of invasion of privacy captured the idea that even the King was not allowed to enter into a private home without invitation. In the 20th century, concern focused on news media disclosure of embarrassing facts, a newsworthiness defense, and notions of community decency (*Sidis v. F. R. Publishing Corp.*, 1940). New technologies of their times—aerial photography and satellite imagery—sparked concerns beyond the traditional on-the-ground photography. At the same time, governmental intrusion by law enforcement raised constitutional Fourth Amendment questions about search and seizure privacy law. Whether or not an intrusion is connected to governmental activities, continuous surveillance may be seen as intrusion upon one's expectation of privacy. Invasion of privacy has a potential to disclose embarrassing information, defame reputation, or commercialize persona. Under current law, privacy protection is judged as "a matter of community mores" (*Virgil v. Time, Inc.*, 1975, p. 1129).

In an era of surveillance and data, the U.S. Supreme Court has held that telephone booth wiretaps violated what courts have defined as a close zone of privacy around a person (*Katz v. United States*, 1967). The Electronic Communications Privacy Act of 1986 criminalized interception of computer data. Additionally, special classes of records, such as health and educational information, are protected under federal statutes (HIPAA, 1996). After the September 11, 2001 terrorist attacks, the PATRIOT Act gave law enforcement agencies new rights to monitor previously private personal data and share it with other police powers seeking to avert future attacks:

> It relaxed restrictions on the sharing of information between domestic law enforcement agencies and intelligence agencies, enhanced the government's subpoena power to obtain and inspect e-mail records of suspected terrorists, expanded bank record-keeping requirements to track transactions of money laundering, and permitted roving wiretaps of suspected terrorists. (Terilli & Splichal, 2014, p. 315)

The National Security Agency (NSA), as was disclosed by former government contractor employee Edward Snowden, has engaged in broad surveillance of online communication, including social media activities. Publication of details by WikiLeaks, *The Guardian*, the *Washington Post*, *The New York Times* and others forced the Obama Administration to defend its practices and review processes. A secret court is assigned the job of reviewing surveillance, but critics have claimed that few safeguards remain to protect personal privacy in an age of big data. Humbach (2012) contends that any right of privacy must defer to First Amendment freedom of expression constitutional rights, and should be treated as exceptions.

The right of social network site users to protect private data on social media sites is not clear because only lower courts, so far, have taken these cases (*Moreno v. Hanford Sentinel, Inc.*, 2009). Facebook was forced to settle with users whose online data was gathered and distributed without consent (*Lane v. Facebook, Inc.*, 2012). The Appeals Court affirmed a $9.5 million settlement approved by a lower court, and a rehearing was later denied (*Lane v. Facebook*, 2013). In the *Lane* case, it was disclosed that Facebook had launched a program in 2007 called Beacon, which involved member sharing of information about website visits away from Facebook. Beacon updated profiles with personal information useful to Facebook's business partners. For example, Blockbuster would give Facebook data about video rentals, and then Facebook would share this with a user's friend network:

> Although Facebook initially designed the Beacon program to give members opportunities to prevent broadcast of any private information, it never required members' affirmative consent. As a result, many members complained that

Beacon was causing publication of otherwise private information about their outside web activities to their personal profile without their knowledge or approval. Facebook responded to these complaints (and accompanying negative media coverage) first by releasing a privacy control intended to allow its members to opt out of the Beacon program fully, and then ultimately by discontinuing operation of the program altogether.

Unsatisfied with these responses, a group of nineteen plaintiffs filed a putative class action in federal district court against Facebook and a number of other entities that operated websites participating in the Beacon program. The class action complaint alleged that the defendants had violated various state and federal privacy statutes. Each of the plaintiffs' claims centered on the general allegation that Beacon participants had violated Facebook members' privacy rights by gathering and publicly disseminating information about their online activities without permission. The plaintiffs sought damages and a variety of equitable remedies for the alleged privacy violations. (*Lane v. Facebook*, 2012, pp. 816–817)

The *Lane* court upheld the settlement as fair, although it may have been too small and directed away from the users who lost their privacy. In a dissenting opinion, a judge pointed out that some go online to shop in order to keep purchases private, but Facebook marketed Beacon to retailers, such as Blockbuster, Zappos and Overstock, to enable brands "to gain access to viral distribution" and "act as word-of-mouth promotion" that "may be seen by friends who are also likely to be interested" in purchasing the products (p. 827). Beacon was implemented over the objections of Facebook users:

> Worse, Facebook made it very hard for users to avoid these broadcasts. The user had to actively opt out. And opting out required video game skills. The user would get a pop-up on his screen asking whether he wanted to opt out, but the pop-up would disappear in about ten seconds. Too slow reading the pop-up or clicking the mouse, and all a user's "friends" would know exactly what he had bought. Since the pop-up disappeared so quickly, someone looking at another window, or answering the phone, or just not paying attention, would likely not even be aware of the opt-out option before it disappeared. (p. 827)

The dissenting opinion made it clear that the settlement money went to lawyers and an educational program rather than those wronged by the privacy invasion. Class members received "no compensation," and they did "not get even an injunction against Facebook doing exactly the same thing to them again" (p. 835).

Feldman (2012) has asked what seems to be a persistent question: "Is privacy dead?" in an analysis published in *The Huffington Post*. "Even in this new exhibitionist environment, anyone doing business utilizing user or customer information should make sure to implement fair and transparent privacy policies" (para. 7). "Is privacy dead? No. But we are changing how we feel about it" (para. 11). Not so, say technology promoters from Palo Alto to New York.

Data aggregators are in the business of selling consumer data. The nearly complete adoption of mobile smartphones presents perhaps the most troubling aspect of the privacy question. Whether or not you check in or broadcast your location,

---

📱 **BOX 8.1 LACK OF PRIVACY AND SOCIAL NETWORKS**

The Social Media Research Foundation's Marc A. Smith (@marc_smith) suggested in 2012 that the United States does little to protect privacy. Germany, for example, has a law protecting employee privacy. U.S. employers may analyze employee email for valuable patterns. The NodeXL software allows for analysis of social networks of Outlook email users.

Computers can now read 130 million tweets per day. Smith has tracked daily snapshots of topics, such as Occupy Wall Street and the Tea Party. "Anytime two people interact in email or otherwise," Smith said, "it leaves a graph."

"Nothing is private," Smith claims. He sees it as similar to an iceberg with about 10% "above the water line" and public. Smith views this as an issue because, for example, an employer may decide to fire an employee for being at the periphery rather than the center of a company email social network.

Source: Lipschultz, J. H. (2012, August 28), Privacy Is Dead?—Really? *The Huffington Post*. www.huffingtonpost.com/jeremy-harris-lipschultz/online-privacy_b_1831956.html

---

telecommunication firms may collect continuous data on your whereabouts. They do not have to tell what they are doing with the data.

The technologies continue to morph with adoption of facial recognition. The U.S. Supreme Court has yet to take on the definition of privacy within a social media context. There are some European safeguards, such as those from the Council of Europe Privacy Convention, that go beyond U.S. law in terms of data protection.

Top Social Media Site Privacy Policies

For this chapter, nine generally accepted top social media platforms in 2013 were selected to study privacy policy language: Twitter, Facebook, Google+, Instagram, LinkedIn, Tumblr, Pinterest, Vine and Snapchat. Some of the policies were difficult to find. Some sites had made recent updates.[1]

Twitter

Twitter is considered one of the most public social media sites. In order to spread content across the network, users must have a public profile. Anyone may follow a user, but she or he may block and/or identify a follower as spreading spam. Twitter encountered a brief conflict with its users in late 2013 when it suspended blocking, only to allow most features again following an online protest. The *Los Angeles Times* (Guynn, 2013) reported:

> The mass protest on Twitter was the first for Twitter as a public company. Executives held an emergency meeting Thursday night to deal with the escalating situation.

Twitter users took to the service to protest under the hashtag #RestoreTheBlock. They said the changes to the block feature would encourage online abuse and harassment on the service. Many women in particular said they would no longer feel safe on Twitter, where they say they receive rape and other threats. (paras. 2–3)

Twitter users complained that, without the ability to block stalkers, they would not feel safe to use the service. Twitter continued to work on ways to avoid the retaliation that sometimes happens following a block. Twitter limits each tweet to 140 characters, and its 2013 policy stated that, "What you say on Twitter may be viewed all around the world instantly" (para. 2). Further, Twitter users agree to allow their data to be used:

When using any of our Services you consent to the collection, transfer, manipulation, storage, disclosure and other uses of your information as described in this Privacy Policy. Irrespective of which country you reside in or supply information from, you authorize Twitter to use your information in the United States and any other country where Twitter operates. (para. 2)

Twitter broadly collects user data and has a right to use it: "This includes not only the messages you Tweet and the metadata provided with Tweets, such as when you Tweeted, but also the lists you create, the people you follow, the Tweets you mark as favorites or Retweet, and many other bits of information that result from your use of the Services" (para. 5). The Twitter default is public data, unless a user deletes information or locks down an account with privacy settings. Users also decide if they want to share their location in tweets and the trend selection. Twitter discloses that the service tracks interaction with links: "We do this to help improve our Services, to provide more relevant advertising, and to be able to share aggregate click statistics such as how many times a particular link was clicked on" (para. 7). Each time a user goes to Twitter, the service collects log data: "Log Data may include information such as your IP address, browser type, operating system, the referring web page, pages visited, location, your mobile carrier, device and application IDs, search terms, and cookie information" (para. 8). Twitter says third-party log data is saved for up to 10 days, and deleting identifiers and converting it to aggregate data may take another week. The policy also makes it clear that there is interaction with third-party advertisers creating tailored ads, and that this feature may be turned off in privacy settings. Critics of online service privacy complain that opt-out procedures should be replaced by opt-in because many users do not realize their choices.

Twitter allows users to delete accounts, but the service holds data for 30 days: "After 30 days, we begin the process of deleting your account from our systems, which can take up to a week" (para. 16). Twitter users must be at least 13 years old, and the service will delete data if it becomes aware that a younger child is using it. As an international SNS, Twitter follows European rules: "Twitter complies with the U.S.-E.U. and U.S.-Swiss Safe Harbor Privacy Principles of notice, choice, onward transfer, security, data integrity, access, and enforcement" (para. 18).

Facebook

Facebook has also received user criticism over changes to its default privacy settings in recent years. Users may not want to share information beyond their friends list, but some data are difficult to protect.

An issue for Facebook users is the data shared by friends: "We receive information about you from your friends and others, such as when they upload your contact information, post a photo of you, tag you in a photo or status update, or at a location, or add you to a group" (para. 8). Facebook may closely track user behavior:

> We receive data about you whenever you use or are running Facebook, such as when you look at another person's timeline, send or receive a message, search for a friend or a Page, click on, view or otherwise interact with things, use a Facebook mobile app, or make purchases through Facebook. (para. 11)

Social media privacy concerns frequently focus on data that have commercial value, as all SNSs seek business models to grow revenue through targeted advertising or other means. Facebook user data, including location, is tapped in a variety of ways: "We may put together your current city with GPS and other location information we have about you to, for example, tell you and your friends about people or events nearby, or offer deals to you in which you might be interested" (para. 17). When a user shares information with the public, rather than just friends, data can be used with third-party services and others off Facebook. Your name, which is required, and profile and cover photographs are always public:

> These help your friends and family recognize you. If you are uncomfortable making any of these photos public, you can always delete them. Unless you delete them, when you add a new profile picture or cover photo, the previous photo will remain public in your profile picture or cover photo album. (para. 27)

User friends and networks also are public data on Facebook, and it retains the right to use data (para. 45):

> While you are allowing us to use the information we receive about you, you always own all of your information. Your trust is important to us, which is why we don't share information we receive about you with others unless we have:
> - received your permission;
> - given you notice, such as by telling you about it in this policy; or
> - removed your name and any other personally identifying information from it.

Facebook accounts may be deactivated, which closes access but stores data for possible reactivation, and accounts also may be deleted: "It typically takes about one month to delete an account, but some information may remain in backup copies and logs for up to 90 days" (para. 51).

Google+

Google's social media service is connected with its massive cloud data operation, which includes many other functions. Google says it uses data to "make those services even better—to show you more relevant search results and ads, to help you connect with people or to make sharing with others quicker and easier" (para. 1). Of course, like other services, Google aims to generate revenue from your use and data.

Google connects user profile data with other data collected, such as from Google Analytics on websites: "We may collect information about the services that you use and how you use them, like when you visit a website that uses our advertising services or you view and interact with our ads and content" (para. 6). Google collects location data through mobile devices and WiFi spots. Google also uses data from browser cookies. While a user may turn off these, some sites do not function without them. Google shares limited data: "We will share personal information with companies, organizations or individuals outside of Google when we have your consent to do so," and uses opt-in for "sensitive personal information" (para. 30). The Google+ environment can be confusing for users, as the company continues to integrate its services. YouTube comments on videos, for example, can be linked to Google+ feeds, and the convergence of platforms offers the largest companies advantages in social media spaces.

Instagram

Instagram was acquired by Facebook in late 2012. Some Instagram users were concerned because of Facebook privacy issues over the years, and Instagram responded: "You still get to choose who can see your Instagram photos, and you still get to choose whether you post your photos on Facebook" (para. 2).

Instagram emphasizes its public sharing platform: "This means that other Users may search for, see, use, or share any of your User Content that you make publicly available through the Service, consistent with the terms and conditions of this Privacy Policy and our Terms of Use" (para. 6). As with other services, friend connection weakens privacy while increasing functionality. Instagram also uses cookies to track user data. Metadata also weakens privacy for Instagram photographs and other content: "If you geotag your photo or tag your photo using other's APIs then, your latitude and longitude will be stored with the photo and searchable (e.g., through a location or map feature) if your photo is made public by you in accordance with your privacy settings" (para. 27). User data may be shared with other businesses: "We may share User Content and your information (including but not limited to, information from cookies, log files, device identifiers, location data, and usage data) with businesses that are legally part of the same group of companies that Instagram is part of, or that become part of that group ("Affiliates")" (para. 30). Public data may be searched by anyone: "Subject to your profile and privacy settings, any User Content that you make public is searchable by other Users and subject to use under our Instagram API" (para. 35). Users retain ownership of their content, although Instagram can use it. Instagram says it attempts to be secure, but cannot guarantee it: "Instagram cannot ensure the security of any information you transmit to Instagram or guarantee that information on the Service may not be accessed, disclosed, altered, or destroyed" (para. 42). As with other privacy policies, Instagram maintains typical age restrictions and other account protocols.

LinkedIn

The professional network application opens its privacy policy by saying LinkedIn's "top priority" is maintaining trust:

> We protect your personal information and will only provide it to third parties: (1) with your consent; (2) where it is necessary to carry out your instructions; (3) as reasonably necessary in order to provide LinkedIn features and functionality to you; (4) as we reasonably believe is permitted by law or regulation; or (5) as necessary to enforce our User Agreement or protect the rights, property, or safety of LinkedIn, its Members, and the public. (para. 2)

LinkedIn discloses the address in California where U.S. user data is stored, and a second address in Ireland for all other users from other countries. LinkedIn profiles serve clear professional purposes: "With your approval, your connections may provide recommendations and endorsements of you" (para. 6). Access to contacts, such as those in email, may also raise privacy issues: "If you grant these products (mobile applications or other LinkedIn applications that sync external email services) permission to access your email accounts, they will access your email header information in order to match it to LinkedIn and other public social media profiles" (para. 8). As with other services, users exchange lower privacy for improved functions. Users must opt-out of third-party data access and use designed to target information and advertising: "LinkedIn will use this information to personalize the LinkedIn-provided functionality on third-party sites, including providing you insights from your LinkedIn network and allowing you to share information with your network (1st and 2nd degree connection on LinkedIn)" (para. 15). LinkedIn is like other services in collecting cookie and log file data. LinkedIn's career focus means that it also offers premium services to employment recruiters. User data also may be subject to subpoena and law enforcement requests.

LinkedIn also requires users to follow their terms of service that emphasize content related to purpose and spirit of its communities—content that does not violate rights of others or is considered offensive. LinkedIn also is bound in California by its Shine the Light Law, which attempts to protect consumer data from direct marketing.

Tumblr

The 2012 Tumblr policies open with the valuable suggestion that users read the rules: "When you use the Services, you are consenting to the collection, transfer, manipulation, storage, disclosure and other uses of your information as described in this Privacy Policy; please read it carefully" (para. 1). A common concern is how people may search for users: "We also allow users to look for their friends by e-mail address; you can, however, opt out of this feature through your Account Settings page, and we do not expose your e-mail address to the public or third parties, except in the limited circumstances set forth in this Privacy Policy" (para. 4). Tumblr's default setting is public: "By default, all sharing through the Services is public, and when you provide us with content it is published so that anyone can view it" (para. 8). Users are warned that, once posted, content copies are likely to exist: "While you are free to remove published pieces of content from or delete your Account, because of the nature of Internet sharing, the strong possibility of Reblogging of your content by others, and technological limitations inherent to the Services, copies of that content may exist elsewhere and be retained indefinitely, including in our systems" (para. 8). As with other services, Tumblr uses cookies and third party services to track and analyze user data.

Vine

In mid-2013, the six-second video app Vine added new privacy settings. Vine is owned by Twitter, which makes it a competitor to Facebook and Instagram. Vine is open about its data collection:

> Vine receives your information through our mobile applications, websites, email notifications, and other interactions with our Services. When using any of our Services you consent to the collection, transfer, manipulation, storage, disclosure and other uses of your information as described in this Privacy Policy. Irrespective of which country you reside in or supply information from, you authorize Vine to use your information in the United States and any other country where Vine operates. (para. 1)

Vine also collects and stores contact information:

> Vine will match the information you provide with the contact information of other Vine users. We do not retain your address book information after displaying these matches. When you connect your Vine account to other services, you are able to post your Content to those services as well. (para. 4)

Vine follows a standard disclosure approach to privacy. It reminds its users that by sharing sites, including the sharing of video and other information, these acts are public:

> Vine is a video sharing platform, so most of the information you provide us is information that you choose to be made public. This includes not only the Content that you post and data provided with such Content, such as when it was posted, but also the accounts you follow, the Content that you like or comment on, and other public interactions on the Services. (para. 5)

Lack of privacy, as with other social media, includes location data, cookies, links, log data and third-party data. By updating a profile or sharing a video, users have consented to allowing Vine to broadly share this information.

Snapchat

This video service is designed to send point-to-point brief videos that appear to disappear after being viewed. Snapchat's privacy policies, though, explain that the data are stored for viewing:

> As mentioned in our previous blog post, Snaps are deleted from our servers after they are opened by their recipients. So what happens to them before they are opened? Most of Snapchat's infrastructure is hosted on Google's cloud computing service, App Engine. Most of our data, including unopened Snaps, are kept in App Engine's datastore until they are deleted. (para. 2)

Snapchat, which tends to have a young group of teen users, explains data retrieval to its users:

> Is Snapchat capable of retrieving unopened Snaps from the datastore? Yes—if we couldn't retrieve Snaps from the datastore, we wouldn't be able to deliver them to their recipients desired by the sender. Do we manually retrieve and look at Snaps under ordinary circumstances? No. The ordinary process of sending Snaps to their recipient(s) is automated. (para. 3)

Snapchat says if Snaps are on their servers, then they must comply with law enforcement requests under the Electronic Communication Privacy Act (ECPA). "Since May 2013, about a dozen of the search warrants we've received have resulted in us producing unopened Snaps to law enforcement," Snapchat discloses. "That's out of 350 million Snaps sent every day" (para. 5). Snapchat claims only two top company officials have access to a tool that may be required to preserve a Snapchat during a law enforcement investigation. Snapchat follows typical terms of service, community and privacy policies.

Overall, the analysis of these privacy policies leads to some clear conclusions: 1) Social media communication tends to be public, except where sites allow users to dial back and opt out of specific features; 2) Social media sites track user data for system improvement, user direction and advertising purposes; 3) Data tend to be stored, retrievable and copied, which makes deletion of uploaded content difficult and time-consuming; 4) Users need to read and understand the implications of privacy policies, opt out of what is possible and not use social media, if they desire complete privacy; 5) Users should consider site purpose and context when deciding to participate; and 6) When it comes to privacy, as with all media in a commercial society, the rule of thumb is "buyer beware."

Big Data and Privacy

There appears to be no standard big data definition, but it is related to predictive analytics, data mining and trends (Nelson & Simek, 2013):

> Facebook has a huge amount of our data. In fact, it has more than some people think because they never read the Terms of Service, which allow Facebook to monitor your online activities while you are logged in. That very valuable data is sold to advertisers so that they can have ads related to your online activities pop up or show on visited web pages. Not so bad if you're searching for a new car, but what if you hang out (while married) in dating sites? Or you frequent pornography sites? What are you doing online that you'd prefer to be kept private? How about searching for help in treating a substance abuse problem? Or how to file a bankruptcy? Perfectly innocent activities certainly deserve to be private but privacy is eroding fast in the big data world.
>
> We just don't think about our digital privacy. We use our car's GPS, we post on Facebook, we buy on Amazon, and we use location service apps on our smartphones. We create our own "big data" cloud about who we are, where we are, what we do, what we like and what we don't. (pp. 34–35)

Allen (2013) considered whether or not individuals have an ethical responsibility to protect privacy within the big data information pool. One challenge is that, "People are giving away more and more personal data to intimates and strangers for a variety of self-interested, altruistic, or civic-minded reasons" (p. 847). Further, there are practical limits to managing data privacy given technological complexities: "I am suggesting a new, richer way to think about the moral relationship of consumers to business and government—as partnerships in ethical goodness" (p. 865). Allen believes that assertive consumers do not give social media businesses and government a pass on privacy and ethics, but rather create the potential for a stronger system of safeguards.

📱 BOX 8.2 GERMANY AND PRIVACY

Germany has been a leader in online data privacy protection since the 1970s. At that time, West Germany passed laws to avoid abuse of personal data, which citizens had experienced under Hitler and saw in East Germany before the fall of the Berlin Wall (Somaskanda, 2013). The scale of the U.S. NSA PRISM spy program, as disclosed by Edward Snowden, fell outside of what is legal under German law:

> Under German data protection law, the BND is not allowed [to] register and store communications data on a wide scale, or randomly tap phone conversations. Instead, they have to use sensors and look for keywords within phone and email conversations—but even there, they are only allowed to scan 10 percent of international communication. (para. 21)

The German government, however, has been unable to use its courts to fully protect social media privacy. Facebook and other sites locate their European operations in Ireland, which has weaker data privacy laws. The German government has expressed the view that Google and other large companies use their size and power to ignore concerns. Some Germans have called for suspension of Safe Harbor rules that allow sharing of European Union banking information with companies in the United States (Overdorf, 2013). Social media privacy is a piece of the larger concerns raised by the NSA disclosures.

Sources:

Somaskanda, S. (2013, July 26). NSA Spying Rankles Privacy-Loving Germans. *The Atlantic.* www.theatlantic.com/international/archive/2013/07/nsa-spying-rankles-privacy-loving-germans/278090/;

Overdorf, J. (2013, November 5). Germany: Privacy Protections Must Go Beyond 'No-Spying Act.' *MINNPOST.* www.minnpost.com/global-post/2013/11/germany-privacy-protections-must-go-beyond-no-spying-act

---

FTC Regulation

In the United States, the strongest privacy protections for social media consumers derive from Federal Trade Commission regulation. The FTC has called upon Congress to enact laws that would address data security, breaches of security and brokering of data (FTC, 2012). The FTC identified three critical areas for businesses to address (paras. 4–6):

Privacy by Design—companies should build in consumers' privacy protections at every stage in developing their products. These include reasonable security for consumer data, limited collection and retention of such data, and reasonable procedures to promote data accuracy;

Simplified Choice for Businesses and Consumers—companies should give consumers the option to decide what information is shared about them, and with whom. This should include a Do-Not-Track mechanism that would provide a simple, easy way for consumers to control the tracking of their online activities.

Greater Transparency—companies should disclose details about their collection and use of consumers' information, and provide consumers access to the data collected about them.

The FTC raised specific concerns about large platforms and mobile use, which would impact social media sites such as Google+ and Facebook. In its full report, the FTC noted enforcement action in 2010 against Facebook:

> Brought enforcement actions against Google and Facebook. The orders obtained in these cases require the companies to obtain consumers' affirmative express consent before materially changing certain of their data practices and to adopt strong, company-wide privacy programs that outside auditors will assess for 20 years. These orders will protect the more than one billion Google and Facebook users worldwide. (p. ii)

The FTC took action with orders against Google, Facebook and online advertising networks, and used fair credit reporting and child online privacy protection laws to force changes. "To the extent that large platforms, such as Internet Service Providers ("ISPs"), operating systems, browsers, and social media, seek to comprehensively track consumers' online activities, it raises heightened privacy concerns" (p. 14). The FTC held workshops to better understand tracking issues and consider the need for tougher regulation. At the same time, "the Commission generally supports the exploration of efforts to develop additional mechanisms, such as the 'eraser button' for social media . . . to allow consumers to manage and, where appropriate, require companies to delete the information consumers have submitted" (p. 29). That idea, however, may conflict with free speech constitutional rights. "While consumers should be able to delete much of the information they place on a particular social media site, there may be First Amendment constraints to requiring third parties to delete the same information" (p. 71, fn. 358).

Privacy and Legal Implications

Social media communication privacy is likely to spawn industry guidelines and standards for self-regulation, future regulation and legislation, and court cases challenging the status quo in the United States. At the international level, there will be continued political and legal pressure on large social media platforms to be transparent and offer users more opportunities to protect their data. Still, the very nature of social media sharing is that social networks negotiate privacy through friend, follower and fan inter-action. The commercialization of social media, sophistication of data collection and tracking, and desire of advertisers to target consumers ready to act present numerous ongoing privacy challenges. Judges and juries will be faced with interpreting legal conflicts over protection of privacy.

While privacy may be seen as a matter of user literacy, site terms of service or govern-ment regulatory protection, it also is connected to the norms of information flow. Tradi-tional journalists seek to access as much information as possible, but there may be a cultural shift. Social media spaces encourage sharing of private stories to an audience. Bloggers, for example, use sometimes-personal narrative storytelling to attract readers. Blogger Tracy Solomon wrote about her daughter's battle with leukemia to increase public understand-ing, and in doing so she and her family voluntarily gave up some of their privacy.

The social norms of privacy will continue to evolve, just as lawmakers and social network sites adjust to new uses of technology. Data protection is a social, political and legal issue. Social media communication by mobile smartphone or other Internet device

(⊙) BOX 8.3 THOUGHT LEADER TRACY SOLOMON

Before I started Katia's blog in November 2002, there had already been identity issues with pictures of others being used to start fake fund-raising cancer sites.

I made it a point to tell many cancer organizations about Katia's blog. Also, the media was covering her story, and I posted links to those articles. There were continuous mar-row drives done nationwide trying to find a match for her over a six-month period in 2002–2003, so her story was widely covered.

Figure 8.1 @tracysolomon.
Courtesy Tracy Solomon.

Internet security is very important to me, and keeping my own name and Katia's name clear is important. We are always willing to share and take part in something when asked. We just prefer to be asked:)

Social media create ease of access to a variety of forms of available information; it challenges journalism to not focus on being first to report something or running a story that is sensationalized—something to grab more followers/viewers. Readers run the risk of having too much information quickly at their fingertips, some sourced and some not. This can cause a great deal of confusion and put people at risk, causing avoidable harm.

Over the next five years, I would like to see a more collabora-tive effort in bringing social media to the forefront of schools, news

(continued)

organizations, emergency services and more. This requires a better understanding of fact checking and the need to provide source information along with what is posted to avoid the misunderstanding of what is opinion versus what is fact. If social media are used correctly, they can save lives. So many can benefit from a tool that ties our world together if it is used in a positive way. We can reach out to people we were never able to before to sell our product, brand or service and/or have a message heard.

Tracy Solomon is active across social media platforms, her Change Happens blog at TracyLSolomon.com and with the Tampa, Florida *Examiner*'s Political Buzz. She has blogged for more than a decade about her daughter's battle with leukemia. Solomon has current interests in the community, nation and world. She uses social media to help others: "Each day has a moment to remember forever. If we are lucky, we'll be watching and realize the moment."

identifies the speaker, and there is no complete online anonymity. Therefore, users must rely upon businesses and government to be more careful with data. At the same time, social media users must act with an understanding of the public nature of most online communication.

■ DISCUSSION QUESTIONS: STRATEGIES AND TACTICS

1. How have your expectations for personal privacy changed, if at all, in the age of social media? What are your most important concerns?
2. What do you think can be done to align United States privacy policies with those in the European Union? What are the advantages and disadvantages of global policies?
3. What are the significant implications for privacy based upon use of mobile smartphones and tablets to access social media sites? Which areas might lead to litigation or changes in law?

Note

1. Search google to find each site's privacy policy: Twitter, https://twitter.com/privacy; Facebook, www.facebook.com/about/privacy/; Google+, www.google.com/policies/privacy/; Instagram, http://instagram.com/about/legal/privacy/; LinkedIn, www.linkedin.com/legal/privacy-policy; Tumblr, www.tumblr.com/policy/en/privacy; Pinterest, http://about.pinterest.com/en/privacy-policy; Vine, https://vine.co/privacy; Snapchat, http://www.snapchat.com/privacy/

References

Allen, A.L. (2013). An Ethical Duty to Protect One's Own Information Privacy? *64 Alabama Law Review* 845.

Bloustein, E.J. (1964). Privacy as an Aspect of Human Dignity: An Answer to Dean Prosser. *39 New York Law Review* 962.

Cooley, T. M. (1888). *Cooley On Torts 2d*, 29.

Electronic Communications Privacy Act (1986). 18 U.S.C. Sec. 2510.

Feldman, M. J. (2012, February 28). Is Privacy Dead? *The Huffington Post*. www.huffingtonpost. com/miles-j-feldman/internet-privacy_b_1306701.html

FTC (2012, March 26). *FTC Issues Final Commission Report on Protecting Consumer Privacy*. Federal Trade Commission. www.ftc.gov/news-events/press-releases/2012/03/ftc-issues-final-commi ssion-report-protecting-consumer-privacy [Full report downloaded at: FTC Report: *Protecting Consumer Privacy in an Era of Rapid Change*. www.ftc.gov/sites/default/files/documents/ reports/federal-trade-commission-report-protecting-consumer-privacy-era-rapid-change-rec ommendations/120326privacyreport.pdf

Guynn, J. (2013, December 12). Twitter reverses changes to blocking feature after mass protest. *Los Angeles Times*. www.latimes.com/business/technology/la-fi-tn-twitter-reverses-changes- to-blocking-feature-after-mass-protest-20131212,0,1607498.story?track=rss&utm_source= dlvr.it&utm_medium=twitter&dlvrit=515009#axzz2nSu22Y1q

HIPAA (1996). Health Insurance Portability and Accountability Act of 1996. 42 U.S.C.A. Sec. 1320d, 4.

Humbach, J. A. (2012). Privacy and the Right of Free Expression. *11 First Amendment Law Review* 16.

Katz v. United States (1967). 389 U.S. 347.

Lane v. Facebook (2013). 709 F.3d 791.

Lane v. Facebook, Inc. (2012). 696 F.3d 811 (9th Cir.).

Lee, L. T (2013). Privacy and Social Media. In A. B. Albarran (Ed.), *The Social Media Industries*, pp. 146–165. New York, NY: Routledge.

Lipschultz, J. H. (1988). Mediasat and the Tort of Invasion of Privacy. *Journalism Quarterly* 65(2), 507–511.

Lipschultz, J. H. (2012, August 28), Privacy Is Dead?—Really? *The Huffington Post*. www. huffingtonpost.com/jeremy-harris-lipschultz/online-privacy_b_1831956.html

Moreno v. Hanford Sentinel, Inc. (2009). 172 Cal. App. 4th 1125.

Nelson, S. D., & Simek, J. W. (2013). Big Data: Big Pain or Big Gain for Lawyers? *39 The Vermont Bar Journal & Law Digest* 33.

Olmstead v. United States (1928). 227. U.S. 438, p. 478.

Overdorf, J. (2013, November 5). Germany: Privacy Protections Must Go Beyond 'No-Spying Act.' *MINNPOST*. www.minnpost.com/global-post/2013/11/germany-privacy-protections- must-go-beyond-no-spying-act

Prosser, D. (1960). Privacy. *48 California Law Review* 383.

Sidis v. F. R. Publishing Corp. (1940) 113 F.2d 806.

Smith, M. (2014, May 3). *Mapping and Measuring Connections*. Slideshare. www.slideshare.net/ Marc_A_Smith/2014-the-next-websmrfnode-xlsnasocial-media-networks

Somaskanda, S. (2013, July 26). NSA Spying Rankles Privacy-Loving Germans. *The Atlantic*.

Terilli, Jr., S. A., & Splichal, S. (2014). Privacy Rights in an Open and Changing Society. In W. W. Hopkins (Ed.), *Communication and the Law, 2014 edition*, pp. 291–316. Northport, AL: Vision Press.

Virgil v. Time Inc. (1975). 527 F.2d 1122 (9th Cir.).

Warren, S., & Brandeis, L. (1890). The Right to Privacy. *4 Harvard Law Review* 193.

9   LAW AND REGULATION

"What a lot of people don't realize is that when they decide to start a blog or post comments ... they are potentially making themselves open to being liable to the laws of that country."

—Anthony Fargo, @AnthonyFargo1 (2012)

Facebook claimed user Christopher Peter Tarquini posted deceptive messages that promised to show others a video of celebrities Justin Bieber and Selena Gomez having sex. Bieber had a whopping 49 million followers, as shown in Table 9.1—second only to Katy Perry—and Gomez had 17.7 million followers at the time.

When people clicked on the link, they were reportedly led to spam that automatically posted the link on their Facebook walls (Crook, 2013). *TechCrunch* learned that Facebook spent $5,000 investigating Tarquini's social media commission scam, which violated its terms of service (paras. 3–5). Facebook went to court to recover its costs and have Tarquini banned for life from the social networking site. Spamming as commercial speech is one form of behavior that may spawn case law. Concern over illegal online behavior in cyberspace is nothing new (Branscomb, 1996), but the openness of social media publishing generates many more cases and concerns. The complexity of social networking also impacts groups of people with every networked communication. In the United States, social media users are governed by the British common law tradition and constitutional development of free expression rights.

Table 9.1   Top Number of Followers on Twitter

Twitter Account	Followers	Following	Tweets
1. @katyperry	49,789,759	129	5,346
2. @justinbieber	48,993,460	123,719	25,957
3. @ladygaga	41,034,003	134,145	4,319
4. @YouTube	38,693,676	566	9,636
5. @taylorswift13	38,513,299	121	2,102

Source: Friend Or Follow (2014, January 24). http://friendorfollow.com/twitter/most-followers/

Free Expression and the First Amendment

The First Amendment of the U.S. Constitution, while not interpreted as providing an absolute right of free expression, remains a strong statement in favor of it:

> Congress shall make no law respecting an establishment of religion, or prohibiting the free exercise thereof; or abridging the freedom of speech, or of the press; or the right of the people peaceably to assemble, and to petition the Government for a redress of grievances.

The *Alien and Sedition Acts of 1798* were not considered before the U.S. Supreme Court, but constitutionality of government action was reviewed beginning with the *Espionage Act of 1917*. Although the Court upheld convictions for publishing and distributing anti-war fliers, a clear and present danger test began to emerge, as well as support for what later became known as the marketplace of ideas. Milton (1644) offered the earliest marketplace of ideas articulation that remains a free speech justification:

> Though all the winds of doctrine were let loose to play upon the earth, so Truth be in the field, we do injuriously by licensing and prohibiting to misdoubt her strength. Let her and Falsehood grapple; who ever knew Truth put to the worse in a free and open encounter?

As the U.S. Supreme Court grappled with 20th-century free speech cases, dissenters offered defenses for speech. Justice William O. Douglas (1951) expressed what became known as the near-absolutist position:

> Unless and until extreme and necessitous circumstances are shown, our aim should be to keep speech unfettered and to allow the processes of law to be invoked only when the provocateurs among us move from speech to action.— *Dennis v. U.S.* (1951, p. 590)

Fifty years ago, *New York Times v. Sullivan* (1964) convinced a majority of U.S. Supreme Court justices to support constitutional protection for political speech, which includes debate on public issues that is "robust" and "wide open" (p. 271). So it is with Twitter and other platforms. Social media pages empower users to be global publishers through blogs, podcasts and social sites. Although anonymity is more "a complicating factor" on Twitter, even for Facebook, LinkedIn and other sites, it challenges attempts to regulate social media:

> Like traditional media, the Internet allows speakers to communicate their messages to a large consuming public. However, because the content providers include independent speakers—whose information may be subject to minimal editing—as well as traditional media speakers—whose information is often verified and edited—defamatory speech has greater potential to reach a widespread audience . . .
>
> Given the speed with which such content can be disseminated and reputations injured as a result, the level of First Amendment protection available for defamatory Internet speech must be critically evaluated . . . Thus, defamatory statements published online have serious potential to cause both reputational injury and economic harm . . . (Sanders & Olsen, 2012, pp. 365–366)

Sanders and Olsen (2012) suggested the need for a psychological sense of community rather than one based upon traditional legal geography. Social media are global (Ali, 2011), and online freedom brings a unique set of legal responsibilities. Social media transform every user through their interaction with others. The international distribution of unfiltered media across a mosaic of legal systems and structures means technological freedom as a trend is colliding with governmental, corporate, organizational and individual desires to control messages. The massive and ubiquitous Internet may be too large to completely control (Fang, 2008), but legal systems and structures attempt to incorporate new cases within traditional rules. Social media have triggered a new set of expectations in journalism (Briggs, 2010), and present new legal challenges (Nockleby et al., 2013).

Internet Libel

Internet Service Providers (ISPs) have protection from liability for libel. America Online, for example, could not be sued for potentially libelous content distributed using its network (*Blumenthal v. Drudge and America Online*, 1998). AOL was protected, a lower court ruled, because of the limited exercise of editorial control and a mostly passive role. In a social media context, it is interesting to think about the use of the RT on Twitter, which may or may not be passive depending upon the context of tweets. In any case, social media make it more difficult to measure economic impact because of the absence of a definable mass media audience. Social media crowds instead are dependent upon individual social networks for distribution. Further emergence of a sharing culture, promoted by sites that encourage users to share content with online friends or fans, introduces a new media model. Content owners who benefit from advertising revenue generated by increased numbers of site visitors must also try to protect property rights. At the same time, some brands use social media to promote valuable content or services that generate revenue (Mathison, 2009). In this model, each user has the power to be her or his own media outlet. It is a world in which sites such as Twitter generate unique content (Pogue, 2009), leverage digital assets (Keller, Levine, & Goodale, 2008; Pavlik, 2008), and internationalize thinking (Groggin & McLelland, 2009).

Facebook, Twitter and the Law

While journalists are, of course, not the only social media users, they have a particular need to verify accuracy of online information (Chow, 2013). Over the last five years, social media sites have gone from being unheard of in the courts to the subject of hundreds of cases each year (Stewart, 2013). Media law scholar Derigan Silver notes that social media law may be eroding First Amendment protections for free speech:

> One of the biggest issues facing non-media users of social media is the distinctions some courts have created between the constitutional protections afforded the media and those afforded to average individuals . . . in effect, lower courts are removing a wide range of speech from constitutional protections at the very time new communication technologies such as email, Facebook, Twitter, and blogs are giving non-media individuals the power to reach wider and wider audiences. (Silver, in Stewart, 2013, pp. 39–40)

For example, in *Tatro v. University of Minnesota* (2012), a state Supreme Court upheld university discipline against a mortuary science student posting what she said were "satirical" comments on her Facebook wall. Amanda Tatro violated student conduct code and program rules designed to professionally respect privileged access to human cadavers. According to court records, the University of Minnesota focused on four Facebook posts:

- **Amanda Beth Tatro:** Gets to play, I mean dissect, Bernie today. Let's see if I can have a lab void of reprimanding and having my scalpel taken away. Perhaps if I just hide it in my sleeve . . . (November 12, 2009)
- **Amanda Beth Tatro:** Is looking forward to Monday's embalming therapy as well as a rumored opportunity to aspirate. Give me room, lots of aggression to be taken out with a trocar (December 6, 2009)
- **Amanda Beth Tatro:** Who knew embalming lab was so cathartic! I still want to stab a certain someone in the throat with a trocar though. Hmm . . . perhaps I will spend the evening updating my "Death List #5" and making friends with the crematory guy. I do know the code . . . (December 7, 2009)
- **Amanda Beth Tatro:** Realized with great sadness that my best friend, Bernie, will no longer be with me as of Friday next week. I wish to accompany him to the retort. Now where will I go or who will I hang with when I need to gather my sanity? Bye, bye. Bernie. Lock of hair in my pocket (Undated, p. 513)

While the postings broke no laws, Tatro was barred from the lab during an investigation of her comments. Meanwhile, two local television newsrooms interviewed her, and this generated public pressure on the university. As the investigation continued, Tatro was allowed to return and take final examinations. Tatro testified at a hearing that she did not understand Facebook posts fell under a rule that prohibited blogging. Anatomy Laboratory Rule #7 specified that, "Blogging about the anatomy lab or the cadaver dissection is not allowable." Tatro's punishment included a grade of "F" in the course, as well as these requirements: that she completes an ethics course, writes a letter to faculty, and completes a psychiatric evaluation. Additionally, she was placed on probation for the remainder of her undergraduate work. Relying primarily on elementary and high school cases, the Minnesota Supreme Court rejected Tatro's First Amendment argument, noting that she had signed a contract to follow lab rules:

> We acknowledge the concerns expressed by Tatro and supporting amici that adoption of a broad rule would allow a public university to regulate a student's personal expression at any time, at any place, for any claimed curriculum-based reason. Nonetheless, the parties agree that university may regulate student speech on Facebook that violates established professional conduct standards. This is the legal standard we adopt here, with the qualification that any restrictions on a student's Facebook posts must be *narrowly tailored* (emphasis added) and directly related to established professional conduct standards. Tying the legal rule to established professional conduct standards limits a university's restrictions on Facebook use to students in professional programs and other disciplines where student conduct is governed by established professional conduct standards . . . we limit the potential for a university to create overbroad restrictions

that would impermissibly reach into a university student's personal life outside of and unrelated to the program. Accordingly, we hold that a university does not violate the free speech rights of a student enrolled in a professional program when the university imposes sanctions for Facebook posts that violate academic program rules that are narrowly tailored and directly related to established professional conduct standards. (p. 521)

As a general rule, social media and other Internet communication are not immune from traditional media law—libel, privacy, copyright and commercial speech. When a user signs on to a site, such as Facebook, she or he agrees to a Terms of Service (TOS) agreement that is essentially a contract. Each Facebook user should explore terms and policies, as these are a legal contract between the social media site and the SNS participant. Too frequently, users click to gain access without reading and understanding terms, which specify rules covering vague areas of the law. Facebook divides its terms into three categories: Rights and Responsibilities, Data Use, and Community Standards.

The 2013 revision (current in May, 2014) of Facebook rights and responsibilities highlights privacy and references its data use policy. "You own all of the content and information you post on Facebook, and you can control how it is shared through your privacy and application settings," the company articulates under its sharing policy. However, photos and videos fall under intellectual property (IP). Users grant Facebook "a non-exclusive, transferable, sub-licensable, royalty-free, worldwide license to use any IP content" posted. The license "ends" when users delete "IP content or your account, unless your content has been shared with others, and they have not deleted it." This effectively makes it difficult to take back control of content once it is shared.

Facebook notes that deleted content "may persist in backup copies for a reasonable period of time (but will not be available to others)." Some computer program applications seek user permission and then use the content that is posted. Additionally, content shared as "public," such as a profile picture, can be seen by "everyone, including people off of Facebook."

Facebook "cannot guarantee" safety, and its TOS has user "commitments" to "not post unauthorized commercial communications (such as spam)," not "collect users' content or information" without prior permission, "not engage in unlawful multi-level marketing," "not upload viruses," and not "access an account belonging to someone else." The Facebook TOS contract also requires that users "will not bully, intimidate, or harass any user," "will not post content that: is hate speech, threatening, or pornographic; incites violence; or contains nudity or graphic or gratuitous violence." So-called "mature" content requires "appropriate age-based restrictions." In general, Facebook is not to be used "to do anything unlawful, misleading, malicious, or discriminatory."

Under the heading "Registration and Account Security," Facebook requires use of "real names and information." As with other TOS provisions, the site relies upon complaints, if a user registers a fake name. Social networking sites rarely require identity verification beyond an email address, and this makes it easy to dodge the rules.

Under the rules, users are to create only one personal account for themselves. Under the TOS, "You will not use your personal timeline primarily for your own commercial gain, and will not use a Facebook Page for such purposes." Convicted sex offenders are not allowed to use Facebook, under the rules. In 2013, Facebook announced it would be updating its rules and processes. The changes in areas such as promoted posts were delayed amid new privacy concerns.

Twitter also presents a number of legal issues.

📱 **BOX 9.1 EMERGING TWITTER LAW**

Tweets, messages of no more than 140 characters on Twitter, are receiving increasing attention from lawyers. *The National Law Journal* reported in 2008 that micro-blogging was a quick way to get an employee or an employer in trouble (Baldes, 2008). Social media interaction can be subpoenaed during a case, and tweets create a legal record of communication and behavior. The tech website Mashable.com (@Mashable; Cashmore, 2008) identified four potential lawsuit areas: company secrets, invasion of privacy/defamation, trademark violations and wrongful employee termination claims.

In 2009, for example, Horizon Group Management, which manages rental property in Chicago, sued tenant Amanda Bonnen for $50,000 after she tweeted as @JessB123: "You should just come anyway. Who said sleeping in a moldy apartment was bad for you? Horizon realty thinks it's okay." Bonnen had just twenty followers on Twitter, but the libel lawsuit claimed the tweet damaged Horizon's reputation. A Cook County judge dismissed the case in finding the tweet was too vague. Other examples of Twitter law include:

- In *U.S. v. Fumo*, 655 F.3d 288 (2011), a Pennsylvania state senator's criminal convictions were upheld, but the appeals court ordered re-sentencing. During deliberations, a TV station reported that a juror had posted on Twitter, as well as on Facebook. After watching the report the night before the verdict, the juror panicked and deleted the postings, which included this tweet: "This is it . . . no looking back now!" On the same March, 2009, evening the juror also deleted this Facebook wall post: "Stay tuned for the big announcement on Monday everyone!" A District Court judge found that the juror violated instructions to avoid discussing the case outside the jury room, but there was no evidence of outside influence. The posts were called "nothing more than harmless ramblings with no prejudicial effect" and that, "They were so vague as to be virtually meaningless." (p. 301)
- The Kentucky Supreme Court cited New York rules that allow a lawyer to search social media sites to research prospective jurors, as long as there is no contact or attempt to "friend" the person. It is also considered ethical for a lawyer to visit public sites during trial evidence and deliberations to monitor but not engage in

discussion. (*Sluss v. Commonwealth*, 381 S.W.3d 215 (2012)) (Lip-schultz, 2014)

- The Florida Bar Association, which regulates attorney advertising, found that, "If access to a lawyer's Twitter postings is restricted to the followers of the particular lawyer, the information posted there is information at the request of a prospective client and is not subject to the lawyer advertising rules under Rule 4–7. l(h)" (Faehner, 2012, p. 36)

In the area of public relations, Hall (2013) suggests that every strategic communication social media policy must address legal concerns that are now central to social media communication on sites, such as Twitter—transparency, privacy, employee control, intellectual property and tone (pp. 223–224). In particular, social media audiences should know who is speaking to them and have some sense of content producer motivation. Social media communication happens within contexts that include employee roles and obligations, content property rights, and normative expectations for personal and company branding.

Sources:

Baldes, T. (2008, December 22). Beware: Your "Tweet" on Twitter Could Be Trouble, *National Law Journal*. www.law.com/jsp/nlj/PubArticleNLJ.jsp?id=1202426916 023&slreturn=20131026150648

Cashmore, P. (2008, December 20). Twitter Lawsuits: 4 Reasons Your Tweets Might be Trouble, *Mashable*, http://mashable.com/2008/12/20/twitter-lawsuits/

Chicagoist (2010, January 21). Twitter Lawsuit Dismissed http://chicagoist.com/2010 /01/21/twitter_lawsuit_dismissed.php

Faehner, M.J. (2012, June). Advertising. *Florida Bar Journal 86*(6), 36–37.

Hall, H.K. (2013). Social Media Policies for Advertising and Public Relations. In D. R. Stewart (Ed.), *Social Media Law, A Guidebook for Communication Students and Professionals*, pp. 212–226. New York, NY: Routledge.

Wang, M. (2009). UPDATED: Rounding up the Buzz. ChicagoNow. http://culture wav.es/public_thought/72990

For Facebook and other sites around the world, the rapid global shift to mobile media through smartphones and tablets has presented new legal challenges. From Asia to the Middle East, high-speed mobile networks opened social media communication and challenged traditional legal restrictions.

International Social Media

Internet access broadened with mobile and real-time applications ("apps"), and social media law and regulation have been evolving with rapid global adoption. Nearly half of the Internet users worldwide are located in Asia (44.8%), and the fastest-growing regions are in Africa and Europe (Internet World Stats, 2012). Within social media, Facebook, LinkedIn and Twitter all had historically large user numbers in 2011 and 2012. Media Metrix reported that overall, Facebook attracted 157.2 million unique visitors in May 2011 and was growing each month. Facebook and MySpace started as equals in 2004, but MySpace has declined since 2008. Social networking, meanwhile, accounts for increasing percentages of user online time. Even China, a country that filters the Internet, has its own social network sites, such as Weibo—a huge Twitter-like application (www.weibo.com).

Global data painted enormous growth on every continent, and it was most dramatic in Asia. While China barely trailed the United States in 2008—with just eight million fewer Internet users than the estimated 218 million in the United States—China's broadband connections of more than 66 million outpaced the United States. With more than four times the population, China's Internet penetration continued to grow dramatically. China took the lead in number of Internet users in 2009. However, freedom continued to be a concern, as China pressured computer manufacturers to pre-install filtering software and resist outside nudging to be more open. China has a huge portion of the world population (more than 56% of all people—3.8 billion—reside in Asia). The U.S. had a diffusion advantage in the 1990s, but rapid global growth is happening almost everywhere across cultures and cybercultures (Bell & Kennedy, 2007).

The 2010 re-licensing of Google in China was contingent upon regulatory limitations. So-called "law-based management" required Google to accept government filtering. In the application letter, Guxiang (Google) pledged to "abide by Chinese law,"

Figure 9.1 In China, hundreds of millions have access to Weibo, but they are officially blocked from Facebook, Twitter and other international sites.

and "ensure the company provides no law breaking content as stipulated in the 57th statement in China's regulations concerning telecommunications" (Xinhua, 2010). The statement says that any organization or individual is prohibited from using the Internet to spread any content that attempts to subvert state power, undermine national security, infringe on national reputation and interests, or that incites ethnic hatred or secession, or transmits pornography or violence. Guxiang also accepted that all content it provides is subject to supervision of government regulators, said the official.

Broad issues of global cyber crime fall under the relatively new area of "Internet governance," which address a variety of activities, including online pharmacies' marketing of nationally regulated medicines:

> Conceptually, it is defined as the establishment of shared principles, norms, rules, decision-making procedures and programs developed by governments, the private sector, and civil society on the use and evolution of the Internet. Reflecting a heretofore decentralized, multi-stakeholder, multi-country, inter-connected, self-governed and autonomous group of actors, the UN has made Internet governance a global priority despite its highly challenging nature. (Mackey & Liang, 2013, para. 36)

A UN-initiated World Summit on the Information Society (WSIS) established the Internet Governance Forum (IGF), and it has begun to address global Internet governance issues, such as the marketing of counterfeit medicines. This involves both technical and behavioral concerns, as stakeholders seek "solutions to issues arising from the misuse of the Internet" (para. 37). Similar to early Internet studies, social media communication presents both challenges and opportunities (Ali, 2011). Former Egyptian President Mubarak, for example, sought to stifle Internet communication at the height of protests in Cairo's Tahrir Square because of "the incredible power of social media" (p. 185). "The story of social media in developing nations so far is one of individual empowerment" (p. 209). In the Arab world, free speech has been challenged because of the need for "state security," which can be weakened as people discuss and debate social change on social media sites:

> The Internet and social media are important because of their intrinsic value and the possibility they create of starting a campaign, spreading news about what is going on, or even starting a movement that demands change. But what is important to remember is that these are only tools used by people who desire change—and want it because of the current situation in which they live. (Abu-Zayyad, 2013, p. 40)

While social networking sites may be used to mobilize protests, more often legal issues arise based upon the power to distribute messages to a wide audience.

Prior Restraint and Terrorism

The post-9/11 world is sensitive to the dangers posed online by terrorists who may use social media to plan violent acts. The law, however, provides centuries of cases highlighting protection of free expression. Blackstone's *Commentaries on the Laws of England* (1765–1769) defines prior restraint doctrine:

> In this, and the other instances which we have lately considered, where blasphemous, immoral, treasonable, schismatical, seditious, or scandalous libels are punished by the English law, some with a greater, others with a less degree of severity; the *liberty of the press,* properly understood, is by no means infringed or violated. The liberty of the press is indeed essential to the nature of a free state: but this consists in laying no *previous* restraints upon publications, and not in freedom from censure for criminal matter when published. Every freeman has an undoubted right to lay what sentiments he pleases before the public: to forbid this, is to destroy the freedom of the press: but if he publishes what is improper, mischievous, or illegal, he must take the consequence of his own temerity.

In Blackstone's widely accepted view, "Every freeman has an undoubted right to lay what sentiments he pleases before the public; to forbid this is to destroy the freedom of the press, but if he publishes what is improper, mischievous or illegal, he must take the consequences for his own temerity." Therefore, the larger social good was achieved by placing responsibility in the hands of individuals. It would be somewhat more likely that individuals would challenge the order with new ideas than that a censor would allow such controversial ideas out. Once available to the public, these could be judged. However, it is not clear that Blackstonian legal theory afforded any protection beyond the point of publication, even under the framers' view. Four types of expression that could be punished under common law were:

- *Seditious libel*—words "designed to bring the government into dispute," meant that truthful criticism was subject to greater punishment.
- *Obscenity*—words that tended to corrupt people through "immoral influences," meant that sexuality was taboo.
- *Blasphemy*—words against the church were seen as "offenses to God," meaning that the state could inflict punishment.
- *Libel*—words against other individuals were thought to threaten peace, meaning that government would punish the offender rather than allow for retribution.

In *Near v. Minnesota* (1931), the Supreme Court established an American prior restraint doctrine. The Court left open the possibility for a narrow class of prior restraints: where national security in time of war was threatened, in times when publication might incite violent overthrow of the government, publishing fighting words or obscenities.

For social media communication, prior restraint law places a burden on government to limit a speaker before online publication, but it does not protect her or him from subsequent punishment through civil lawsuit or the criminal justice system. The Web over time was less revolutionary than first predicted and more an extension of traditional media in terms of American communication law. A difficult challenge is how to define offensive material. For example, Senator Joseph Lieberman in 2008 complained to Google about the existence of YouTube videos posted by terrorist organizations, such as al-Qaeda. Google operates YouTube, and it protects free speech for legal, nonviolent and non-hate speech videos.

📱 BOX 9.2 SOCIAL MEDIA TERRORISM

Professor Gabriel Weimann (2010) recounts the exchange between two Palestinians—one with homemade explosives asking for instructions, and the other explaining how to make a bomb on the public site, *Izz al din al Kassam*:

> The internet has enabled terrorist organizations to research and coordinate attacks; to expand the reach of their propaganda to a global audience; to recruit adherents; to communicate with international supporters and ethnic diasporas; to solicit donations; and to foster public awareness and sympathy for their causes. (p. 46)

Beginning with the chat room and electronic forum, and developing within social media communication, there is a "cyber-jihad" movement (p. 46). The U.S. has warned that Twitter could be "an effective communication tool for terrorists trying to launch military attacks" (p. 48). Wary that Facebook and similar sites do not guarantee anonymity, terror groups look for apps that are not focused on individual identity. On the other hand, there have been examples of recruiting on Facebook.

YouTube is one of the oldest social media sites, and it is the most popular global video space. Since its launch in 2005, terrorist groups "realized the potential of this easily accessed platform for the dissemination of their propaganda and radicalization videos" (p. 51). One user posted more than 100 such videos in 2009 alone (p. 52). YouTube videos considered "jihadist content" have been spread "far beyond traditional jihadist websites" (p. 52). Social networking is an effective tool for those wishing to fuel political sympathies and even convert individuals to a cause by luring them to extremist messages.

Source: Weimann, G. (2010). Terror on Facebook, Twitter, and YouTube. *Brown Journal of World Affairs 16*(2), 45–54.

The U.S. First Amendment perspective tends to promote freedom of expression by limiting government action against media—including social media. In most countries, though, there are few protections for freedom of speech and publication. Consider the 2013 conviction of Jeremy Forrest in the United Kingdom. Authorities investigated tweets that named his victim, which were against the law. Sussex police said the Crown Prosecution Service monitors social media sites for violation of law designed to protect the identity of sexual assault victims. The British law provides for lifetime anonymity. *The Guardian*'s David Banks (@DBanksy) observed that the identity of the victim had been made public at the time of her abduction, and this may have confused some, but not all, Twitter users:

> Others clearly knew the legal position, but were intent on defying it because it did not make sense to them, or somewhat disturbingly, they did not think the

victim had deserved anonymity in this case. One taunted the authorities to sue him for it if they dared (apparently unaware that this is not a civil matter, it is a criminal one; naming a victim of a sexual offence is itself a sexual offence). (Banks, 2013, para. 8)

In the U.K., there are guidelines of the Crown Prosecution Service (CPS) for prosecution of social media communication. These attempt to strike a public interest balance between protecting individuals and allowing for balanced freedom of speech. British common law made through cases is a foundation for U.S. law, which also provides constitutional First Amendment protection. Nevertheless, the British social media guidelines offer instructive principles to consider.

▢ BOX 9.3 CPS GUIDELINES ON PROSECUTING CASES INVOLVING SOCIAL MEDIA

The British guidelines offer prosecutors "clear advice" on making consistent decisions in social media cases. U.K. law applies to all social media, including "to the resending (or retweeting) of communications."

General principles test two stages of a case: "the first is the requirement of evidential sufficiency and the second involves consideration of the public interest." Cases require "sufficient evidence to provide a realistic prospect of conviction," and this "means that an objective, impartial and reasonable jury (or bench of magistrates or judge sitting alone), properly directed and acting in accordance with the law, is more likely than not to convict."

* * * *

An initial assessment is made of "the content of the communication and the conduct in question so as to distinguish between,"

1. Communications which may constitute *credible threats* of violence to the person or damage to property.
2. Communications which *specifically target an individual or individuals* and which may constitute harassment or stalking within the meaning of the Protection from Harassment Act 1997.
3. Communications which may amount to a *breach of a court order*. This can include offences under the Contempt of Court Act 1981, section 5 of the Sexual Offences (Amendment) Act 1992, breaches of a restraining order or breaches of bail. Cases where there has been an offence alleged to have been committed under the Contempt of Court Act 1981 or section 5 of the Sexual Offences (Amendment) Act 1992 should be referred to the Attorney General and via the Principal Legal Advisor's team where necessary.
4. Communications which do not fall into any of the categories above and fail to be considered separately (see below): i.e., those which may be considered *grossly offensive, indecent, obscene or false*.

* * * *

The guidelines distinguish "credible threats of violence," referencing Lord Chief Justice in *Chambers v DPP* [2012]: *". . . a message which does not create fear or apprehension in those to whom it is communicated, or may reasonably be expected to see it, falls outside [section 127(i)(a)], for the simple reason that the message lacks menace."* (para. 30)

Threats should not be prosecuted if they are not credible. The guidelines urge prosecutors to look for "evidence of hostility or prejudice," and criminal law encourages an "increase in sentences for racial and religious aggravation," as well as "increase in sentences for aggravation related to disability, sexual orientation or transgender identity."

* * * *

The British are concerned about "targeting specific individuals through harassment or stalking, which are defined as "repeated attempts to impose unwanted communications or contact upon an individual in a manner that could be expected to cause distress or fear in any reasonable person" and "contacting, or attempting to contact, a person by any means." Courts in the U.K., as is the case in the U.S., may issue a restraining order against an individual engaged in online stalking. British law also restricts "grossly offensive, indecent, obscene or false" communication. At the evidence stage of an investigation, the guidelines call for a "high threshold" because of the millions of daily social media messages, which create "the potential that a very large number of cases could be prosecuted before the courts" and "the potential for a chilling effect on free speech." Prosecutors are urged to "exercise considerable caution before bringing charges."

The British also reference Article 10 of the European Convention on Human Rights: Everyone has the right to freedom of expression. This right shall include the freedom to hold opinions and to receive and impart information and ideas without interference by public authority and regardless of frontiers . . .

Article 10 "protects not only speech which is well-received and popular, but also speech which is offensive, shocking or disturbing" (citing *Sunday Times v UK (No 2)* [1992].

The U.K. standard is "communication that is *grossly* offensive" for there to be criminal charges. "Just because the content expressed in the communication is in bad taste, controversial or unpopular, and may cause offence to individuals or a specific community, this is not in itself sufficient reason to engage the criminal law." The context of a social media communication is considered, as in the case of an Internet bulletin board . . .

. . . Instead, prosecutors should focus on cases "where a specific victim is targeted and there is clear evidence of an intention to cause distress or anxiety, prosecutors should carefully weigh the effect on the victim, particularly where there is a hate crime element."

(continued)

Interestingly, age is also considered because children and young people "may not appreciate the potential harm and seriousness of their communications and a prosecution is rarely likely to be in the public interest."

Source: The Crown Prosecution Service (2012). Guidelines on prosecuting cases involving communications sent via social media. www.cps.gov.uk/legal/a_to_c/ communications_sent_via_social_media/

The emphasis on a public interest standard is similar to what is found under U.S. broadcast regulation. While the Federal Communication Commission (FCC) reconsiders its regulation of electronic media, the U.S. Supreme Court has rejected public interest regulation for Internet communication, which now includes social media.

U.S. Internet Indecency

A portion of the *Telecommunications Act of 1996*, called the *Communications Decency Act* (*CDA*), set the stage for several attempts to regulate the Internet and social media communication by making it explicitly illegal to knowingly send or make available to minors any indecent or obscene material. The U.S. Supreme Court, however, found part of the CDA's indecency provisions unconstitutional. In *Reno v.* ACLU (1997) it acknowledged Congress' concern with preventing children from being the targets of, or having access to, sexually explicit communications, but it said the CDA's ban on indecency was vague and overbroad.

The Internet uses nearly unlimited digital space, which makes it very different from the limited broadcast public spectrum. Further, people are not as likely to be exposed inadvertently to sexually explicit material on the Internet as they might be on broadcast stations. Still, obscene material may be banned from the Internet because the First Amendment does not protect any obscene messages, regardless of medium. Website operators act as publishers: "Publishers may either make their material available to the entire pool of Internet users, or confine access to a selected group, such as those willing to pay for the privilege" (p. 853). The Court has consistently called for narrowly tailored restrictions on Internet speech and application of traditional obscenity law. From a legal perspective, the Internet has been viewed as similar to print media. Social media communicators have First Amendment rights, but they also are subject to its narrow restrictions. In the *Reno* case, former Justice Sandra Day O'Connor was ahead of her colleagues on the bench in calling for zoning the Internet by using .xxx domain names—it was a technological solution that took more than a decade to begin to materialize.

Courts use *Miller v. California* (1973) to define obscenity across all media—including social media. An early computer bulletin board operator in California, for example, was charged in Memphis under federal law with transmitting obscene content, and the conviction of two people was upheld (*United States v. Thomas*, 1996). When judging obscenity, a jury must examine three parts of the *Miller* legal test for media content:

1. *Prurient Interest.* An average person, applying contemporary local community standards, must find that the work, taken as a whole, appeals to prurient interests.

2. *Patently Offensive.* The work must depict in a patently offensive way sexual content specifically defined by applicable state law.

3. *Value of Work.* The work lacks serious literary, artistic, political or scientific value.

The *Miller v. California* approach to obscenity requires all three items to be satisfied for a jury to find that the media content is obscene. Justice John Paul Stevens observed in one case, though, that prurient appeal is a problem by potentially forcing the most puritanical village standards on everyone. For social media, it may be quite difficult to identify "the work" in the context of "a whole," as mobile social platforms such as Snapchat are brief and temporary. Likewise, it is unclear how state law can be applied within the international context of social media. Finally, the value test is a matter of generational and cultural definition that is very challenging for judges and juries. Online pornography remains profitable, and commercial interests often clash with restrictive local community standards (*Nitke v. Gonzalez*, 2005). Pornography spammers continue to be a problem, and Facebook is among those social media sites filing lawsuits to stop it (Crook, 2013).

Regulated Media Technologies

The growth of media technologies and a free market economic system helped generate a 20th-century information economy that included commercial newspaper "metropolitan distribution networks" (Pool, 1983, p. 20). It is easy to see how potentially powerful social networks are now replacing the importance of newspaper networks.

Likewise, United States global media "imperialism" through traditional channels (Innis, 1972, p. 169) also is being weakened in the 21st century by social media. Printing presses gave way to the Internet, and social media sites that offered anyone access destroyed professional journalism norms of gatekeeping.

Despite the weakening of controls over media communication, the U.S. government maintains a regulatory interest in information accuracy and consumer perception of claims.

((•)) BOX 9.4 THOUGHT LEADER MISTY MONTANO

The relationship between the journalist and the news consumer has had the greatest impact from social media. The basic rules of journalism—who, what, where, when, why and how—will always be the backbone of good, solid reporting. However, journalism has been greatly impacted by social media when applied to each person who engages with the story. Journalists have found themselves being the "who" because readers expect them to actively talk with people about their stories on social media. The witness on the scene of a breaking news situation who tweets it or posts it anywhere on social media is now the one who "breaks" the news and is often thrown into a citizen journalist role.

(continued)

Journalists and news organizations use social media as a tool in every part of the story process, from finding the story to determining the angle of it. Journalists learned how to let their social communities actively engage with the process before and after the story is finished. This in itself can be dangerous in the sense that information can be misinterpreted in 140 characters or can change between Facebook posts. Social media requires journalists to have a transparent relationship with news consumers, and this includes attribution of information and editorial process.

Figure 9.2 @Misty-Montano.

Courtesy Misty Montano.

News travels to family and friends through their social networks even though many of these people wouldn't normally seek out news items. News organizations now have an integrated social media marketing plan to engage regular and new audiences to move them to the end product: TV, online and mobile news.

While millions of people use social media, in my opinion, a large majority of them do not understand how the social networks actually work. Many do not understand why they see what they see in their news feed on Facebook. Many do not understand that Facebook is constantly changing based upon user behavior. Many who have Twitter accounts don't know how to make Twitter useful in their lives other than being forced into using it to participate in favorite TV shows or to find out emergency information from local law enforcement or news agencies.

Journalists do not understand much of this either. They've been asked or required to use social media, but have limited understanding of how it works. What every journalist is told, and many believe, is that social media can be the reason a person chooses their story over the story of another journalist. Without understanding how different social sites work, many journalists begin to use them only to find that just using them doesn't mean the audience follows.

Social media can be the reason a journalist becomes a trusted source of information; however, many do not know how to find the right, ethical balance as a journalist. Many journalists don't know the answer to these questions: When is opinion allowed? When is commentary appropriate? How do I respond to questions from viewers or readers?

News organizations, which expect employees—from the reporter to the behind-the-scenes employee like an editor, producer or photographer—to use social media but provide little to no training or guidelines, will end up in a situation where either the social communities aren't developed or one action of an employee on social media could harm the organization.

For those who work in television, one of the most important oppor- tunities over the next five years is to develop true social TV engage- ment with the audience. Social TV has already been created through sharing comments of viewers, live polls, running commentary of view- ers, but social TV is just in its infancy. When developed further, social TV will make local TV a news destination for viewers.

Journalists and news organizations have new opportunities through the continued development of digital and mobile products that make it easier for the news consumer to access and engage with the story. Digital and mobile apps need to focus on social sharing and user- generated content. Social sharing of news content is vital in keeping and creating loyal news consumers. Viewer/reader generated content not only helps build out a story, but it also can be the motivator for someone to choose one news report over another.

I believe an often-overlooked opportunity is that of partnerships. People want information that will impact their lives in some way. People want resources, ideas, and information that help them with their day-to-day actions, as well as help keep them safe and informed during an emergency situation. The community a news organization serves is filled with many experts, from the hyper-local community- based publications to the person who manages a website focusing on one specific area, such as special needs children. These are resources that news organizations can partner with to provide expertise, ideas and information to have an impact on their audience. These partner- ships will not only create new, useful content for a news organization, but will tap into the social communities of their partners.

Weaving one's personal life with his work and public life on social media is truly an art form. Anything posted on social media can have an impact on one's employment.

Disclaimers in "about me" and "bio" sections with phrases like "views are my own" and "RTs are not an endorsement" provide no protection to someone whose actions on social media are seen as dam- aging to the company for which that person works.

The law protects an individual's right to free speech and protects an individual from being forced to give their social network pass- words to their employers; however, nothing is truly private on social media and the right to have a job is not protected by law. One's use of social media becomes one's personal brand. Employers have the right to protect their company profile and brand. Employers have the right to search the digital footprint of its employees. Often employ- ers don't seek out what their employees are actively doing online. Instead employers find out what has been said or done because of others' sharing their reaction to it. When the public reaction to what one has done on social media snowballs or turns into a social mob mentality, an employer has the right to determine if what is

(continued)

happening is damaging to the company and to take actions against that employee.

The main rule I preach wherever I go is this, "Don't BE the news." This simply means to think first and be smart in all you do. Behave on social media the way you would behave in front of the important people in your life—managers, colleagues, parents, teachers, grandparents, etc. If you wouldn't say or do it in front of these people, then don't do it on social media.

Misty Montano is the Digital Content Manager for 9NEWS in Denver, Colorado. She is an Emmy award-winning journalist who supports and teaches others to use and develop social media communities. Montano works to create social TV in which TV, digital and social all work together to engage the 9NEWS journalists with the audience. She previously was Assignment Editor at KCNC-TV and received her B.A. in Media Communication from Hastings College.

Commercial broadcasters, such as Misty Montano, rely upon advertising revenues to pay the bills and turn a profit. Media businesses and their advertising are governed in the U.S. by commercial speech law and regulation.

FTC Regulation: Advertising, PR and Social Media

The Federal Trade Commission (FTC) regulates advertising in the United States utilizing a "clear and conspicuous" legal standard. Commercial speech, defined by Supreme Court Justice John Paul Stevens as "expression related solely to the economic interests of the speaker and its audience," (Hayes, 2013, p. 264) is a special class of communication under the law. The FTC has as its mission: "To prevent business practices that are anticompetitive or deceptive or unfair to consumers; to enhance informed consumer choice and public understanding of the competitive process; and to accomplish this without unduly burdening legitimate business activity" (FTC, 2014a, para. 1). The FTC seeks "vigorous competition among producers and consumer access to accurate information, yielding high-quality products at low prices and encouraging efficiency, innovation, and consumer choice" (para. 2). Their top strategic goal is consumer protection: "Prevent fraud, deception, and unfair business practices in the marketplace" (para. 3). The FTC has jurisdiction over a variety of privacy and identity concerns in the digital age: limiting unwanted calls and emails; computer security; online safety of children; protection of identity from theft; and repairing identity after theft (FTC, 2014b). After Typhoon Haiyan, for example, the FTC urged consumers "to do some research to ensure that your donation will go to a reputable organization" rather than "fraudsters" (Tressler, 2013, paras. 2–3).

The FTC has used a *reasonable consumer* standard as the legal test for deception since 1983, when a policy statement defined this:

> The Commission believes that to be deceptive the representation, omission or practice must be likely to mislead reasonable consumers under the circumstances.

The test is whether the consumer's interpretation or reaction is reasonable. When representations or sales practices are targeted to a specific audience, the Commission determines the effect of the practice on a reasonable member of that group. In evaluating a particular practice, the Commission considers the totality of the practice in determining how reasonable consumers are likely to respond. (FTC, 1983)

Advertising is considered deceptive, if it lacks a reasonable basis (*Firestone*, 1973). The FTC determines deception based upon false advertiser claims that would give a consumer a false impression (Ibid., fn. 5). In particular, disclosure needs to be written, clear and conspicuous.

The FTC also has investigated complaints about the Yelp review site (Eater, 2013). Questions persist about whether or not Yelp offered search benefits to those restaurants advertising on the site—an allegation that Yelp firmly denies. Still, at sites such as Yelp and Amazon, the influence of reviews opens the possibility that some may try to "game" the system in their favor by encouraging positive reviews or promoting placement of negative reviews against competitors. This is a very difficult social media environment to control or regulate because it is fluid and dispersed.

The FTC clear and conspicuous standard is reflected through the guidance to be prominently placed using easily understood words. Disclosures need to be located in places where they will be seen, as well as near a review or claim that is being made. A social media site that buries important details in fine print would not be following FTC standards. Font size is an issue because of the use of small, mobile devices and various operating systems or device settings.

In 2004, the FTC investigated Amazon.com's online Toy Store because of concerns over protection of child privacy. The FTC responded to complaints by finding that the purpose of the site was to sell toys to adults, Amazon used adult language and there were no activities targeted at kids: "Thus, the FTC staff does not believe the overall character of those websites indicates that they are targeted at children" (FTC, 2004, p. 2). Children under 13 are protected under the COPPA online privacy law, but the FTC found that a "Kid's Review Form" was not promoted to attract children. The FTC also has been concerned with the issue of paid blogging. The FTC issued guidelines reflecting truth-in-advertising principles (FTC, 2010, p. 1):

- Endorsements must be truthful and not misleading;
- If the advertiser doesn't have proof that the endorser's experience represents what consumers will achieve by using the product, the ad must clearly and conspicuously disclose the generally expected results in the depicted circumstances; and
- If there's a connection between the endorser and the marketer of the product that would affect how people evaluate the endorsement, it should be disclosed.

Although the principles and guidelines are not new, the FTC revised these to emphasize that they apply to social networking sites and social media marketing:

The FTC revised the Guides because truth in advertising is important in all media—including blogs and social networking sites. The FTC regularly reviews its guides and rules to see if they need to be updated. Because the Endorsement

Guides were written in 1980, they didn't address social media. The legal principles haven't changed. The FTC revised the examples to show how these standards apply in today's marketing world. (p. 2)

The FTC said financial arrangements between paid bloggers and advertisers may not be apparent to readers, and the law defines deceptive practices as those misleading " 'a significant minority' of consumers" (p. 2). FTC enforcement focuses on advertisers rather than endorsers. The FTC has authority to regulate deceptive advertising as commercial speech, which does not have full First Amendment rights. "If you have a relationship with a marketer who's sending you freebies in the hope you'll write a positive review, it's best if your readers know you got the product for free" (p. 3). The guidelines emphasize transparency in communication.

On a personal Facebook page, for example, FTC urges identifying an employer, if products are mentioned: "People reading that discussion on your Facebook page might not know who you work for . . . readers might not realize the products you're talking about are sold by your company" (p. 4). The onus is on advertisers and marketers to train people, monitor content and review "questionable practices" (p. 6).

In one case, the Bureau of Consumer Protection notified Hyundai Motor America that gift certificates given to bloggers encouraging links to Hyundai videos or comments on Super Bowl advertisements may have run afoul by failing to disclose the relationship. The law "requires the disclosure of a material connection between an advertiser and an endorser when the relationship isn't otherwise apparent to consumers" (Fair, 2011a, p. 1). A staff letter read: "An advertiser's provision of a gift to a blogger for posting specific content promoting the advertiser's products or services is likely to constitute a material connection that would not be reasonably expected by readers of the blog" (p. 1).

Still, the FTC closed its investigation without further action. The FTC found that Hyundai may not have known in advance about the arrangement, "a relatively small number of bloggers received the gift certificates," and some bloggers did disclose the payments (p. 1). Hyundai had hired a media firm, which developed the blogging campaign, as noted by FTC staff:

> Although advertisers are legally responsible for the actions of those working directly or indirectly for them, the actions at issue were contrary both to Hyundai's established social media policy, which calls for bloggers to disclose their receipt of compensation, and to the policies of the media firm in question. Moreover, upon learning of the misconduct, the media firm promptly took action to address it. (p. 2)

It is important to recognize the responsibilities of all parties. The advertiser has ultimate responsibility for its social media campaigns, and the correct path is compensation disclosure. While the company received some initial cover for having hired a firm to run the campaign, its social media policies also were relevant. The FTC draws three rules from its Endorsement Guides: 1. Mandate a disclosure policy that complies with the law; 2. Make sure people who work for you or with you know what the rules are; and 3. Monitor what they're doing on your behalf (p. 2).

More recently the FTC has become interested in the so-called "blurred lines"—"the blending of ads with news, entertainment, and other content in digital media—sometimes called 'native advertising' or 'sponsored content' " (Fair, 2013a, p. 1). As public relations firms venture into advertising work, previous divisions between traditional PR earned media and sponsored or paid media become difficult to separate. In all areas, the FTC calls for disclosure and transparency.

Privacy also continues to be a regulatory issue. The FTC issued a complaint against Facebook for "deceptive or unfair" privacy practices (Fair, 2011b, p. 1). The FTC-proposed order stated that information "from or about" individual consumers, such as names, addresses, email addresses and telephone numbers, are covered by privacy rules. FTC staff (pp. 1–2) said that:

- Facebook can't misrepresent what covered information it collects or discloses.
- When Facebook offers privacy settings on its site, it has to honor them. For example, it can't offer settings that restrict information to "Only Friends" and then share it with others.
- Facebook can't mislead people about the extent to which it shares covered information with third parties, like apps or advertisers.
- Facebook can't mislead people about the steps it takes to verify the privacy or security that third parties provide—for example, apps used on its site.
- Facebook can't mislead people about the extent to which their covered information is accessible after they've deactivated or deleted their accounts.
- Facebook can't mislead people about the extent to which the company complies with the government or third-party privacy programs—like the US-EU Safe Harbor Framework.

The FTC says Facebook needs to "clearly and prominently" disclose data sharing and receive consent from its users. The guidance called for severing control of user data within 30 days of account terminations, as well as independent assessment, monitoring and compliance reporting.

One other developing FTC concern is the use of Internet "spycam" technologies (Fair, 2013b, p. 1). Some software has offered "detective mode" settings that triggered webcams without awareness and consent. The FTC concludes, "Technologies that track or monitor consumers can raise privacy and security eyebrows" (p. 2). In business settings, the FTC urges "appropriate notice and consent safeguards" (p. 2). Some employers, for example, monitor employee social media usage or prohibit it. If spyware is used for monitoring, then employees should know this within a set of clear rules. The FTC may attempt to impose broad liability through its lawsuits, including software developers, corporate officers and companies using monitoring. Beyond the FTC, courts also rule on commercial property rights within social media communication.

Copyright Infringement, File Sharing and Fair Use

Social media communication have extended intellectual property rights issues beyond the early Internet cases. Copyright protects original material upon its creation, and the creator has exclusive rights to reproduce and distribute it, as well as the right to create other works derived from the original. Therefore, uploading a document or media file such as a photograph, copying a posting and re-transmitting it without permission all could violate copyright and digital theft statute law (*Digital Theft Deterrance Act*, 1999). Content owners may exercise rights for specific periods of time, which have been extended under U.S. law to sometimes more than a century. At some point content falls into the public domain and can be copied and shared without restriction.

Social media, which emphasizing creative content sharing on sites, such as You-Tube, raise numerous important legal issues. When a user sees a posting, the computer temporarily loads the file, which might be considered illegal copying. Of course, downloading the file by taking a screen shot or saving it more clearly reflects copyright infringement under U.S. law.

The *Digital Millennium Copyright Act of 1998* eliminated loopholes by addressing streaming media and licensing fees for music and videos (*Eldred v. Ashcroft*, 2003). There is a long history of copyright cases against illegal use of media content. From music bootleggers to video thieves, the U.S. government has attempted to protect the property rights of copyright owners. Social media, however, generate holes in these enforcement efforts by dispersing illegal activity across user networks and sites. Given these enforcement challenges, corporate owners seek to manage and control use and payments through social media sites, such as iTunes and YouTube. The **Digital Rights Management (DRM)** approach seeks to collect user payments for media, control downloading/uploading and sharing. To some extent, social media sites make it easier to track, charge and restrict illegal copying than the earlier websites. However, DRM has proven difficult to enforce. Some critics believe that a better system may emerge over time, based upon user behavior.

Social Perspectives on Law

Social media communication, as with earlier computer and Internet law, has raised new concerns about free expression. From hopes to fears, the marketplace of ideas brings with it norms expressed in the law. Freedom of expression is at odds with, for example, a general right of privacy or right to be forgotten:

> The concept of a privacy interest arising out of the obscurity of information, as a socio-normative principle, and the right to be forgotten, as a legal mechanism concerned with the European idea of dignity-based privacy, are both fundamentally at odds with the established theories that undergird the American First Amendment right of freedom of speech . . . It appears that the differences between the long tradition of vigorously protecting free speech and the concepts of obscurity and the right to be forgotten are irreconcilable. (Larson III, 2013, pp. 119–120)

Normative theory within a social context has been defined as how media *ought* to operate based upon values (Lipschultz, 2008). Normative legal theories, including classical liberalism, are tested through cases and case law. As a function of technology, social media communication challenges traditional industrial assumptions about control. Normative laws restrict prior restraint on publication, including the types happening in social media communication, but also enable subsequent punishment for harmful speech through libel suits. Economic forces influence which cases are brought, as well as outcomes. In its simplest form, libel involves damage to reputation.

In a libel case, a plaintiff must prove publication, identification, falsity, fault and damages. Proving publication on the Internet, in some cases, could be more difficult than earlier mass media forms. Unless the offending pages were downloaded and saved or printed, it is possible that the defamation could vanish in cyberspace. Assuming the social media communication content was saved, identification of the plaintiff should be fairly straightforward and not unlike other media forms. The plaintiff's evidence that the material in question is false is always one of the most difficult aspects of a libel suit, regardless of media form. The Internet might pose some special problems because of the ability to "cut and paste" images and words digitally. The standards of fault depend upon whether the plaintiff in a libel suit is a public figure or not. For most people alleging libel, they merely must show that the social media publisher was negligent with the facts. Because most content providers are not trained journalists, it would seem that standards for negligence might be lower and more difficult to prove in court. For public figures and officials, the standard is "actual malice"—defined legally as reckless disregard for the truth and entertaining serious doubts about the information. If all of these elements can be shown, a plaintiff in a libel suit must still make the case for economic damages. For example, a tweet would have to show to cost an individual or organization a specific amount of money. Or, if a Facebook post led to someone being fired, a court could examine actual damages of lost wages, as well as additional costs.

Once a plaintiff has made his or her case, the defendant in a libel suit has several defenses to follow. Had someone published a libel on a social media site, the simplest defense would be that the information was the truth. That judgment depends upon Internet communication of millions of people. Baym (1995) was an early observer of the nature of online culture and communities:

> If language use is an important locus of cultural meaning making in traditional cultures, it is only more so for Usenet cultures, which are so heavily linguistic in nature . . . There are few if any shared spaces, face-to-face encounters, or physical artifacts to provide cultural foundations. Thus, the discourse, shaped by the forces of the system and object of interest as well as the idiosyncrasies of the participants, carries inordinate weight in creating a group's distinct environment. (p. 33)

But the once-isolated online communities began to take on traditional qualities within social networking sites. Facebook, for example, offered the possibility for political opponents to confront each other amid the heat of a contested political campaign. Top social media communication sites at any given time represent "self-sustaining" forms of interaction (Rogers, 1995, p. 313). Legal rules may encourage a marketplace of ideas, but they exist within a much broader set of social, political and economic constraints. Stevenson (1995) viewed modern media as a form of radical democratization with "a plurality of voices" in a "fragmented culture" (pp. 68–69). Early computer-mediated communication norms were harbingers for social media communication. Although global in nature, users in the United States tend to adopt a First Amendment perspective. On the one hand, social media provide a platform for free speech and access to potentially large audiences. On the other, use leads to loss of personal privacy.

Social Media Privacy Issues

Social media users continue to express concerns about protection of their privacy on sites such as Facebook. At the same time, Facebook is among those sites that attempt to protect users from spammers. YouTube owner Google continues to make technological changes in an attempt to limit, if not eliminate, spam email and comments. The site also has banned some videos, targeting those intended to promote illegal activities or incite violence.

Employees at work also have very limited privacy rights while online. They are subject to company social media policies, which vary greatly in the level of restrictiveness. A very real legal question remains about whether or not First Amendment rights extend into the workplace, as other constitutional rights do.

New technologies also threatened to erode traditional common law views about the sanctity of privacy in one's own home. Privacy becomes a question when law enforcement authorities tap into computer transmissions. While a court order is required, it may be possible for computer users to encrypt transmissions. In 1993, the National Security Agency (NSA) proposed a clipper chip to allow decoding. The government's homeland security efforts since September 11, 2001, to fight terrorist threats also have caused new privacy concerns. The U.S. Court of Appeals, District of Columbia Circuit, for example, upheld the Federal Communications Commission decision that law enforcement agencies require wiretap compatibilities to listen in on mobile telephone and network use (*Am. Council of Educ. v. FCC*, 2006). The NSA has come under scrutiny in recent years for accessing large stores of social media and other data through orders of a secret court. The global nature of emerging spy centers in various countries make it likely that virtually every email and other social media communication may be tracked by governments. In the U.S., the Fourth Amendment protections against illegal search and seizure have been seriously weakened by the emerging security state. Documents released in 2013 by ex-NSA contractor Edward Snowden and published in *The Washington Post* and *The Guardian* raised concerns about the widespread government surveillance of communication networks, including social network sites. The media coverage was shared across social media and generated a public backlash. The ongoing WikiLeaks release of classified government information offers a new model of networked news (Beckett, with Ball, 2012).

Changing social and political conditions created from the September 11, 2001, terrorist attacks presented a new level of complexity. New communication technologies may be used for good or evil, and regulators struggle to allow for advancements without making it easier to harm people. Within sites such as Facebook, the company warns users about data it collects on postings and even user locations. As Facebook (2014) tells users: "Remember, when you post to another person's timeline, that person controls what audience can view the post. Additionally, anyone who gets tagged in a post may see it, along with their friends." User settings may limit public viewing, but data are saved for use by the company for advertising purposes and for the government, if subpoened.

The boundaries and limitations of communication and business in cyberspace remain unsettled. As one scholar of computer-mediated communication has noted, digital and Internet technologies present a paradox: "Utopian and dystopian views about the future of the Internet describe two very different future scenarios" (Barnes, 2003, p. 331). Increasingly, events such as the 2014 Olympics in Sochi offer contexts controlled by a hosting government and economic entity focused on profits rather than free speech

(Dickey, 2013). For athletes and even audience members, there may be social media restrictions when entering controlled venues.

As Pool (1983) noted: "The onus is on us to determine whether free societies in the twenty-first century will conduct electronic communication under the conditions of freedom established for the domain of print through centuries of struggle, or whether the great achievement will become lost in a confusion about new technologies" (p. 10). It remains to be seen what happens now that the powerful must deal with potentially billions of social media "publishers" communicating through complex and unpredictable computer networks. These can be seen as part of a larger technological system driving social change and resistance to it (Ellul, 1980). These new media force examination of social and legal assumptions (Lievrouw & Livingstone, 2006). The emerging social media communication environment is mobile and wireless (Raychaudhuri & Mario, 2011), and it is ahead of the legal rules designed to protect individuals, social systems and political actors.

The challenge for us is to see concepts such as "marketplace of ideas," "social responsibility" and "public interest" in light of social, political and economic factors. If we do this, it will follow that new technologies such as the Internet may not fundamentally change the tilt of power. Nowhere can this be seen more than among bloggers who speak their minds and sometimes exert influence (Rettberg, 2008). Social media communication technology can encourage open international communication (Thussu, 2009). It also may activate meaningful exchanges, collaboration and social change. Social media communication law mirrors older media law in that it remains fluid as policies and regulation adapt to change (Wiley, Abernathy, & Wadlow, 2007). The ambiguity of law in this environment leaves space for behavior evaluated in terms of values and ethical norms.

The global nature of social media communication presents many challenges going forward. The online publication *The Daily Beast*, for example, noted that tweeting from the U.K. "racist or otherwise libelous bile can land you in jail" (Moynihan, 2014, para. 1). A 44-year-old Staffordshire shopkeeper, for example, "was arrested, fingerprinted, and had his computer seized by police when he made a pair of tasteless jokes about Nelson Mandela" (para. 12). Although newspapers reprinted the tweets, only the Twitter user was targeted by authorities. Likewise, in the area of U.S. libel law, users can be sued for defamation, but Facebook and other social network sites are immune from liability (*Finkel v. Facebook*, 2009) under provisions of the *Communications Decency Act* of 1996 (47 USC 230). Nevertheless, journalists using social network sites to source their reporting that turns out to be inaccurate may be sued for libel (Chow, 2013). Social media law is an evolving legal landscape that requires understanding by users. In the end, as legal scholar Kimberly Chow warns, social media communication should be handled with care.

■ DISCUSSION QUESTIONS: STRATEGIES AND TACTICS

1. How are social media a significant change for U.S. and global rules of law? In this redefinition, what are important limitations on free expression?
2. How are social media rules applied within workplaces? What differences exist between government restrictions on use and those limits imposed by others?
3. What can we conclude about the existence of social media privacy? How does interest in having access to content and wanting to share it conflict with privacy?

References

AbuZayyad, Z. K. (2013). Human Rights, the Internet and Social Media: Has Technology Changed the Way See Things? *Journal of Politics, Economics & Culture* 18(4), 38–40.

Ali, A. H. (2011, Summer). The Power of Social Media in Developing Nations: New Tools for Closing the Global Digital Divide and Beyond. *Harvard Human Rights Journal* 24(1), 185–219.

Am. Council of Educ. v. FCC, U.S. App. LEXIS 14174 (2006).

Baldes, T. (2008, December 22). Beware: Your "Tweet" on Twitter Could Be Trouble. *National Law Journal*. www.law.com/jsp/nlj/PubArticleNLJ.jsp?id=1202426916023&slreturn=20131026150648

Banks, D. (2013, June 26). Jeremy Forrest Case: Twitter Users Could Have Broken the Law. *The Guardian*. www.theguardian.com/media/2013/jun/26/jeremy-forrest-twitter-users.

Barnes, S. (2003). *Computer-Mediated Communication, Human-to-Human Communication Across the Internet*. Boston, MA: Allyn and Bacon.

Baym, N. (1995). The Emergence of Community in Computer Mediated Communication. In S. G. Jones (Ed.), *CyberSociety: Computer-Mediated Community and Communication*. Thousand Oaks; CA: Sage.

Beckett, C., with Ball, J. (2012). *WikiLeaks, News in the Networked Era*. Cambridge, UK: Polity Press.

Bell, D., & Kennedy, B. M. (Eds.) (2007). *The Cybercultures Reader, second edition*. London: Routledge.

Blackstone, W. (1769). *Commentaries on the Laws of England* (1765–1769). The University of Chicago. http://press-pubs.uchicago.edu/founders/documents/amendI_speechs4.html

Blumenthal v. Drudge and America Online, 992 F. Supp. 44 (D.D.C. 1998).

Branscomb, A. W. (1996, June). Cyberspaces: Familiar Territory or Lawless Frontiers. *Journal of Computer-Mediated Communication*, 2(1). http://onlinelibrary.wiley.com/doi/10.1111/j.1083-6101.1996.tb00178.x/full

Briggs, M. (2010). *Journalism Next*. Washington, DC: CQPress.

Cashmore, P. (2008, December 20). Twitter Lawsuits: 4 Reasons Your Tweets Might be Trouble. *Mashable*. http://mashable.com/2008/12/20/twitter-lawsuits/

Chicagoist (2010, January 21). Twitter Lawsuit Dismissed. http://chicagoist.com /2010 /01/21/ twitter_lawsuit_dismissed.php

Chow, K. (2013, Fall). Handle with Care: The Evolving Actual Malice Standard and Why Journalists Should Think Twice Before Relying on Internet Sources. 3 *N.Y.U. Journal of Intellectual Property & Entertainment Law* 53–75.

Communications Decency Act (1996). Pub. L. 104, Tit. 5, 110 Stat. 56.

Constitution of the United States, Bill of Rights (1789). www.archives.gov/exhibits/charters/bill_of_rights.html

Crook, J. (2013, November 21). Don't Spam Facebook with Fake Bieber Porn Unless You Want to Get Sued. *TechCrunch*. http://techcrunch.com/2013/11/21/dont-spam-facebook-with-fake-bieber-porn-unless-you-want-to-get-sued/

The Crown Prosecution Service (2012). Guidelines on prosecuting cases involving communications sent via social media. www.cps.gov.uk/legal/a_to_c/communications_sent_via_social_media

Dennis v. U.S., 341 U.S. 494, 590 (1951).

Dickey, J. (2013, August 12). Express Yourself. Or Not. *Sports Illustrated*, p. 20.

Digital Theft Deterrence Act, 17 U.S.C. § 504(a), (c)(1)(1999).

Eater (2013, January 23). FTC Complaints About Yelp Allege Extortion, Libel, More. http://eater.com/archives/2013/01/23/ftc-complaints-about-yelp-allege-extortion-libel-more.php

Eldred v. Ashcroft, 537 U.S. 186, *reh'g denied,* 538 U.S. 916 (2003).

Ellul, J. (1980). *The Technological System, Translated from the French by Joachim Neugroschel.* New York: Continuum.

Facebook, Rights and Responsibilities. 2. Sharing Your Content and Information. www.face book.com/legal/terms

Facebook (2014). *Choose Who You Share With.* https://m.facebook.com/help/www/459934584 025324

Faehner, M.J. (2012, June). Advertising. *Florida Bar Journal* 86(6), 36–37.

Fair, L. (2011a, December 22). *Using Social Media in Your Marketing? Staff Closing Letter Is Worth a Read.* Washington, DC: Federal Trade Commission.

Fair, L. (2011b, December 1). *Facebook's Future: What the FTC Order Means for Consumer Privacy.* Washington, DC: Federal Trade Commission.

Fair, L. (2013a, November 18). *Blurred Lines.* Washington, DC: Federal Trade Commission.

Fair, L. (2013b, October 22). *How Aaron's Erred: What Your Business Should Take from the Latest Spycam Case.* Washington, DC: Federal Trade Commission.

Fang, I. (2008). *Alphabet to Internet, Mediated Communication in Our Lives.* St. Paul, MN: Rada Press.

Federal Trade Commission (FTC) (1983, Oct. 14). Policy Statement on Deception: Appended to Cliffdale Associates, Inc., 103 F.T.C. 110, 174 (1984). www.ftc.gov/ftc-policy-statement-on-deception

Federal Trade Commission (FTC) (2004, November 24). Letter to Marc Rotenberg, Electronic Privacy Information Center. Washington, DC: Federal Trade Commission.

Federal Trade Commission (FTC) (2010, June). *The FTC's Revised Endorsement Guides: What People Are Asking.* Washington, DC: Federal Trade Commission.

Federal Trade Commission (FTC) (2014a). *About the FTC.* www.ftc.gov/about-ftc

Federal Trade Commission (FTC) (2014b). *Consumer Information. Privacy & Identity.* www.con sumer.ftc.gov/topics/privacy-identity

Finkel v. Facebook (2009). N.Y. Misc. LEXIS 3021, NY Slip Op 32248(U).

Firestone, 81 F.T.C. 398, 1972, *aff'd,* 481 F.2d 246, 6th Cir., *cert. denied,* 414 U.S. 1112 (1973).

Groggin, G., & McLelland, M. (Eds.). (2009). *Internationalizing Internet Studies, Beyond Anglophone Paradigms.* New York, NY: Routledge.

Hall, H.K. (2013). Social Media Policies for Advertising and Public Relations. In D. R. Stewart (Ed.), *Social Media Law, A Guidebook for Communication Students and Professionals,* pp. 212–226. New York, NY: Routledge.

Hayes, A.S. (2013). *Mass Media Law, The Printing Press to the Internet.* New York, NY: Peter Lang.

Innis, H. A. (1972). *Empire and Communications.* Toronto: University of Toronto Press.

Internet World Stats (June, 2012) www.internetworldstats.com/stats.htm

Keller, B.P., Levine, L., & Goodale, J.C. (2008). *Communications Law in the Digital Age 2008,* three volumes. New York: Practicing Law Institute.

Larson III, R.G. (2013, Winter). Forgetting the First Amendment: How Obscurity-based Privacy and a Right to Be Forgotten are Incompatible with Free Speech. *Communication Law & Policy* 18(1), 91–120.

Lievrouw, L.A., & Livingstone, S. (Eds.) (2006). *The Handbook of New Media, Updated Student Edition.* London: Sage.

Lipschultz, J.H. (2008). *Broadcast and Internet Indecency, Defining Free Speech.* New York, NY: Routledge.

Lipschultz, J. H. (2014). *Communication and the Law 2014 Edition,* W.W. Hopkins (ed). Northport, AL: Vision Press.

Mackey, T. K., & Liang, B. A. (2013). *Globalization and Health 2013, 9*(45). www.globalization andhealth.com/content/9/1/45

Mathison, D. (2009). *Be the Media*. New Hyde Park, NY: Natural E Creative Group.

Miller v. California, 413 U.S. 15 (1973).

Milton, J. (1644). *Areopagitica: A Speech for the Liberty of Unlicensed Printing to the Parliament of England*. Project Gutenberg. http://gutenberg.readingroo.ms/6/0/608/608-h/608-h.htm

Moynihan, M. (2014, January 23). Can a Tweet Put You in Prison? It Certainly Will in the UK. *The Daily Beast*. www.thedailybeast.com/articles/2014/01/23/can-a-tweet-land-you-in-prison-it-certainly-will-in-the-uk.html

Near v. Minnesota, 283 U.S. 697 (1931).

New York Times v. Sullivan, 376 U.S. 254, 271 (1964).

Nitke v. Gonzalez, 413 F. Supp. 2d 262 (S.D.N.Y. 2005), *affd.*, 547 U.S. 1015 (2006).

Nockleby, J. T., Levinson, L. L., Manheim, K. M., Dougherty, F. J., Gold, V. J., Ides, A. P., & Martin, D. W. (2013). *The Journalist's Guide to American Law*. New York, NY: Routledge.

Pavlik, J. V. (2008). *Media in the Digital Age*. New York, NY: Columbia University Press.

Pogue, D. (2009). *The World According to Twitter*. New York, NY: Black Dog & Leventhal.

Pool, I.d.S. (1983). *Technologies of Freedom*. Boston, MA: Harvard University Press.

Raychaudhuri, D., & Mario, G. (Eds.) (2011). *Emerging Wireless Technologies and the Future Mobile Internet*. New York, NY: Cambridge University Press.

Reno v. ACLU, 521 U.S. 844 (1997).

Rettberg, J. W. (2008). *Blogging*. Cambridge, UK: Polity Press.

Rogers, E. M. (1995). *Diffusion of Innovations*, fourth edition. New York, NY: Free Press.

Sanders, A. K., & Olsen, N. C. (2012, Autumn). Re-defining Defamation: Psychological Sense of Community in the Age of the Internet. *Communication Law & Policy 17*(4), 355–384.

Stevenson, N. (1995). *Understanding Media Cultures*. London, UK: SAGE.

Stewart, D. R. (Ed.) (2013). *Social Media and the Law, A Guidebook for Communication Students and Professionals*. New York, NY: Routledge.

Tatro v. University of Minnesota, 816 N.W.2d 509 (2012), Minn. LEXIS 246.

Thussu, D. K. (Ed.) (2009). *Internationalizing Media Studies*. London, UK: Routledge.

Tressler, C. (2013, Nov. 12). *How to Help Victims of Typhoon Haiyan in the Philippines*. www.consumer.ftc.gov/blog/how-help-victims-typhoon-haiyan-philippines

United States v. Fumo, 655 F.3rd 298, 301 (2011).

United States v. Thomas, 74 F.3rd 701 (6th Cir. 1996).

Wang, M. (2009). UPDATED: Rounding up the Buzz. ChicagoNow. http://culturewav.es/public_thought/72990

Weimann, G. (2010). Terror on Facebook, Twitter, and YouTube. *Brown Journal of World Affairs 16*(2), 45–54.

Wiley, R. E., Abernathy, K. Q., & Wadlow, R.C. (Eds.) (2007). *25th Annual Institute on Telecommunications Policy & Regulation*. New York, NY: Practicing Law Institute.

Xinhua (2010, June 30). *Google Says to "Abide by the Chinese Law" in Order to Renew License*. http://news.xinhuanet.com/english2010/china/2010-07/01/c_13377786.htm

10   SOCIAL MEDIA ETHICS

"Hyping transparency distorts media ethics in several ways: It misunderstands the basis of media ethics, while blurring crucial differences among concepts; it wrongly implies that transparency can replace other principles and can resolve ethical issues created by new media."

—*Stephen J. A. Ward (@MediaMorals, 2013)*

Social media communication raises important ethical issues because it can be perceived as anonymous—crossing borders and cultures worldwide. From its computer-mediated communication origins to state-of-the-art PR and advertising campaigns, a lack of transparency and communication independence may trigger a social media response.

The new media landscape has some wanting to say that transparency is more important than other values, but it is not "a magical idea—a norm with seemingly magical powers to restore democracy" (Ward, 2013a, para. 6). Ward suggests that "responsible publication for democracy," not transparency, is the ethical foundation in journalism, and "editorial independence" also is a basic idea (para. 11)—especially in an era of non-professional journalists:

> Without a stress on independence, and without a constant critical eye for conflicts of interest, I fear that questionable, non-independent journalism will fly under the flag of transparent journalism. One can be a transparent journalist, yet still be inaccurate or care little for minimizing harm. But more than this, even if a journalist is transparent, accurate and minimizes harm, we still are left with a crucial question for her: How free are you to tell the stories that the public needs to hear? Telling people "where you come from" as a journalist is to be commended. But it is not enough for journalism ethics. (para. 32)

Editorial independence may be compromised when special interests override larger public interests. Ward suggests that lack of independence leads to "propaganda" or "narrow advocacy," if "non-professional journalists" do not "make a strong ethical argument for ignoring considerations of independence" (paras. 29–30). In the online world, the speed of information distribution, for example, leads to incorrect information distributed on Twitter about nearly every breaking news national story—from the Boston Marathon bombings to the shootings in 2013 at the Los Angeles airport. In Ward's view, "irresponsible reporting" happens when we ignore some values, "such as verification and minimizing harm," and instead emphasize being first with the story.

185

Social media communication tools and practices are beginning to mature, so it makes sense to discuss and debate values that underlie behavior. Journalists, PR and advertising managers and marketers must confront changing norms. Ward has made the case for "radical" change in the view of journalism ethics and global practices. Beyond the implications of an interconnected world, Ward is concerned with the proliferation of activist journalism:

> But when are activist journalists not propagandists? When are journalists partisan political voices and when are they journalists with a valid cause? Rather than simply dismiss activist journalism on the traditional ground of objectivity, how can we develop a more nuanced understanding of this area of journalism? (Ward, 2013b, para. 21)

This relates to the problem of real-time public sourcing on Twitter of the separation of rumors from story facts—particularly when journalists work across cultural norms.

It comes down to credibility and trust. In Ward's view, "independence, not transparency, distinguishes journalism from propaganda, journalism from narrow advocacy." He challenges a key point in *The New Ethics of Journalism* (2014), a volume edited by Kelly McBride and Tom Rosenstiel (@tbr1)—Ward wants to reform independence rather than replace it. To be fair, McBride and Rosenstiel discuss transparency within the context of 20th-century mass media scale and neutral voice:

> These two precepts, which grew out of both an economic and a democratic imperative, led to an ethical principle of *independence*: the notion that the organization and the individuals who create the news should not advocate for outcomes or slant the news in favor of a particular point of view. (pp. 89–90)

Figure 10.1 A large screen at Edelman PR in New York merged social and mass media information for viewers seeking the latest news.

Reading further, their perspective values "independent observers" and not lowering standards because "true transparency is more than disclosure" requiring "producing the news in ways that can be explained and even defended." The book explains this in Adam Hochberg's (@adamhochberg) chapter discussing the Wisconsin Center for Investigative Journalism's concerns related to non-profit news organizations: donor transparency, editorial independence, the firewall between journalism and fundraising, and conflicts of interest (Hochberg, 2014, p. 132).

We should also recognize that independence has always been an ideal, and local news organizations regularly struggle with the need to keep advertisers happy. This has not changed in the digital era. If a newspaper uses its official news brand on Facebook and Twitter to promote a grand opening, it sacrifices a degree of editorial independence. There is a conflict of interest, if it fails to report a problem, such as a traffic jam, that affects the public interest.

But do not limit thinking to journalism. Failure to disclose interests is a huge social media communication problem with public relations, advertising and marketing. From sponsored content to native advertising, the lines between content and vested interests are crossed in ways that promote neither transparency nor independence. On LinkedIn, for example, Felix Salmon (@felixsalmon, 2013) notes that "there is very little distinction between editorial and advertising" because it "is all just posts" (para. 13):

> LinkedIn is about people more than it is about companies, but that really only helps—it makes everything feel more personal and less corporate, and that in turn makes the message more likely to be well received. No one cares about the editorial/advertising divide: the very concept seems silly. Indeed, if any disclosure is needed, readers would much rather know whether a certain CEO wrote a given post himself, or whether he had it written for him. (Good luck finding that out.) (para. 13)

Therein lies the deeper issue of social media communication ethics. Real-time interaction and engagement happens within the context of individual social networks and marketing strategies. CEO's are now being called upon to be social media participants, according to one study, in order to show innovation, build media relationships, provide a human face for the company and other aspects of reputation management. Joe Mathewson (@joemathewson) boils down the challenge of our time to "seek the truth, verify, and be fair" (Mathewson, 2014, p. 198). Corporate executives, meanwhile, worry about their participation in social media communication—even within the professionally oriented LinkedIn platform, where their specific concerns include (Toomey, 2013, p. 8):

1. Can I keep my contacts private? "Contacts can be visible only to you, or to all of your connections."
2. Do I have to connect with everyone who asks me to? "Your connections should be people you know personally and/or have done business with, and who you might be able to refer to others."
3. What types of content should I share on LinkedIn? "Share your company's news, thought leadership and blog posts."

4. What are the differences between Endorsements and Recommendations? ". . . an Endorsement is a one-click way for your connections to validate your Skills & Expertise . . . A Recommendation is a detailed, written statement . . ."

5. When should I connect with new contacts? "Growing your network is an ongoing process"

Information verification goes a long way toward finding an ethical path. Fairness is more challenging because we make subjective judgments. It owes a lot to traditional ethical concerns about morality, justice, virtue and safety of others. In journalism, for example, media ethics regarding traditional roles are stressed by the lack of social media control:

> The public is swamped with information through more traditional sources as well as via the Internet, and its social media "children," the bloggers, Facebook updaters and tweeters . . . It is our contention that this new "role" of the mass media is to sift through all that information . . . The gate-keeping role of journalists has not ended, but the number of non-journalistic gates is increasing and editors are competing against more sources, more outlets and more voices. (Patching & Hirst, 2014, p. 218)

Social media communication should not alter fundamental values and ethical principles, but we must be open to differing values, principles and practices that we encounter within global social networks. The early debate about ethics is not a threat. It is healthy and serves our desire to promote democracy, community and freedom.

Theories and Philosophies

Media ethics developed as a field within the context of issues surrounding 20th-century mass media. Christians, Rotzoll, & Fackler (1991) used the Potter Box as a way to think about morality within "a systematic process" (p. 2). Potter's moral reasoning box moves a person through a process of definition, values, principles and loyalties (p. 4). For example, media may decide to publish "even if some people get hurt or are misunderstood," (p. 4) if they value the information as representing truth. The first definition stage of the process begins with a "situation" (p. 8). There are a variety of ethical principles, such as:

- Aristotle's Golden Mean is that which lies "between two extremes" (pp. 11–12).
- Kant's Categorical Imperative is that "moral law is unconditionally binding" (p. 14).
- Mill's Principle of Utility is that "happiness was the sole end of human action" (p. 15).
- Rawl's Veil of Ignorance seeks to have the "most vulnerable party" receiving "priority" (p. 18).
- Judeo-Christian Persons as Ends is the ethics of loving "your neighbor" (p. 19).

Media ethicists have advanced thinking to bring it into a global and digital media context, which may create an "open media ethics" (Ward & Wasserman, 2010, p. 276). Opening media ethics is a matter of "meaningful participation" and "significant influence on the course of discussion" (p. 277), "content determination and revision" (p. 278), and transformation related to "citizen-based new media" with a "potential to create a global ethics discourse" (p. 281). Social media communication may be media critiques or activism that may be understood within the framework of "mobilization efforts" (p. 282). Consider what Ward and Wasserman (2010) describe as "peer-to-peer ethics" on a global scale:

> This peer-to-peer accountability can take the form of comments or blog posts, responses to Twitter feeds, or exchanges that take place parallel to citizen journalism posts . . . citizen journalists are held accountable for misrepresentations or inaccuracies by fellow commentators or visitors to the site." (p. 286)

Drawing upon the work of Habermas, Ward and Wasserman (2010) suggest that ethical processes and "reasoning should aim at an ideal mode of inclusive and equal discourse" (p. 288), which aligns with the veil of ignorance. A global context within journalism ethics addresses, for example, cultural sensitivities in "times of grief and trauma" (Motlagh, Hassan, Bolong, & Osman, 2013, p. 1). There is initial evidence that media credibility is related to "role conceptions of professional journalists while social trust was positively associated with both professional and citizen journalists' role conceptions" (Chung & Nah, 2013, p. 274). Transformative credibility standards and role perceptions may represent the beginning of more open ethical processes.

Idealism and Relativism

Ethical idealism of truth, independence and minimization of harm has been altered by digital media realities. While truth remains an ideal principle, emerging values include transparency and community engagement: "Clearly articulate your journalistic approach, whether you strive for independence or approach information from a political or philosophical point of view" (McBride & Rosenstiel, 2014, p. 3). Shirky (2014) wrestles with the Internet dilemma of beliefs, facts and "post-fact" assertions:

> The Internet allows us to see what other people actually think. This has turned out to be a huge disappointment. When anyone can say anything, we can't even pretend most of us agree on the truth of most assertions any more. (p. 15)

The fundamental shift is from a world in which media function within a structure that offered a degree of scarcity and exclusivity. "What does change, enormously, is the individual and organizational adaptations required to tell the truth without relying on scarcity and while hewing of ethical norms without reliance on a small group of similar institutions that can all coordinate around those norms" (p. 20). As a new expectation of transparency is offered by open ethics, the very fact that storytellers are confronted in real time with their audience members suggests a philosophical level of social media communication ethics ambiguity:

> What's harder to gauge is the power—and tension—that social media interaction will bring to this kind of storytelling. As journalists tell their stories via Twitter, they will certainly also receive questions and comments from their followers. Some of that interaction will no doubt interrupt and change the course of the storytelling. (Huang, 2014, p. 50)

Social media storytelling, journalism and other forms, is likely to align with practices of collaboration in which communities contribute to its development. The shift from professional ethical norms to small group behavioral rules could replace the need for normative ethical rules with the engaged community desires to crowdsource and correct story narratives.

Moral Development

While traditional ethics seeks to cultivate individual moral development through its principles, rules, codes and processes, the emergence of fluid community narratives might be a function of interpersonal and small group communication and agreement. Typically, codes of ethics serve to guide media professionals, including those engaged in social media communication (Roberts, 2012). Tension exists, as codes may blur "distinctions between minimal expectations and ideal standards" (p. 115). It is debatable that media ethics codes are effective in training new employees, or even that they serve a valuable public relations function for media industries. Yet, research has found that codes reflect values: "Decision makers need to identify their values to understand the reasons behind their actions" (p. 116). Based upon Rohan's (2000) dimension contrasting individual and social context outcomes, Roberts (2012) identifies key concerns. While an individual may seek "achievement" or "power," society may be driven by "universalism" (i.e., "tolerating") and "benevolence" (i.e., "enhancing the welfare") (pp. 117–18). Likewise, an organization may be concerned with "tradition" (i.e., "commitment"), "security" and even "conformity," at the same time that opportunity is stimulating (p. 117–118). After examining 15 ethics codes, Roberts (2012) confirmed that they tend to emphasize social context rather than individual values:

> These values make fundamental claims about the interdependent relationships among media, society, and the environment. The reliance upon benevolence and universalism themes is not surprising, given that nearly all of these codes were created by organizations that espouse some level of social responsibility . . . and desires by the code-writing organizations to reflect values that society would respect. (p. 122)

The values, while important ideals, may present difficult challenges for social media communicators. The search for truth, for example, is highly valued across media fields. Yet, social media communication may blur truth by valuing subjectivity and opinion. Further, personal branding places pressures on individuals to differentiate themselves from the social media crowd, while ethical guidelines urge caution. Within such an environment, it is not clear how the process of moral development advances individual and organizational thinking.

Trust and Transparency

Social media communications practitioners may assume that by being as transparent as possible, they will build trust. The examination of conflict between individual and social values, however, suggests that transparency alone will not be effective. Bowen (2013) lists fourteen other values—fairness, avoiding deception, dignity and respect, eschewing secrecy, reversibility, viewpoint identification, rationality, clarity, disclosure, verification, responsibility, intention, community good and consistency: "Consistency allows publics to know and understand you, and you can meet their expectations" (p. 126). If we build trust through consistency rather than transparency alone, then social media ethics needs to be understood within a very broad context.

Social media may replace traditional media communication in areas such as political discussion, as distrust of institutions leads to new forms of "interaction and information consumption" (Himelboim, Lariscy, Tinkham, & Sweetser, 2012, p. 106):

> Whereas trust of one's *outer circle* was a good predictor for a variety of online behaviors and attitudes, political openness was found to be more sensitive to differences between types of spaces preferred for gaining political information. Trust in the *outer circle* predicted use of all types of online media (consumption and interaction), where political openness successfully predicted only the use of social media. (p. 107)

In other words, social media behavior is more aligned with expressing political opinions or support for a candidate than it is trust in information coming from others. Social media communication spaces may be useful to people with a need to express opinions, even when they may be controversial or even potentially harmful in an ethical sense.

At a fundamental level, CMC anonymity may cultivate a different form of communication, which breaks down social taboos or reaffirms narrow social norms (Leonard & Toller, 2012). In a study of MyDeathSpace.com communication, several themes emerged: sympathy for deceased and loved ones, suicide method, judging the deceased and others, explanations for suicide, regret for death, and loved ones' response to posters (pp. 392–399): ". . . we found that the Web site MyDeathSpace provided a setting for individuals to write in and discuss the death of an individual due to suicide rather than a site for the bereaved to commiserate and make sense of the death of their loved one" (p. 400). Such CMC may serve individual more than social needs. This site did not "serve as a venue where survivors of suicide can reach out to others for social support and encouragement" (pp. 400–401). "Online spaces that allow for primarily absolute and pseudo anonymity appear to encourage extremely disinhibited communication that demonstrates no regard for others involved in the communication" (p. 402). As an ethical issue, individuals had the freedom to discuss the frequently avoided issue of suicide, but the anonymous communicators did so without regard for potential harm inflicted on family and friends. Clearly, social media communication raises ethical issues of human dignity.

(( )) BOX 10.1 THOUGHT LEADER CRAIG NEWMARK

Some years ago I started reading some history about large-scale social change, since it felt like something big is happening right now, as regular people learn to work with each other via the Internet.

In high school American history, we dug into our own revolution and how that was affected by the leaders of the British "Glorious Revolution" about a century before. Much more recently, I've read about

(continued)

the Protestant Reformation, the rise of Christianity, and how the Roman Republic became the Roman Empire.

It dawned on me, and many others, that the leaders of dramatic change were very effective doing what we'd now consider blogging. Tom Paine and Ben Franklin blogged compellingly that the Colonies should declare their independence. John Locke (not the guy from LOST) blogged about individual rights in the context of British representative democracy, and Martin Luther blogged about his vision of Christianity.

Saint Paul described his vision of Christianity in the form of "epistles," not that differ-

Figure 10.2 @craignewmark.

ent from the warblogs written by Julius Caesar in the conquest of Gaul. (Caesar had arguably invented journalism previously.)

These bloggers used the best technologies of their time, usually involving paper or parchment, and either copyists or, later, the printing press. Networked distribution involved what we now call "store and forward" methods, via network nodes, including churches or coffee houses.

A number of folks have made these observations, best documented by Tom Standage, of *The Economist*, in his recently published "The Writing on the Wall."

Looks like massive social change involves tipping points that are inspired by the most compelling voices of their time. Victor Hugo said something like "there's nothing so powerful as an idea whose time has come." Compelling bloggers both manifest and articulate those ideas, creating those tipping points.

For you biology nerds, society and culture evolve a la "punctuated equilibrium" where not much happens until something triggers a tipping point.

Tom eloquently points out that, "history retweets itself."

That's happening now, where people use the Internet and social media to get people to work together.

That's to say that the Internet provides everyone with their own printing press and the means to distribute their work . . . and to possibly influence large numbers of people.

Some people have specific agendas in mind; others are a little more meta, hoping to give voice to the voiceless, by writing about it in essays like this.

After all, a nerd's gotta do what a nerd's gotta do.

Craig Newmark is founder at craigconnects.org, a site created "to give the voiceless a real voice and the powerless real power." Newmark holds undergraduate and graduate degrees in Computer Science from Case

Western Reserve University. The native of New Jersey lives in San Francisco. He worked at IBM for 17 years, as well as GM, Bank of America and Charles Schwab. His 1995 project to help friends promote events in San Francisco became Craigslist—now among the top English-language web platforms. He does customer service for the site, which is "run by a small group of very smart people who have stayed loyal to the idea that it should be simple, fast, mostly free, and 'bottom-up' oriented," Newmark says. "I've learned a lot that can be applied to the common good."

Human Dignity Frameworks

Bowen (2013) utilized the 2006 case of a fake blog—a "flog" created by Edelman PR for Wal-Mart—which posed a personal and positive RV couple interacting "with happy Wal-Mart employees" (p. 126). By concealing the identities of paid bloggers and its source, "the website does not respect the dignity of the public, nor does it respect their intellectual need for open and honest information to form independent judgments" (p. 127). Deception is an ethical violation of human dignity. "Deliberately concealing sponsorship, astroturfing, and flogging are practices that violate the moral duty communicators have to society to be universally honest, to communicate with dignity and respect, and act with good will" (p. 127).

Practical Social Media Ethics

As social media have developed in recent years, traditional media organizations adapted to the new interaction with audience members. National Public Radio, in response to ethical concerns, has offered its journalists specific rules of engagement.

▢ BOX 10.2 NPR SOCIAL MEDIA GUIDELINES

NPR has emphasized that real-time breaking news coverage of events "present new and unfamiliar challenges" and has urged reporters to "tread carefully." The guidelines have urged that online behavior—"just as you would in any other public circumstances"—means treating people with "fairness, honesty and respect." NPR has emphasized verification of information: "Verify information before passing it along."

Under an accuracy heading, NPR has told its reporters to be "careful and skeptical." A social media team was created for consultation on difficult challenges. "Its members have expertise in collecting information from a variety of sources, in establishing to the best of their ability the credibility of those voices and the information they are posting, and in analyzing the material they use." The guidelines connect trust and credibility to transparency: "And to the greatest extent practical, spell out

(continued)

how the information was checked and why we consider the sources credible." Crowdsourcing, while not determining what would be reported, is considered useful.

The guidelines have expressed concern about false online identities. Under an offline follow-up heading, NPR again urged caution. "So, when appropriate, clarify and confirm information collected online through phone and in-person interviews."

Likewise, NPR has expressed concern about manipulated photographs and old video that are distributed online: "bring a healthy skepticism to images you encounter, starting with the assumption that all such images or video are not authentic."

The guidelines also address honesty, including avoiding political partisanship, a lack of Web privacy and independence:

It's important to keep in mind that the terms of service of a social media site apply to what we post there and to the information we gather from it. Also: The terms might allow for our material to be used in a different way than intended. Additionally, law enforcement officials may be able to obtain our reporting on these sites by subpoena without our consent—or perhaps even our knowledge. Social media is a vital reporting resource for us, but we must be vigilant about keeping work that may be sensitive in our own hands.

NPR reminds reporters that their "standards of impartiality also apply to social media." The traditional rules apply to personal pages and joining groups—whether or not the employee identity is "readily apparent."

"In reality, anything you post online reflects both on you and on NPR." The guidelines also address the important issue of media accountability. Social media happen in "public spaces." NPR adds, "don't behave any differently online than you would in any other public setting." The standard is a conservative one in recommending that reporters avoid online norms that sometimes may be looser than the face-to-face world.

As such, reporters are asked to consider legal implications, "regardless of medium." In respecting community norms, there is a need for awareness: "Our ethics don't change in different circumstances, but our decision might." Finally, the NPR guidelines conclude: "Social media are excellent tools when handled correctly."

Source: NPR (2012, May 2). *NPR Ethics Handbook.* Social media. http://ethics.npr.org/tag/social-media/

Equality and Fairness

Lack of disclosure to the public raises issues of fairness. Paid tweets by celebrities, for example, earn some thousands of dollars. Bowen (2013) concluded that failure to be transparent about sponsorship violates fundamental ethical principles:

Be transparent; paid speech should be identified as such. Identify communication as personal, individual speech and opinion versus speech as a representative of the organization, so that publics have the information to evaluate it appropriately. Check relevant facts. A rational analysis should examine messages from all sides and viewpoints. (p. 129)

While deception through failure to disclose sponsorship may not lead to harmful outcomes, it runs the risk of creating public misperception that could be influential. For example, if a healthy-looking movie star is paid to promote an unhealthy product on Twitter, the social media communication may lead some to buy and consume it.

Natural Law and Harm

Beyond legal implications of potentially harmful social media communication, it is ethically fundamental to follow the principle to do no harm. "Communication professionals who implement social media initiatives would be well advised to consider the harm to their reputations that can be caused by ignoring ethics in the technological space" Bowen (2013, p. 132). Particularly when young people are present in social media spaces, which may be difficult to know, safety is a concern: "In response to concerns about online predators, illegal downloading, and imprudent posting of content online, a number of cyber safety initiatives have emerged online and in schools around the country" (James et al., 2010, pp. 218–219). Core and salient issues include: "identity, privacy, ownership and authorship, credibility, and participation" (p. 219), and one research group calls for the use of "good play" rules to address ethical online behavior from a positive perspective to encourage "meaningful and engaging" participation within a community:

> . . . definitions of responsible or ethical conduct in online spaces may differ markedly from offline definitions. Here we consider the new digital media as a playground in which the following factors contribute to the likelihood of good play—(1) technical literacy and technology availability; (2) cognitive and moral person-centered factors (including developmental capacities, beliefs, and values); (3) online and offline peer cultures; and (4) presence or absence of ethical supports (including adult or peer mentors, educational curricula, and explicit or implicit codes of conduct in digital spaces). Our approach to ethics does not focus solely on transgressions but strives to understand why, how, and where good play happens. (p. 226)

The approach emphasizes media literacy rather than rules to cultivate and "develop ethical reflection and conduct as a key foundation for youth empowerment" (p. 277). While the application of moral development through online play may be appropriate in an educational learning context, social media communication practitioners are expected to adhere to organizational standards and industry guidelines. Privacy, such as that when a user is on Facebook or adjusts settings, is a fundamental expectation: "Crucially, these rights and obligations hold regardless of the perceptions that users have of their online interactions" (D'Arcy & Young, 2012, pp. 535–536).

Reconsidering Community

Ethical issues are all around us in social media communication, which offer competing values to the traditional world of journalism and media. As the NPR social media guidelines mentioned earlier say, "Realize that different communities—online and offline—have their own culture, etiquette, and norms, and be respectful of them." Respect for others is an important community value. Too often, organizations run into online and offline difficulties because of a breakdown of respect for others.

New social media tools, such as Storify, create spaces that are not as limited by space as Twitter. At the same time, organizations across the social media communication landscape are developing understanding about the need to provide employee guidance, support and ongoing feedback.

The global nature of social media has challenged ethicists "to account for a diversity of ethical perspectives globally, while avoiding cultural relativism" (Wasserman, 2011, p. 791). Post-colonial criticism of traditional media ethics is that "constructs such as freedom and responsibility, which are often presented as having universal validity, are themselves 'local' in that they have originated from particular epistemological traditions rooted in Western thought and experience" (p. 792). In Africa, for example, there is "a contested terrain" of "development journalism," "indigenization" and "professionalization and social responsibility" (p. 800). While media practitioners in the U.S. push for First Amendment freedoms, a global perspective must take into account stages of development and cultural assumptions within the language used to describe normative ethics.

Limitations of Ethics

Social media ethics typically are applied as a set of professional guidelines. Formal law rarely governs them. Organizations have attempted to incorporate traditional ethical guidelines based upon a set of values, even though social media norms may differ among online communities. There will continue to be tension between the practice of social media communication and the constraints desired by media organizations.

Social media communication tends to follow traditional media in testing our ideals about freedom and social responsibility within a democratic context (Christians, Rotzoll, & Fackler, 1991). Beyond a desire to avoid harm to others, ethics assumes accountability to others within a social context. Each decision made has implications within society. The best hope is to align individual notions of morality and ethics with industry and organizational values and practices. By communicating with others, including online communities, it is hoped that greater understanding emerges over time.

■ DISCUSSION QUESTIONS: STRATEGIES AND TACTICS

1. Is there a proper role for activist journalists within social media? How should traditional or mainstream journalists differentiate their work?
2. Which values are most important for ethical behavior within social media? In what ways may it be difficult to be governed by traditional ethical guidelines?
3. How are global norms of ethics a challenge to U.S. rules? In what ways will global social media communication influence future directions in ethics?

References

Bowen, S. A. (2013). Using Classic Social Media Cases to Distill Ethical Guidelines for Digital Engagement. *Journal of Mass Media Ethics* 28(1), 119–133.

Christians, C. G., Rotzoll, K. B., & Fackler, M. (1991). *Media Ethics, Case & Moral Reasoning, third edition.* New York, NY: Longman.

Chung, D. S., & Nah, S. (2013). Media Credibility and Journalistic Role Conceptions: Views on Citizen and Professional Journalists Among Citizen Contributors. *Journal of Mass Media Ethics 28*(4), 271–288.

D'Arcy, A., & Young, T. M. (2012). Ethics and Social Media: Implications for Sociolinguistics in the Networked Public. *Journal of Sociolinguistics 16*(4), 532–546.

Himelboim, I., Lariscy, R. W., Tinkham, S. F., & Sweetser, K. D. (2012). Social Media and Online Political Communication: The Role of Interpersonal Informational Trust and Openness. *Journal of Broadcasting & Electronic Media 56*(1), 92–115.

Hochberg, A. (2014). Centers of Investigative Reporting. In K. McBride & T. Rosenstiel (Eds.), *The New Ethics of Journalism*, pp. 123–135. Los Angeles, CA: Sage.

Huang, T. (2014). Centers of Investigative Reporting. In K. McBride & T. Rosenstiel (Eds.), *The New Ethics of Journalism*, pp. 39–59. Los Angeles, CA: Sage.

James, C., Davis, K., Flores, A., Francis, J., Pettingill, L., Rundle, M., & Gardner, H. (2010). Young People, Ethics, and the New Digital Media. *Contemporary Readings in Law and Social Justice 2*(2), 215–284.

Leonard, L. G., & Toller, P. (2012). Speaking Ill of the Dead: Anonymity and Communication About Suicide on MyDeathSpace.com. *Communication Studies 63*(4), 387–404.

Lipschultz, J. H. (2012, August 28), Privacy Is Dead?—Really? *The Huffington Post.* www.huffingtonpost.com/jeremy-harris-lipschultz/online-privacy_b_1831956.html

Mathewson, J. (2014). *Law and Ethics for Today's Journalist: A Concise Guide.* Armonk, NY: M. E. Sharpe.

Motlagh, N. E., Hassan, M. S. B. H., Bolong, J. B., & Osman, M. N. (2013). Role of Journalists' Gender, Work Experience and Education in Ethical Decision Making. *Asian Social Science 9*(9), 1–10.

McBride, K., & Rosenstiel, T. (Eds.) (2014). *The New Ethics of Journalism.* Los Angeles, CA: Sage.

NPR (2012, May 2). *NPR Ethics Handbook.* Social media. http://ethics.npr.org/tag/social-media/

Patching, R., & Hirst, M. (2014). *Journalism Ethics, Arguments and Cases for the Twenty-first Century.* London, UK: Routledge.

Roberts, C. (2012). Identifying and Defining Values in Media Codes of Ethics. *Journal of Media Ethics 27*(2), 115–129.

Rohan, M. J. (2000). A Rose by Any Name? The Values Construct. *Personality and Social Psychology Review 4*(3), 255–277.

Salmon F. (2013, March 15). Too Many Flavors of Native Content. *Reuters Opinion.* http://blogs.reuters.com/felix-salmon/2013/03/15/the-many-flavors-of-native-content/

Shirky, C. (2014). Truth Without Scarcity, Ethics Without Force. In K. McBride & T. Rosenstiel (Eds.), *The New Ethics of Journalism*, pp. 9–24. Los Angeles, CA: Sage.

Toomey, K. (2013, September). 5 Questions Executives Ask About LinkedIn. *Public Relations Tactics 20*(9), 8.

Ward, S.J.A. (2013a, November 4). Why Hyping Transparency Distorts Journalism Ethics. *PBS Media Shift.* www.pbs.org/mediashift/2013/11/why-hyping-transparency-distorts-journalism-ethics/

Ward, S.J.A. (2013b, August 19). Why We Need Radical Change for Media Ethics, Not a Return to Basics. *PBS Media Shift.* www.pbs.org/mediashift/2013/08/why-we-need-radical-change-for-media-ethics-not-a-return-to-basics/

Ward, S.J.A., & Wasserman, H. (2010). Towards an Open Ethics: Implications of New Media Platforms for Global Ethics Discourse. *Journal of Mass Media Ethics 25*, 275–292.

Wasserman, H. (2011). Towards a Global Journalism Ethics via Local Narratives, Southern African Perspectives. *Journalism Studies 12*(6), 791–803.

11   BEST PRACTICES IN SOCIAL MEDIA

"I love Twitter. Sure it is noisy. Yes, it has quite a few spammers and bots and 'push' marketers . . . but just about everything good that has happened in my business has had its origin in Twitter. It is surreal quite frankly."

—*Kim Garst (@kimgarst, 2013)*

Kim Garst is CEO of Boom Social in Tampa, Florida. Her blog (http://kimgarst.com) was among the *Social Media Examiner*'s top sites, and Forbes has called her a social media power influencer. On Twitter, Garst has more than 200,000 followers, and she follows more than 150,000, yet she attempts to respond and thank all engaging with her content. She has posted more than 170,000 tweets. Social media "has invaded the very core of the way we communicate," Garst said at the 2012 IBM Global Summit in Orlando. "It affords you the opportunity to connect with people you would never in the ordinary course of life connect to." In search of online business opportunities for more than two decades, Garst sees social media as the direction ahead. She added Pinterest to her list of key sites, with traffic second only to Twitter. Clients interested in personal or company branding also need to be on Facebook, YouTube and LinkedIn for marketing purposes. These sites are increasingly visual, so photographs, graphics and video are very important to be effective within social media. Test engagement with various approaches to see which content is "sticky" on specific sites. Live video sites, such as Spreecast (http://spreecast.com) offer the lure of video connected to real-time chat and engagement. This is a potentially powerful combination as a way to promote ideas, products and services. The mobile new media environment presents distinct challenges and opportunities for each communicator and medium.

Mobile Media

It is clear that users of smartphones and tablets are beginning to have a major impact on social media, and this trend will continue. The "new forms of sociability" may reinforce or work against traditional communication, as "mobile communication, along with other network technologies, is associated with increased face-to-face engagements with network ties, bringing people together physically as well as psychologically" (Campbell & Ling, 2011, p. 325). However, the "flip side" of networked communication is that it may emphasize "social divisions" through member boundaries "when mobile media are used for network configuration" (p. 325).

The organization of mobile apps reflects "a fingerprint of sorts" in that these show "the combination of interests, habits, and social connections that identify that person" (Gardner & Davis, 2013, p. 60). Social networking and social media sharing through apps "becomes an integral part of the way" people in general—and particularly youth— "choose to express themselves online" (p. 61). Hunsinger (2014) contends that computer connections along with social media immediacy created communal perceptions:

> It is the interactivity that generates the sense of presence and thus community that enables most people to engage with social media. However, it is also this interactivity that encourages people to use it with friends and communities . . . the interfaces are mediations of data . . . Social media interfaces engage us through interactivity and the appearance of co-presence, community, and in the end, the appearance of social connection. (p. 9)

Appearance or reality, these online connections are useful for all forms of media communication. Those seeking to engage with a dispersed media audience can find many of its members now using mobile media devices to access social media platforms.

Newspapers, Magazines and Journalism

Social media interest is high among journalists. In terms of best practices, the following are popular:

- Live tweet from a news event and create a Storify summary of a curated list of the best engagement and information.
- Send out links to stories across social media sites to drive traffic to websites.
- Use great photography to spark audience interest in coverage and promote the brand.
- Engage online with people in the community to identify news sources and seek verifiable information.
- Search social media platforms for story ideas and possible new trends.
- Monitor government operations and behavior of politicians.
- Cultivate personal brands of star journalists.
- Respond to criticism of coverage.
- Promote advertisers' events with sponsored posts.
- Curate content from credible news sources to clarify and correct bad information circulating as social media rumors.
- Post photographs from publication archives and offer to sell popular prints.
- Take advantage of convergence opportunities by publishing audio, video and streaming events in real-time.
- Thank fans for engaging and sharing content.
- Answer questions from readers.

Steve Buttry has posted dozens of ideas for journalists on Slideshare.net. He suggests that news organization community engagement equates to making a "top priority to listen, to join, lead & enable conversation to elevate journalism" (Buttry, 2013). This happens across many evolving social media platforms, including Tout mobile video and Instagram. Journalists can use social media as a reporting tool by looking for blogs and content in their local communities. Social media offer the opportunity to connect with comments and commentators. Journalists also use crowdsourcing in the search for *verified* news content. From live tweeting to tracking hashtags, journalists using social media may have an advantage over those ignoring sources and content. Across all forms of journalism, mobile apps and social media create new opportunities and possibilities.

Radio and Mobile Apps

Internet podcasts initially created some competition for local radio stations, as did the movement toward purchasing online song libraries from iTunes. In the social media era, online services such as Spotify and Pandora allowed music listeners to share playlists with friends.

A recent trend is the creation of news and information apps that cater to an increasingly smartphone-oriented audience. All-news radio, for example, has survived and prospered for decades in large media markets. In an age of mobile smartphones and social media, radio is again changing to meet new habits.

Rivet Radio News, a Chicago start-up, launched in late 2013 with an iPhone app, and its developers are coming after the all-news audience. Rivet is targeting people on the go and wanting to personalize story selection in categories such as breaking news, business, sports, arts & entertainment, technology and lifestyle. The app allows users to pause, rewind and skip stories. Newscasters emphasize conversational style, even as they keep pace with breaking news.

Rivet also uses listener location to provide on-demand stories, including hyper-local traffic updates. "It shows the power of being free from the tyranny of the clock," General Manager Cindy Paulauskas said. "We can make our traffic reports as long or as short as they need to be, and we can create updated reports whenever the situation changes." Rivet uses the flexible approach with all of its recorded stories grouped in categories selected by the user instead of a clock-driven live radio format.

Figure 11.1 Rivet News Radio sought to engage mobile smartphone users with an app that distributed hyperlocal traffic reports and customized news. Courtesy Rivet News Radio.

Across at the other end of the Loop, Chicago's WBBM Newsradio 780 is mobile on the award winning CBS Radio.com app. It allows users to select favorite stations and has a built-in sleep timer and alarm. Users can read online stories while listening to live radio, and there is some basic Twitter and Facebook sharing.

News Director Ron Gleason believes that live radio audiences come and go, and he is not convinced they will take the effort to select and navigate recorded content. Gleason sees social media as impacting all of journalism:

> The good: more and more people are getting valuable information faster and faster. The bad: you can't always trust what you see—because the information is only as good as the source. As a credible source on which Chicagoans rely, we are actively involved in the use of social media to let people know about the stories we're reporting. We reach people with our AM and FM signals, through our stream, at CBSChicago.com, through the CBS local YourDay app, via Twitter, Facebook, etc. The more ways we can reach out, the more people we'll reach. The good news for WBBM: there's still no medium more immediate than Newsradio, and the ability for broadcast outlets to reach the masses during breaking news stories and emergencies is second to none. (Gleason, 2013)

The Newsradio 780 format follows its consistent model that has been successful over several decades. It is a strong media brand with news, sports, weather, and traffic built around quarter hours and immediate updates.

While WBBM has "trained" listeners over the years to keep an eye on the clock, Rivet News Radio is building brand loyalty through engaging content. "Our key metric now is Repeat Users," Paulauskas said. "We hope that continues to trend upward, and are doing everything we can to create an engaging experience that makes listeners want to tune in again and again." The Rivet mobile app model has been called a **Pandora**-like service for news because it plays news like a streaming music service. While music services pay for rights to play music, news and information may be created much less expensively. Radio news must continue to evolve to become a form of mobile news that includes the frequent convergence of photographs and video. The larger social media shift demands a visual presence and interaction with fans.

(((•))) BOX 11.1 THOUGHT LEADER CHARLIE MEYERSON

The leveling of the playing field between journalist and, as Jay Rosen has dubbed them, "the people formerly known as the audience" has had astonishing impact. Reporters are subject now more than ever to analysis, criticism and correction by those who once had to content themselves with letters to an editor—who may or may not have chosen to publish them. And a reporter's success (as gauged by audience reach) depends as never before on readers', listeners' and viewers' decision to share . . . or not to share.

The challenge will be finding journalists whose ability to engage an audience matches their ability to gather and report facts.

I've been saying this for years, and I'll say it again here: Hard though some journalists may find it to believe, I think this is the best time in history to become a journalist. Yes, times are tough for some media companies. But, as I told students at the University of Illinois, we are closer now than ever to the ideal advanced by Justice Oliver Wendell Holmes, who said, "the best test of truth is the power of the thought to get itself accepted in the competition of the market." These days, if you have something true to say—and I mean "true" here broadly: not just "truthful" or "factual," but also "truly funny," or "truly moving," or "truly beautiful"—this new digital world empowers you to communicate it to anyone, anywhere, regardless of medium. You don't need a printing press. You don't need an antenna. All you need is a way with words or sound or pictures and a library card to use a computer.

Figure 11.2 @Meyerson. *Photograph by Lila M. Stromer, courtesy Charlie Meyerson.*

Source: Meyerson, C., as interviewed by R. Kaempfer. (2007, February 18). http:// chicagoradiospotlight.blogspot.com/2007/02/charlie-meyerson.html

Charlie Meyerson is a journalist based in Chicago. He is head of news for HearHere's startup, Rivet News Radio. He's also an adjunct professor of journalism at Roosevelt University and an occasional contributor to WBEZ-FM, Crain's Chicago Business and WXRT-FM. He has been an adjunct lecturer in the graduate program at Northwestern University's Medill School of Journalism and at Columbia College Chicago. Meyerson holds undergraduate and graduate journalism degrees from the University of Illinois, where he began his broadcasting career. He consults in content strategy through his practice, Meyerson Strategy.

Television, Branding and Live from the Scene

As a major October snowstorm headed into the Denver area, reporter Kevin Torres and his live truck operator headed outside the newsroom on assignment to cover impact, which included accidents. For decades, live and local television news produced predictable content. What is new and exciting is the blending of backpack journalism, mobile media technologies and social media strategies.

As snow fell in advance of a 9 p.m. live news report, Livestream viewers of Torres' channel went along with him behind the scenes. Much as popular sociologist Erving Goffman might have described "front stage" and "backstage" life, the video stream and chat room offered a backstage glimpse into the workings of TV news. Torres became noticeably tense as his truck operator was unable to bounce a signal into the station. With all of the drama of reality TV, our viewpoint was carried back inside the truck for a quick drive to the Golden, Colorado, exit.

Even for those who have met Torres, it still may have felt like a parasocial inter-action—a sociological term coined to describe how media personalities seem like our friends—while typing into the chat room. The video stream had an Apollo 13 feel and sound. A duct tape joke didn't go over that well, although Torres did let viewers know that this was an older live truck. Once on air from Golden, tension subsided. The 10 p.m. live shot went off on time and with professional ease. Viewers could monitor the backstage streaming video, as well as the on-air broadcast. After Torres finished, he was back with his online audience for a quick wrap-up and goodbye for the night.

Torres was willing to share with online fans most of his side of cellphone calls to the station, which ended once by unfortunately dropping what he said was a new phone. This live and unrehearsed aspect to the online stream helped magnify authenticity and strengthen engagement because viewers could see Torres' engaging off-air personality. He also let them know that he was checking Facebook, Twitter and email at different points in and out of the broadcasts.

Few reporters and stations are sharing this much about what happens away from the bright lights of TV cameras. Television has an opportunity to be experimenting with this innovative social media approach. It offers the opportunity to drive audience traffic online, on the air and back online. While this may not be *the* future of local news, it is an

Figure 11.3 Backpack journalist Kevin Torres has taken viewers behind the scenes with "backstage" TV news preparation, including experiencing a ride in the live truck. Courtesy Kevin Torres.

attractive real-time model that follows the rules of computer-mediated communication: identity (branding), interaction (two-way) and community building (online). If Web 2.0 demonstrated the tools of social media, Web 3.0 will be about refining communication.

At the national level, television programming from *The Voice* (#TheVoice) to a live performance of *The Sound of Music* (#SoundOfMusicLive) leveraged online engagement. While musical theatre is challenging on network television, NBC decided that by engaging social media fans, program interest could be magnified. In fact, despite negative comments, NBC's audience of 21.3 million viewers in 2013 was the largest for a non-sporting event in four years (RTT News, 2013; Lane, 2013).

Top Media Sites on Social Media

Most readers would be able to identify Facebook and Twitter among the top social media sites, but there are many media sites that benefit from Facebook likes, Twitter re-tweets and overall social media exposure. Table 11.1 is a list of the top fifteen media sites based upon Facebook likes.

A top site, such as *The Huffington Post*, has more than one million likes and typically more than 150,000 Facebook users talking about it at any given time. By posting links that get shared, some users will click and visit sites to read stories. The deck is shuffled a bit in terms of the top Twitter tweets: 1. BBC; 2. Mashable; 3. *The New York Times*; 4. *The Huffington Post*; and 5. CNN (Thompson, 2013). While the data are far from precise, it is clear that traditional media and new media are competing across the social media platforms for leadership in audience size and user activity. Blogging, which has dramatically grown in importance because of sites such as *The Huffington Post*, is one of the best practice drivers that is used to promote ideas and brands.

Table 11.1 Most Overall Facebook Likes

1. *The Huffington Post*
2. Buzzfeed
3. Upworthy
4. CNN
5. Daily Mail
6. *New York Times*
7. BBC
8. ABC News
9. *The Guardian*
10. NBC News
11. *The Blaze*
12. Fox News
13. Yahoo
14. NPR
15. Mashable

Source: Thompson, D. (2013, December 10). I Thought I Knew How Big Upworthy Was on Facebook: Then I Saw This. *The Atlantic*. www.theatlantic.com/business/archive/2013/12/i-thought-i-knew-how-big-upworthy-was-on-facebook-then-i-saw-this/282203/

Blogging

Activities identified as blogging may take many forms. An individual may operate a WordPress, Blogger or other site with complete editorial control and decision-making. At the same time, sites such as *The Huffington Post* maintain a blog team that exercises an editorial review process. Blogs published there must conform to style and other publishing rules. Beyond submission of a post and receiving an editorial decision, bloggers typically have little contact with the blog team.

On the other hand, the *Chicago Tribune* hosts *ChicagoNow*, a blog site that promotes wide-open community discussion from many bloggers who do not sign opinions with their names. Editors at this site promote a local blogger community by hosting regular social hours called "blatherings" and other events. One is called "Blogapalooz-Hour" in which bloggers are given a topic in the evening and have one hour to publish. Following the event, *ChicagoNow* community managers create a Storify summary of the monthly topical posts. The topics are very general, such as, "Write about a great challenge faced by you or someone else" (ChicagoNow, 2013).

Beyond full-length blog posts, which may run 500 to 1,000 words or more, micro-blogging on Twitter, Tumblr and other social media sites is seen as a way to regularly communicate ideas without the effort and time required by more traditional blogging.

Blogs for Public Relations and Social Media Marketing

Blogging and micro-blogging developed from early Internet discussion boards. The principle is the same in that online publishing gives authors exposure to a global audience. In some cases, the combination of blogging and PR alter careers and generate large amounts of interest. Creating, developing and maintaining a blog are important best practice steps for anyone launching a career or seeking to further develop awareness.

((•)) BOX 11.2 THOUGHT LEADER ROBERT P. MILES

Back in the olden days of yore (the mid-1990s), tech life was hard. You young'uns think it's rough when you can't get Wi-Fi, drop your tablet, lose your cellphone? Piffle!

"Networking" meant the office computers were linked through a mainframe that filled an entire hermetically sealed room. (Heaven forbid you entered without authorization! Why, a speck of dust could take the whole system down!). And connecting to the Internet? We had to *dial* a hard-wired modem through a telephone line (the signal had to climb uphill both ways! Through the snow!),

Figure 11.4 @valueinvestorNE.
Courtesy Robert Miles.

waiting entire *minutes* for the call to connect. World Wide Web sites? No graphics! No video! Just *words*.

The words "social" and "media" were never linked —if they were, it meant a group of people watching a *television* show together (suffering through commercials, no less!). No Facebook, no LinkedIn, no Twitter, no blogs! I know, such deprivation. Ah, but we did have "bulletin boards."

Not like Pinterest. Bulletin boards, back in the days of yesteryear, allowed people to post messages that could be read by others who intentionally sought them (no pushed content, can you imagine? Of course you can't). As sites such as AOL (get this: known then as America Online) and Yahoo! emerged, it was on just such a bulletin board that I, unwittingly, became an early adopter of what became social media marketing.

In 1993, AOL hosted *The Motley Fool*, a new investment newsletter founded by brothers David and Tom Gardner. Owning a 25-employee business events company meant investing my employee's retirement funds. Believing it as important to know how to invest as what to invest in, I studied strategies. *The Motley Fool* and its bulletin board caught my eye.

One thing I wanted to know was, who was the most successful investor and would he manage my investments? It may have been *The Motley Fool* that led me to Roger Lowenstein's 1995 book, *Buffett: The Making of an American Capitalist*. Already considered "the Oracle of Omaha," Buffett was then a 65-year-old business magnate raised and living in Omaha, Nebraska. I was then a 38-year-old with a 12-year-old company, who'd been raised and lived near Detroit, Michigan. Though Buffett most certainly was not available to manage my investments, his Midwestern perspective and humor resonated with me, another Midwesterner.

But, I realized, a third alternative was available: investing in Buffett himself. After purchasing Berkshire Hathaway stock, I attended my first "Woodstock for Capitalists" the first Saturday in May of 1996, one of 8,000 shareholders and guests (today that number exceeds 30,000) in Omaha to absorb his sage advice.

The more I learned about and from Buffett, the more enamored I was of his principles. Becoming something of a Buffett geek, I waxed enthusiastic to anyone who would listen. And then I decided to share my enthusiasm more widely, by committing to post "101 Reasons to Own Berkshire Hathaway" on *The Motley Fool* bulletin board dedicated to Buffett's company.

Using the screen name SimpleInvestor, the first post, on December 9, 1998, read: "INVEST WITH THE BEST—There is simply no better investment than Berkshire Hathaway, and no better investment manager than Warren Buffett. I have been investing in the stock market for

(continued)

30 years and I have done just about everything imaginable . . . I have searched high and low throughout this country and abroad. And my search has led me to the single greatest investment that I have ever made . . . I invite you to sit back and read my 101 REASONS TO OWN BERKSHIRE HATHAWAY. Please feel free to debate, agree or even add your own reasons why you own Berkshire. Fortunately there are more than 101 days until the next annual meeting. . . ." The post drew a whopping eleven recommendations.

Although not posted daily, all 101 reasons were finished before the May 1999 shareholders meeting. "Recommendations" increased and messages rolled in from readers around the world, including a European economist who urged me to publish the posts. That sounded like a good idea.

Being naive about publishing, I printed out the posts into a booklet style, then had 500 copies produced between tape-bound covers. The finished "book," with its manila cover and back, had all the sophistication of a college dissertation.

Not being naive about social courtesies, I wrote Mr. Buffett to inform him of this project. Surprisingly, he wrote me back. Even more surprising, he informed me that as a *Motley Fool* reader, he'd read all 101 of the reasons. Topping things off, he included a check for 10 copies to give his board of directors.

Reality quickly set in as libraries and bookstores refused to carry the "book." It was self-published, had no LOC number, no ISBN, no bar code. The best option for promotion seemed to be where it started, on *The Motley Fool*. Sales were brisk and soon more books were printed. Then I posted a different message: I'd buy shareholders an ice cream cone at the Omaha Dairy Queen the evening before the May 2000 annual meeting, even if they didn't buy the book.

People showed up in droves. The local and worldwide news media appeared. So did Warren Buffett. When he put an arm around my shoulder, flashbulbs (yes flashbulbs) lit up. The book-signing event caught the eye of a John Wiley & Sons publishing company representative attending the reception.

Before I knew it, I was in New York City, receiving an offer for this book and for my next one. To which I said, "I didn't know I was going to write another book." Of course you are, I was told. A check was pushed toward me. A tape-bound copy of "The World's Greatest Investment: 101 Reasons to Own Berkshire Hathaway" was pushed back in return.

Little did I know this Simple Investor's decision to share my enthusiasm on a bulletin board would forever alter my career path. Three books later, I travel the world speaking about Buffett's investment strategies, appear regularly on cable news, host the annual "Value Investor Conference," and teach an Executive MBA course at the University of Nebraska at Omaha's College of Business Administration. If it hadn't been for the "newfangled" online communication that ultimately grew into social media, my enthusiasm for Warren Buffett would never have enthused millions, but only bored my friends to tears.

Robert P. Miles is an author, founder and host of the Value Investor Conference (www.valueinvestorconference.com/) and teaches a one-of-a-kind course at the University of Nebraska at Omaha Executive MBA program, titled *The Genius of Warren Buffett.*

The lessons learned by Bob Miles during the early Internet offer hints as to how social networking and social media may create new opportunities with new people and businesses. By jumping into what some would consider risky social media spaces with ideas and passion, an individual connects with others seeking similar information and interests.

Helpful Tools

Social media users typically spend a lot of time in an array of spaces, so there is a great need for planning, strategies and development of best practices that cultivate efficient use of new tools. Social media dashboards offer content managers an opportunity to synthesize the most relevant and important data in real time.

For example, it may be important to track the top influencers on Twitter, which can be viewed from different perspectives. As we have explored, a social network can be visualized in terms of who is near the center of it, and who is at the periphery. Likewise, we may want to track hashtags, audience size, mentions or linked websites. The sheer size of global social media present information and data management challenges— content duplication, content access, timeliness of content, relevance of content to a particular platform and discussion, and efficiency within large networks.

Beyond these issues, businesses worry about the bottom line of social media activities. Evidence has begun to emerge suggesting that Twitter has a meaningful value, particularly for smaller companies with less access to mainstream media and a desire to break through the clutter (Andrews, 2013).

Brandwatch blogger and community manager Ruxandra Mindruta (@Ruxandra-Rux; 2013) in Brighton, U.K., published an excellent list of top free tools used to monitor social media, shown in Table 11.2.

Social media best practices require community brand managers to hone content by utilizing social media metrics and analytics to gauge interaction responses and feed results into future decisions.

Getting Ahead of the Social Media Pack

There are clear leaders in social media, if one looks only at large numbers of followers and engagement measures. Garst (2013) is listed as the tenth in a list of top people (shown in Table 11.3) for re-tweets by marketers, according to the *Marketing Profs* (2013) site.

Table 11.2 Top Free Social Media Monitoring Tools

1. **Hootsuite** allows users to manage multiple social media accounts, collaborate with teams and analyze weekly reports.
2. **TweetReach** measures impact and influence of followers by tracking movement of tweets.
3. **Klout** is a controversial measure of brand engagement, but it offers some sense of community perception.
4. **SocialMention** monitors more than 100 sites and tracks influence along four dimensions: Strength, Sentiment, Passion and Reach.
5. **Twazzup** is a first stop for Twitter users seeking real-time updates, keywords and top influencers.
6. **Addictomatic** monitors brand reputation across key social media platforms.
7. **HowSociable** users track 12 sites, including Tumblr and WordPress.
8. **IceRocket** monitors sites across 20 languages with a database of 200 million blogs.
9. **TweetDeck** is a popular tool for scheduling posts and monitoring activity across several sites.
10. **Reachli** (formerly Pinerly) measures and optimizes video and images, and it has Pinterest analytics.

Source: Mindruta, R. (2013, August 9). Top 10 Free Social Media Monitoring Tools. Brandwatch. www.brandwatch.com/2013/08/top-10-free-social-media-monitoring-tools/

Table 11.3 Top Marketing Sources for Re-tweets

1. @barackobama
2. @jowyang
3. @darrenrovell
4. @guykawasaki
5. @jack
6. @dannysullivan
7. @jeffbullas
8. @billclinton
9. @corybooker
10. @kimgarst

Sources: Marketing Profs (2013, August 6). Digital Marketers on Twitter: What They Share, Whom They Retweet. www.marketingprofs.com/charts/2013/11340/digital-marketers-on-twitter-share-retweet#ixzz2nxONt2jN
Garst, K. (2013, August 15). Twitter "Business Killers" to Avoid. http://kimgarst.com/twitter-business-killers

Social media best practices require users to go beyond attracting followers and fans, and it can be argued that the quality of interaction is much more important than the numbers over time. Garst (2013) identifies a formula for success, which includes avoiding common mistakes. She prefers offering social media tips, repeating motivational quotes, answering questions and general conversation over selling. Garst agrees with most successful social media practitioners who lead with valuable content. Secondly, Garst urges users to remain focused on target demographics in deciding whom to follow, what to say and when. She clears a lot of social media noise by using tools such as Hootsuite to manage and filter conversations.

Friedman (2013) listed six key trends that emphasize growing social and mobile media use: 1. Social media's "meteoric rise in influence" (para. 2); 2. Mobile accounts for 15% of all Internet traffic, half "of average global mobile web users now use mobile as . . . primary or exclusive means of going online" (para. 3); 3. Older people like brands on Facebook, but younger users "favor Instagram, SnapChat, and Tumblr" (para. 4); 4. Facebook and Instagram advertising worked to produce significantly "higher click-through rates" (para. 5); 5. People and brands shared photographs on Instagram and Pinterest; and 6. Google+ expanded features, and some brands experimented with it.

From Vine videos to amazing photography, best practices continue to redefine the nature of online social media storytelling and influence. Social media are fast and sometimes prone to quick viral sharing of content. Mobility and location drive social networking toward authentic real-time engagement, but social media branding and marketing rely heavily upon the features of entertainment. As was the case before social media, entertainment interest is likely to divide along traditional demographic group differences.

Perils

Social media communication may backfire on a user. Some consider social media a sword with two edges that when combined with snarky comments may lead a user to be suspended or fired from work, or worse (Nathanson, 2013).

In general, one of the social media perils is that trust for anything considered an advertisement is very low. Consumers, however, listen to friends for most recommendations. Marketers, for example, try to appeal to and even reward potential influencers. They also use social media sharing and collaborative game-like experiences. They hope to remain authentic rather than having the public turn on them with negative sentiment.

Social media branding, re-branding and community building typically link messages to research findings used to create strategic media campaigns. While it is not that difficult to generate interest and buzz through a hashtag, it is impossible to completely control users, including those who may try to hijack the campaign for their own purposes. Still, the best practices involve building relationships—the kind that may lead some followers, fans or friends to come to your defense amid a social media crisis. In this sense, social media best practices align with traditional media relations that use the power of celebrities and the excitement of events.

For business owners, it makes sense to start slow in social media and seek advice from those with experience. Social media consume time, and they are an expense. Best practices suggest that business may benefit from having a Facebook page, which then generates weekly insights data. Individuals should create a LinkedIn profile, monitor key Twitter sources, and consider the value of YouTube videos or Google+ options. The list of social media sites will quickly grow, which means that it is problematic to enter these spaces without a clear plan, strategies, goals, objectives and tactics. It also is a problem to jump into social media spaces without first considering the value of creating a website or blog. By doing this, users really must begin to have an understanding of SEO and analytics before creating value from online relationships. By using social media to communicate with people and businesses, it is possible to raise awareness and interest in relationships. As has been the case with email for more than two decades, online interaction must be timely and relevant to avoid being ignored.

IT, Collaboration, Virtual Teams and Other Trends

Information Technology (IT) offers new ways to explore technological capabilities, best practices, and learning through use of shared mental models and other perspectives. Much of the quality work in social media is a function of teamwork, and these collaborative teams can also help personal and organizational brands avoid making mistakes caused by decisions made without thought. Collaboration happens when groups work toward common purposes, which typically take into account stakeholders. The field of collaboration science is emerging through engineering of the ways in which people think and work (Morgeson, Reider, & Campion, 2005). Collaboration is concerned, then, with the composition of group members within a social media team, as well as the ways that leadership may promote creativity and encourage individuals to act in the interest of the larger good (Day, Gronn, & Salas, 2004). Collaborative communication within social media seeks to foster mutual understanding through coorientation (Lin & Cheng-His, 2006). As individuals seek agreement and understanding, there may be perceived performance, financial, physical, convenience, social and/or psychological risks that deter potential group success (p. 1208). Coorientation within a team would allow leaders to measure whether or not the group can accurately predict orientations of other group members (Christen, 2005).

Hollingshead and Contractor (2006) found that adding new communication media to existing capabilities can, in fact, enhance communication and interaction in small groups: "Collaboration among group members entails cognitive as well as emotional and motivational aspects of communication" (Hollingshead & Contractor, 2006, p. 115). Technologies may enhance within-group communication, provide additional information to the group, or alter tasks. Theoretical concerns include the degree of media richness and potential effects. Mediation may increase anonymity, increase task-centeredness, make communication less personal or even have an effect on the consensus-building process.

Social media communications for older and new media are becoming products of mobile media platforms and apps. The development and refinement of best practices requires team collaboration and constant learning about new tools and ideas.

■ DISCUSSION QUESTIONS: STRATEGIES AND TACTICS

1. How do mobile media devices and mobile-friendly platforms impact social media communication? What are the major changes and trends?
2. How do newspapers, radio and television journalists need to change to adapt to a social media environment? What are the potential rewards and risks?
3. What role may collaboration and teamwork play in improving the quality of social media and refining best practices?

References

Andrews, E. L. (2013, April 1). The Bottom Line on Corporate Tweeting. Graduate School of Stanford Business. www.gsb.stanford.edu/news/research/bottom-line-corporate-tweeting?utm_source=twitter&utm_medium=social-media&utm_campaign=boundaries

Buttry, S. (2013, December). Better Journalism Through Engagement. Slideshare. www.slideshare.net/stevebuttry

Campbell, S. W., & Ling, R. (2011). Conclusion: Connecting and Disconnecting Through Mobile Media. In S. W. Campbell and R. Ling (Eds.), *Mobile Communication*, pp. 323–330. New Brunswick, NJ: Transaction.

ChicagoNow (2013). ChicagoNow's Blogapalooza 3.0. Storify. http://storify.com/ChicagoNow/chicagonow-s-blogapalooza-3-0

Christen, C. T. (2005). The Utility of Coorientational Variables as Predictors of Willingness to Negotiate," *Journalism & Mass Communication Quarterly 82*(1), 7–24.

Day, D., Gronn, P., & Salas, E. (2004). Leadership Capacity in Teams. *Leadership Quarterly*, *15*(6), 857–880.

Friedman, P. (2013, December 19). 6 Social Media Trends of 2013 and What They Mean for the Future. *The Huffington Post*. www.huffingtonpost.com/peter-friedman/social-media-trends-of-2013_b_4463802.html

Gardner, H., & Davis, K. (2013). *The App Generation*. New Haven, CT: Yale University Press.

Garst, K. (2013, August 15). Twitter "Business Killers" to Avoid. http://kimgarst.com/twitter-business-killers

Gleason, R. (2013, December 18). Personal email, WBBM Newsradio 780 news director.

Hollingshead, A. B., & Contractor, N. S. (2006). New Media and Small Group Organizing, in L. A. Lievrouw & S. Livingstone (Eds.), *The Handbook of New Media*, pp. 114–133. London: Sage.

Hunsinger, J. (2014). Interface and Infrastructure of Social Media. In J. Hunsinger and T. Senft (Eds.), *The Social Media Handbook*, pp. 5–17. New York, NY: Routledge.

IBM (2012, September 6). Smarter Commerce Conversations—2012 Orlando—Kim Garst. http://youtu.be/1oVolmYybHU

Lane, E. (2013, December 9). Social Media Alive With *The Sound of Music* on NBC. www.huffingtonpost.com/eden-lane/social-media-alive-with-t_b_4401085.html

Lin, T. M. Y., & Cheng-His, F. (2006). The Effects of Perceived Risk on the Word-of-Mouth Communication Dyad. *Social Behavior & Personality 34*(10), 1207–1216.

Marketing Profs (2013, August 6). Digital Marketers on Twitter: What They Share, Whom They Retweet. www.marketingprofs.com/charts/2013/11340/digital-marketers-on-twitter-share-retweet#ixzz2nxONt2jN

Mindruta, R. (2013, August 9). Top 10 Free Social Media Monitoring Tools. Brandwatch. www.brandwatch.com/2013/08/top-10-free-social-media-monitoring-tools/

Morgeson, F., Reider, M., & Campion, M. (2005). Selecting Individuals in Team Settings: The Importance of Social Skills, Personality Characteristics, and Teamwork Knowledge. *Personnel Psychology*, *58*(3), 583–611.

Nathanson, R. (2013, December 9). Social Media: Perils and Payoffs for Public Officials. *Albuquerque Journal*. www.abqjournal.com/316631/news/social-media-perils-and-payoffs.html

RTT News (2013, December 16). *The Sound of Music Live!* Ratings Higher Than First Reported. www.rttnews.com/2239727/the-sound-of-music-live-ratings-higher-than-first-reported.aspx?type=ent

Thompson, D. (2013, December 10). I Thought I Knew How Big Upworthy Was on Facebook: Then I Saw This. *The Atlantic*. www.theatlantic.com/business/archive/2013/12/i-thought-i-knew-how-big-upworthy-was-on-facebook-then-i-saw-this/282203/

12 FUTURE OF SOCIAL MEDIA AND INFORMATION LITERACY

"In many ways I consider my Twitter activities a giant, distributed, never-ending media literacy project."

—Andy Carvin, (@acarvin, 2013)

In the 24/7, real-time world of social media, users need the ability to quickly make good decisions. Media literacy is the skill of deconstructing messages and understanding context. This is important for social media novices, as well as communication professionals, who may become caught up in a social media moment.

Justine Sacco was a public relations professional, but she said something on Twitter that cost her a very good job. She was in London getting ready to board a long flight to Africa when she tweeted:

@JustineSacco: Going to Africa. Hope I don't get AIDS. Just kidding. I'm white! (December 20, 2013).

Those twelve words caused a global uproar on social media while she was in the air for more than 10 hours. There were parody accounts and critical tweets with #HasJustineLandedYet on Twitter. By the time her flight landed in Cape Town, South Africa, her name had been removed from the InterActiveCorp website—a PR firm with many large clients. IACA issued an apology, calling the tweet offensive and outrageous. At first, Sacco deleted the tweet, but it had already been captured in screen shots and virally spread across the Net. Her initial action drew more criticism, and she took down the Twitter account. Sacco was fired from her executive job as communications director for the racist remark, and many found it difficult to understand how a professional could make such a huge mistake. Her apology even called it "a huge stupidity" (Dimitrova, 2013, para. 1). Sacco should have had better media literacy skills, but she also had a previous history of questionable tweets. The case is also noteworthy because the tweet sparked a social media "mob" reaction likened to "trial by social media," which is similar to the more traditional notion of "pillory of the press" (Bowcott, 2011). It is understood that media exposure—traditional or social—may generate an immediate penalty of mass public ridicule.

One way to view social media is through the metaphor of "the stream," which reflects the idea that information flows and may even crest (Madrigaldec, 2013, para. 1). The idea of a stream emphasizes real-time data, such as that on Twitter, which has no beginning or end. A premium is placed on sharing of current information, and the conversation is *"permanently unfinished"* (para. 13). Such a stream may not lend itself to quality content or media that remain fresh for very long. In a media literacy sense, users and fans must understand these characteristics, deconstruct what they are viewing and make conscious decisions about how to spend time.

The lure of the social media stream is also a problem within schools. Teachers, who can be seen using their cellphones, do so even though this activity by students often is prohibited during the school day:

> It turns out that this is a hotly debated issue. Many schools have policies that do not allow students to use cellphones during the school day; some even have policies that forbid students to have phones with them in school, at all. But these policies do not necessarily extend to teachers. (Dobrow, 2013, para. 4)

A media literacy approach would be to develop good teacher and student use habits, rather than restricting access to the devices, because prohibition misses learning opportunities.

In this book, social media have been explored from a variety of perspectives and within different contexts. From computer-mediated communication concepts to the applied fields of journalism, public relations, advertising and marketing we can identify a desire for online engagement and influence. In this chapter, we look at how social media may be important in driving social change. Media and information literacy address what we know and how we know it. It is a perspective that urges us to become smarter social media users.

(((•))) BOX 12.1 THOUGHT LEADER SAMMI HE

The most significant change in the PR industry is due to widely adopted social media usage. Public relations practitioners get substantially shorter periods of time to react to an issue or crisis. The general public, journalists, investors, employees and other related parties can now follow the development of any event online through various social media tools, such as Twitter and Facebook.

In the next five years, we should see more "freelancers," who have significant followers on their blog or Twitter account, and write for many different publications. They may not necessarily be primarily journalists, as there are fewer so-called "disciplines" now in traditional media outlets. The changes make it more dif-

Figure 12.1 @SammiHe.
Courtesy Sammi He.

ficult for PR professionals to pitch stories and also require us to have greater knowledge in more areas. It is hard for us to identify who the true experts are in a certain area. Also, despite many attempts to measure "engagement" or "ROI," there still is no industry standard to measure the efforts of social media at the corporate or personal level. In addition, information, especially false information like rumors, more easily flies around through social media. Lastly, brands or individuals can be easily "brandjacked" or manipulated, as others take their user names or domains and assert themselves as someone else.

Bloggers, Twitterers and LinkedIn groups usually build audiences with like minds and interests, which give PR professionals an advantage of targeting the right audiences more efficiently and effectively. They have their own virtual circle, which allows the messages to be circulated without too much promotion. Done right, social media also may help clients reduce the cost for a campaign, yet generate more positive and effective results.

Sammi He is a member of the Corporate/Financial Practice of Burson-Marsteller. Sammi has more than three years of experience in communications, with an emphasis in media relations, event planning, strategy development and executive positioning. She is also a member of B-M's U.S.-China Specialty Group, where she acts as a core member of the team, seeking insights into how to reach all forms of media and audiences in Asia. Additionally, she helps Chinese clients establish and increase awareness in the U.S. through various activities. She received her undergraduate and graduate degrees from the University of Nebraska at Omaha.

Media Literacy

Literacy skills are a fundamental requirement of an elementary and secondary education, yet media literacy may not be emphasized within traditional early education. Further, life-long learning by adults about the nature of global media corporations; framing of media messages; potential effects on children and adults; and application of this knowledge in the role of active, deliberative citizenship is crucial (Tewksbury & Rittenberg, 2012). George Takei, for example, went from being known as Sulu on the *Star Trek* television show to a social media star. More importantly, he used his connection to fans to attack negative stereotypes about Asians and gays. Takei told *The Daily Beast*:

> Ours is a people's democracy, and it can be as great as a people can be, but it's also as fallible as people are. So, this democracy is vitally dependent on good people to be actively engaged in the process. (Stern, 2014, para. 17)

Through his website, Oh My! memes and a play about his life, Takei blends entertainment and political activism that is powered by social media communication. His content may be seen as a form of social media literacy education in response to the ignorance that also is spread online in the social media marketplace of ideas.

The social media environment presents a challenge that young, middle-aged and older people alike have not faced in the history of civilization—to exercise personal responsibility in an unprecedented era of open communication and access to a global audience. Whether we know it or not, we all have the power to be publishers, yet few of us are formally trained to do so. Consider high school students in the United States who find the freedom the Internet offers an attractive method of expression. However, mass media are full of accounts of the dangers of predators using this information (Coronado,

2006). In the years during social media development, the problem of inappropriate and illegal online communication has become widespread. The general issue led the state of Massachusetts in the early days of social media to urge MySpace.com, a website devoted to personal pages and groups, to raise the minimum age of users from 14 to 18. Age restrictions imply that teens do not or cannot be *taught* to exercise sophisticated media and information literacy skills. The soaring popularity of personal websites is only one part of the larger social media literacy issue.

📱 BOX 12.2 MYSPACE ONLINE COMMUNITIES

MySpace Describes Its Definition of an Online Community

MySpace is an online community that lets you meet your friends' friends.
    Create a private community on MySpace and you can share photos, journals and interests with your growing network of mutual friends!
    See who knows who, or how you are connected. Find out if you really are six people away from Kevin Bacon.

MySpace is for everyone:

- Friends who want to talk Online
- Single people who want to meet other Singles
- Matchmakers who want to connect their friends with other friends
- Families who want to keep in touch—map your Family Tree
- Business people and co-workers interested in networking
- Classmates and study partners

Anyone looking for long lost friends! This MySpace online community description falls short of taking a media literacy approach, but it does suggest creation of "a private community" for photograph sharing. Too often, the marketing and business interests of social network sites emphasize use and encourage it without development of users' critical thinking skills. A social responsibility perspective would offer specific examples of private and public communication.

Source: Techterms (2007, Mar. 6). MySpace. www.techterms.com/definition/myspace

---

It is unfair to see social media sites only as potentially harmful to young people. Clearly, they also provide socialization and interaction opportunities. When a missing person report is posted on Facebook, for example, it can assist law enforcement in an investigation. The key is how social networking is used. A media literacy perspective allows us to examine content and technology from a variety of angles, not just one.

From a computer-mediated communication perspective, Huffaker and Calvert (2005) examined issues of online identity and language among teenage blog users. They found that a majority of teen bloggers presented extensive personal data, including first names, age, and contact information. One in five teens revealed a full name.

The integration of media and information literacy produces an emphasis on schools and education, library usage, intercultural communication and global media. Culture and stereotypes have been found to exist within social media, as they do in society.

Developments in social media presented new questions about how the public processes information and entertainment. Peter Levine, Deputy Director of CIRCLE, The Center for Information and Research on Civic Learning and Engagement, discussed the proliferation of unreliable information and the challenges posed by it: "Some prominent individuals and institutions are calling for schools to prepare young people to identify reliable information online" (Levine, 2005, p. 1). In this context, there is a call for formalized information literacy education in the schools, but U.S. K–16 education has been slow to respond. One important issue for schools is the examination of media use in different environments, such as during social free time and within different cultural contexts (Vered, 2001; Hart, 2001; Lealand, 2001). Educators need to respond to the larger framework of student media and social media use in a global and multimedia environment. In such a world, media and information literacy must be placed within an emerging multicultural education framework. Public and private elementary and secondary school teachers appear to support the goals and values of media education, but the constraints of curricula, time, and resources limit their willingness to expand instruction and include media education. While media literacy education has spread throughout the United States, it has not been fully adopted by educators (Yates, 2004). So media and information literacy education have yet to reach a mature status as an integral and essential part of school curricula. Schools present one set of concerns for those wishing to understand media and information literacy, but libraries are a different context. The role of media librarianship has been transformed by technological and social change. Librarians and library patrons are increasingly likely to be in interaction with one another, likely to be utilizing technology, and likely to approximate pedagogical structure. This blending of classroom, library online and social media contexts will continue to evolve, as online interaction grows in popularity.

Life-Long Learning and Media Literacy

Social media and information literacy is a dynamic field of study, which is being dramatically influenced by social and technological change (Briggs, 2010). For example, the introduction and diffusion of the video iPod made it possible for people to download media content and take it for viewing anywhere. Thus, such portable media messages competed for attention with ubiquitous place-based television (i.e., TV screens in supermarkets, schools, doctor's offices, gas stations, etc.) and traditional print media. The rapid diffusion of smartphones and tablets followed, creating a media-rich environment. Everyone is challenged to exercise more sophisticated media literacy skills. Increasingly, it is not enough to be able to read and understand text-based messages. The prevalence of multi-media requires people to exercise advanced visual literacy skills.

Aging baby boomers—those born between 1946 and 1964—are a key group headed toward their retirement years. Interesting issues have emerged about whether this group, raised on television, would behave as their parents did in terms of traditional media usage. In fact, this group quickly embraced social media sites, such as Facebook, as well as online media usage on sites such as Twitter. Newspapers and television remain important sources for boomers, yet inexpensive tablets encouraged the shift away from traditional media uses. Awash in new media choices, boomers are set to make lifestyle choices that break the mold of previous generations. From a global media literacy perspective, boomers can be thought of as users and fans who critically examine consumer content (Hilt & Lipschultz, 2005). In this sense, the media literacy approach directly challenges critical theorists who argue that consumers are passive and easily manipulated—especially when users have the tools at their fingertips (Mathison, 2009).

The Internet led some authors to emphasize the importance of digital literacy skills, information literacy skills, technology literacy, and visual literacy as significant elements in understanding media literacy. Shapiro and Hughes (1996) asked what would individuals need to know to be considered competent and literate in an information society:

> As we witness not only the saturation of our daily lives with information organized and transmitted via information technology, by the way in which public issues and social life increasingly are affected by information-technology issues—from intellectual property to privacy and the structure of work to entertainment, art and fantasy life—the issue of what it means to be information-literate becomes more acute for our whole society. (p. 1)

The stream of social media content makes it difficult to precisely define literacy, much less social media literacy. Silverblatt (1995) organized media literacy around four prime aspects of message interpretation: process, context, framework, and production values. He builds upon this through a definition of media literacy that has five elements— awareness of impact on individuals and society; understanding media processes; message analysis strategy development; content as cultural indicators; and enhancement of media enjoyment and appreciation. Silverblatt's framework may work for social media users in allowing them to step back from the social stream and understand cultural significance of the communication in a way that he describes as critical awareness (Silverblatt & Zlobin, 2004). Within social and mobile media, messages vary in form and content. Instead of following narrow professional content rules, any user may produce content using any set of production rules. The optimistic view is that social media promote citizen decision-making, collaboration and compromise, yet there also continues to be anecdotal evidence that users tend to retreat to conversations with like-minded individuals and organizations.

Global Media Corporations

One concern has been that traditional media ownership is increasingly highly concentrated in the hands of a few major global corporations (Bagdikian, 2000). Beyond the homogenous messages distributed by these large corporations, most users have been educated without the media literacy tools to challenge media values of violence and blind consumerism. McChesney (1999) saw media literacy as a movement designed to increase education, skepticism and knowledge:

> It is fueled by the large public discontent with the hypercommercialism, banality, and assininity of corporate media fare, as well as the commercialization of

education and every possible facet of social life. Media literacy has considerable potential as long as it involves explaining how the media system actually works and does not posit that the existing system is by definition good, democratic, and immutable. (p. 301)

Social media seem in one sense to liberate individuals from corporate control by offering new communication options. Still, large corporate social media sites, such as Facebook, Twitter and Google+ continue to dominate much of the landscape. Social media offer a paradox of freedom and control—users are free to communicate, but they do so within systems designed by large media industries (Albarran, 2013).

Framing of Media Messages

Relatively little structured education exists to prepare viewers to deconstruct and critically examine complex media messages. One example would be the innovative undergraduate program at Webster University. This field of study views media literacy as "a critical thinking skill that focuses on the source of much of our information: the media." Programs such as this address media literacy through:

- awareness of media impact on individuals and the society;
- understanding of mass communication processes;
- developing critical approaches to analyze media messages;
- media content awareness of text, sound, and images; and,
- exploration of cultural and social constructions, depictions, and presentations of diverse groups by media.

Further, some campuses use information literacy in education curricula to address issues related to instruction design, web page development, and website evaluation. Educational institutions reflect dramatic and relevant changes in society.

Traditional media, such as radio and television, also are adapting to this new environment. Where once the nightly network newscast was king, the lines have blurred between news and entertainment. For example, cable television programs like *The Colbert Report* employ satire and actual news video to make fun of the political and social landscape at the same time as they critique it.

MSNBC's *Countdown with Keith Olbermann* (2006), which mixed serious and humorous news until it was dropped from cable, once suggested that the public and news sources can become confused about reality:

Number three, Stephen Colbert. When I was on his show, I told him, you're too good. Some conservatives will not realize you're destroying them. Like Tom DeLay, it turns out. The DeLay Defense Fund has e-mailed a critique of a new anti-DeLay documentary. It credits Colbert's interview with the filmmaker as "cracking the story," with such questions as, Who hates America more, you or Michael Moore?

At its core, media literacy (Media Literacy, 2003) is the ability to pay close attention to content (including the visual) and make sense of a wide range of media messages and presentations (Green, Lodato, Schwalbe, & Silcock, 2012). The critical examination of text, photographs, audio, and video requires awareness, education, and practice.

In one example, a tourist photo was altered to include what appears to be a jet heading toward the World Trade Center. The image was widely distributed in the weeks following September 11, 2001. In fact, a close examination of the lighting, color, clothing, sky, and angles reveals it is a fake. Likewise, the e-mail stories disseminated about the image did not withstand critical scrutiny. The **Snopes** website is one dedicated to debunking false Internet information, and this content is widely shared via social media. One great advantage of the emerging social media world is that each shared item can be scrutinized by participants within social networks to assist a user in discovering whether or not content is authentic.

Potential Effects from Media Literacy

In order to understand the emerging field of media and information literacy, attention must be paid to a wide range of interdisciplinary studies. Media research frequently addresses literacy concerns as they relate to dynamic news construction, audience perception of stories and cultivation of long-term beliefs (Dominick, 2009). At the same time, library studies have been at the heart of questions related to how people seek, find, process, and use new information. Thus, media and information literacy draws from traditional disciplines, but it forges a new way of looking at how people use media (Barnes, 2003; Baran & Davis, 2000).

Social media literacy urges users to reflect upon content ownership, privacy invasion and other issues addressed in this book. Podcasting was one early form that helped democratize media by allowing anyone with a computer to participate.

Application of Knowledge

As people adopt new and different media, including social media through SNS platforms, studies will need to be grounded in what we already know about the development of visual and computer literacy skills (Kupianen, 2013). Media audiences are known to possess complex schemas—ordered information that offers cognitive explanations (Graber, 2006). Potter (2001/2008) aligned media literacy as a perspective related to media exposure and meaning making from messages. Meaning making is cognitive and affective—capable of generating emotional response (Rodman, 2001).

Media and information literacy matter because people of all walks of life need to be able to deconstruct media messages and critique the quality of information sources. For example, many days after 9/11 there came a moment when morning network TV shows left coverage and returned to the mundane: cooking recipes, review of the latest popular music artist CD, and the following of sensational murder cases. Likewise, we could have predicted the shift away from Hurricane Katrina coverage. While some light has been shed on the ebb and flow of news cycles, viewers armed with media and information literacy knowledge and skills would immediately recognize what is happening and why. From organizational routines to individual behaviors, news and information are important. Media tactics help explain content from a political and economic perspective. This level of understanding about media behavior needs to diffuse into media and information literacy education for all ages. From WikiLeaks (Beckett, with Ball, 2012) to virtual relationships (Brown, 2011) and political change (Garrett & Danziger, 2011), social media present literacy challenges and opportunities.

Media and information literacy remains in most places outside the definition of what elementary and secondary school age students *need* to know. This is even the case in most higher education requirements. If everyone seems to agree that we live in a media and information age, why have educators been so slow to respond? Is it because of politics, economics, or some other macro explanations? Media and information literacy remains somewhat on the edge of more traditional disciplines. This, however, must and will change in the global media and information age. Globalization is likely to place increasing importance on cultural theory, democratic theory, and development of new social movements. This may be related to development of new media as technological tools for social change. As individuals are empowered by their media and information literacy skills, it is possible that these abilities will be harnessed as cultural tools in grassroots battles to maintain local and national identities.

Social media literacy extends to policy questions and issues. When a University of Kansas media professor spoke out following the Navy Yard 2013 shootings in Washington, DC, he received death threats and personal attack. The university placed the professor on leave and revamped its disciplinary policies to include social media. The following social media policy amendments were made by the Regents in the weeks following the event.

📱 BOX 12.3 UNIVERSITY OF KANSAS SOCIAL MEDIA POLICY

The Kansas Board of Regents in 2013 added social media language to a section of their suspension, termination and dismissal policies, which were under review in 2014.

The chief executive officer of a state university has the authority to suspend, dismiss or terminate from employment any faculty or staff member who makes improper use of social media. "Social media" means any facility for online publication and commentary, including but not limited to blogs, wikis, and social networking sites such as Facebook, LinkedIn, Twitter, Flickr, and YouTube. "Improper use of social media" means making a communication through social media that:

  i. directly incites violence or other immediate breach of the peace;
  ii. when made pursuant to (i.e. in furtherance of) the employee's official duties, is contrary to the best interest of the university; . . .
  iv. subject to the balancing analysis required by the following paragraph, impairs discipline by superiors or harmony among co-workers . . .

In determining whether the employee's communication constitutes an improper use of social media under paragraph (iv), the chief

(*continued*)

executive officer shall balance the interest of the university in promoting the efficiency of the public services it performs through its employees against the employee's right as a citizen to speak on matters of public concern, and may consider the employee's position within the university and whether the employee used or publicized the university name, brands, website, official title or school/department/college or otherwise created the appearance of the communication being endorsed, approved or connected to the university in a manner that discredits the university. The chief executive officer may also consider whether the communication was made during the employee's working hours or the communication was transmitted utilizing university systems or equipment.

Source: University of Kansas, Board of Regents (2013). Suspensions, Terminations and Dismissals (6)(b) Other. www.kansasregents.org/policy_chapter_ii_c_suspensions

Social media literacy skills might have led the professor to pause and reflect on the need to inject into a Twitter controversy, or at least the manner of the communication. Likewise, a social media literacy perspective should have kept the Kansas Board of Regents from revising policy so quickly after an incident. Rather than focusing on communication restrictions and punishment, the board might have been able to generate a statement that respected free expression and balanced it against the need for public safety. The vague nature of several of the policy provisions is a problem. It translates to a policy that could lead to termination for nearly any use of a social networking platform and opens the door to arbitrary actions. Social media use could be used as an excuse to fire an employee when other reasons could be more easily challenged in court. It is believed that the Kansas policy in its original language would not survive a First Amendment review by the federal courts.

Global social media literacy will continue to generate new questions (Lipschultz & Hilt, 2005). Computer and visual literacy skills must evolve with constant technological change (Potter, 2001/2008). Individuals, for example using mobile and social media, face literacy issues in the interaction between people, messages, sounds and visual images (Hobbs, 1997). Social media literacy needs to be connected and understood as social activity (Vered, 2001), cultural experience and knowledge (Hart, 2001). Beyond simple access and use (Lealand, 2001), social media users will face critical multicultural challenges (Haynes Writer & Chávez Chávez, 2001; Yates, 2004). Social media literacy experts will need to keep up on issues and educate users (Widzinski, 2001), as few people have adequate time to devote to the fluid environment that has political significance (Best, 2005). Old and new media alike present information and other content in a variety of forms. Mass media and information literacy is a way of thinking about theories, skills and practices utilized to make better judgments. The field is one approach that assists consumers of social media.

(ᚚ) BOX 12.4 THOUGHT LEADER CAROL FOWLER

Social media have given access to the tools of mass communication once only held by journalists and brands (through advertising). This has had a profound impact on the influence and profitability of traditional news media, and the change is ongoing, although I think the biggest shift has taken place and now the lords of traditional media understand there is no "putting the genie back in the bottle." Anyone with a Twitter account can be a reporter. Social media also created an environ-

Figure 12.2 @carolfowler.
Photograph by David Klobucar, courtesy Carol Fowler.

ment in which it is permissible and even encouraged for journalists to share personal opinions about politics and religion. Objectivity, while ideal, is no longer essential. There are a handful of examples of reporters getting fired for what they shared in social media, but usually it is because they crossed the line of good taste, rather than because they let their personal feelings about an issue they're covering be known.

The credibility of information is in question, in ways like never before. Can you believe what you read? Those trained in the principles of journalism follow a code of ethics, but what's the code of ethics in sharing news and content on Facebook? It's up to the public to be more discerning than ever. The rise of social media has created a demand for education in media literacy. I hope that in the next five years, parents and educators take a more active role in teaching young people what sources of information they should trust.

Social media tipped the scale by creating a powerful mechanism for consumers to hold brands accountable, whether that be a restaurant, auto dealer, appliance maker or mortgage lender. The idea of calling a lawyer or taking your complaint to the Better Business Bureau? How old-fashioned!

As of this writing, about 70% of people read consumer reviews before making an important purchase. Those reviews have real value, and over the next five years, I see brands reaching out to individual customers in the social space more respectfully and strategically. The consumer reviews website where I work, Viewpoints.com, is responding to this paradigm shift by creating a mechanism for manufacturers and brands to "claim" their reviewed products and respond directly to a consumer on our site

(continued)

immediately after a review is posted. We've named it Viewpoints Pulse because it allows brands to keep their fingers on the "pulse" of what people are saying. I'm excited about this because it creates a fuller picture of a product for those who are shopping. If a consumer hated something, it helps to know the brand's response (i.e. maybe the user wasn't following the directions) or conversely other consumers and the manufacturer will get an early heads-up on a problem.

In its highest use, social media should be a conversation, not a one-way rant. Over the next five years, I am most excited about coming up with new ways to facilitate greater understanding on all sides.

Carol Fowler is a senior digital content strategist and technology entrepreneur who is co-founder of Queue Digital, a start-up that helps local news organizations develop an integrated mobile strategy to expand their audiences. With decades of experience as a major market television news manager, Fowler has led editorial, sales and marketing teams in providing content for new audiences, with shorter attention spans, who self-select while on-the-go. Fowler brings expertise in SEO practices, media operations, storytelling, social media and editorial decision-making. From 2012 to 2014, she was Vice President of Content—Digital and Social Media for a leading consumer reviews site, Viewpoints.com. Fowler is an alumna of the University of Missouri School of Journalism.

Social media literacy skills empower users to examine the technology values that exist within much of what is shared and discussed. There are corporate benefits when we buy and use the latest technologies. In 2014, wearables, technologies that are connected to various parts of a user's body, open the possibility of sharing data across social networks. Clearly, there are issues that go beyond personal privacy, yet social media messages tend to promote how cool this use will be. At the same time as the wealthy developing world uses the latest social media technologies, the poor have little or no access, may be exploited in the manufacturing processes, and may be the victims of environmental disasters caused by unrestrained development. If we reduce social media to consumer satisfaction, then this postmodernism may be a "hedonistic" search for needs that will never be fully met (Stevenson, 1995, p. 149). Such issues force us to consider the largest social media literacy question of all: Are we making progress?

Engagement, Networked Communicators, Trust and Influence

This book began by exploring how the entrepreneur businesses culture promotes social media change. By recognizing the challenges of big data privacy, media organization power and control, user best practices must be informed by knowledge about the networked world. We can learn to critically examine data, platforms and policies. We can effectively use social media without being forced to surrender our identities, interactions and communities.

Trust should be earned over time. Social media offer the opportunity for users to evaluate the influencers rather than accept media agenda setting. Responsible social media conversation takes ownership of communication. Users should be able to tell their own stories and judge those of others. Rather than a reflex, social media sharing should be a thoughtful activity. From professional strategies and tactics to simple user interaction, a media literacy approach offers the potential to use social media in promoting a better society.

From Dubai to Shanghai, social networking has become a normal behavior for individual users desiring to present a version of the self by interacting through online communication and cultivating a sense of community—sometimes across great distances. At the same time, global social media communication features commercial marketing and advertising that is very similar to what developed in the United States.

The future of social media communication is likely to feature continued improvement of smaller and lighter hardware driven by advances in software programming. The key questions must focus on how people, organizations and businesses will use these new technologies to communicate across SNS and other social online spaces. For journalists, public relations professionals, advertisers and marketers, social media communication defines what Microsoft's Bill Gates once called "The Road Ahead." The challenges and opportunities involve understanding key concepts, defining best practices, examining data, operating within a legal framework and striving to be ethical. For those willing to take the time to master social media communication, individual and professional rewards are likely to follow. It is not that social media communication

Figure 12.3 College students browse Apple laptop computers on a city campus in Hangzhou, China, where mobile smartphones were also very popular by early 2012.

offers a utopia, for there are clearly important concerns about data privacy, socially responsible behavior and media literacy. In the end, though, it is not possible to reverse the technological momentum of the last three or four decades. The best we may hope for is to harness capabilities, think about best uses and make reasoned decisions about the future.

■ DISCUSSION QUESTIONS: STRATEGIES AND TACTICS

1. How would social media literacy improve the quality of communication within your social network?
2. Is there a balance between free expression and responsible social media communication? How does media literacy promote user understanding?
3. In what ways are social media promoting social change or the status quo? How do you think this might be different going forward?

References

Albarran, A. B. (Ed.) (2013). *The Social Media Industries*. New York, NY: Routledge.

Bagdikian, B. H. (2000). *The Media Monopoly, sixth edition*. Boston, MA: Beacon Press, pp. 239, 241.

Baran, S. J., & Davis, D. K. (2000). *Mass Communication Theory: Foundations, Ferment, and Future*. Belmont, CA: Wadsworth/Thomson

Barnes, S. B. (2003). *Computer-Mediated Communication, Human-to-Human Communication Across the Internet*. Boston, MA: Allyn and Bacon.

Beckett, C., with Ball, J. (2012). *Wikileaks, News in the Networked* Era. Cambridge, UK: Polity Press.

Best, K. (2005). Rethinking the Globalization Movement: Toward a Cultural Theory of Contemporary Democracy and Communication. *Communication and Critical/Cultural Studies, 2*, 214–237.

Bowcott, O. (2011, July 5). Contempt of Court Rules are Designed to Avoid Trial by Media. *The Guardian*. www.theguardian.com/law/2011/jul/05/contempt-court-rules-trial-media

Briggs, M. (2010). *Journalism Next*. Washington, DC: CQ Press.

Brown, A. (2011, March-April). Relationships, Community, and Identity in the New Virtual Society. *The Futurist*, 29–31, 34.

Coronado, R. (2006, April 27). Man Pleads No Contest to Molesting Girl, *Sacramento Bee*, p. B2.

Dimitrova, K. (2013, December 21). Tweet on AIDS in Africa Sparks Internet Outrage. ABC News. http://abcnews.go.com/International/tweet-aids-africa-sparks-internet-outrage/

Dobrow, J. (2013, December 4). Do as I Say, Not as I Do: Teachers, Cellphones and Media Literacy. *The Huffington Post*. www.huffingtonpost.com/julie-dobrow/do-as-i-say-not-as-i-do-t_b_4379085.html?utm_hp_ref=media&ir=Media

Dominick, J. R. (2009). *The Dynamics of Mass Communication, tenth edition*. New York, NY: McGraw-Hill.

Garrett, R. K., & Danziger, J. N. (2011, March). The Internet Electorate. *Communications of the ACM 54*(3), 117–123.

Graber, D. A. (2006). *Mass Media & American Politics, seventh edition*. Washington, DC: CQ Press, p. 196.

Green, S. C., Lodato, M. J., Schwalbe, C. B., & Silcock, B. W. (2012). *News Now, Visual Storytelling in the Digital Age*. Boston, MA: Pearson.

Hart, A. (2001). Researching Media Education in Schools in the United Kingdom. *Studies in Media & Information Literacy Education 1*, 1–5. www.utpjournals.com/simile

Haynes Writer, J., & Chávez Chávez, R, (2001). Storied Lives, Dialog—Retro-reflections: Melding Critical Multicultural Education and Critical Race Theory for Pedagogical Transformation. *Studies in Media & Information Literacy Education 1*, 1–4. www.utpjournals.com/simile

Hilt, M.L., & Lipschultz, J.H. (2005). *Mass Media, an Aging Population, and the Baby Boomers*. Mahwah, NJ: Lawrence Erlbaum.

Hobbs, R. (1997). Expanding the Concept of Literacy. In Robert Kubey (Ed.), *Media Literacy in the Information Age*, pp. 163–183. New Brunswick, NJ: Transaction Publishers.

Huffaker, D.A., & Calvert, S.L. (2005). Gender, Identity, and Language Use in Teenage Blogs. *Journal of Computer-Mediated Communication 10*(1), http://jcmc.indiana.edu/vol10/issue2/huffaker.html

Kupianen, R. (2013). *Media and Digital Literacies in Secondary School*. New York, NY: Peter Lang.

Lealand, G. (2001). Some Things Change, Some Things Remain the Same: New Zealand Children and Media Use," *Studies in Media & Information Literacy Education,* 1, 1–4. www.utpjournals.com/simile

Levine, P. (2005). The Problem of Online Misinformation and the Role of Schools. *Studies in Media & Information Literacy Education, 5*(1), 1–11. www.utpress.utoronto.ca/journal/ejournals/simile

Lipschultz, J.H., & Hilt, M.L. (2005). Media & Information Literacy Theory and Research: Thoughts from the Co-Editors. *Studies in Media & Information Literacy Education 5*, 1. www.utpress.utoronto.ca/journal/ejournals/simile

Madrigaldec, A.C. (2013, December). 2013: The Year 'the Stream' Crested. *The Atlantic*. www.theatlantic.com/technology/archive/2013/12/2013-the-year-the-stream-crested/282202/

Mathison, D. (2009). *Be the Media*. New Hyde Park, NY: Natural E Creative Group.

McChesney, R.W. (1999). *Rich Media, Poor Democracy, Communication Politics in Dubious Times*. Urbana, IL: University of Illinois Press, p. 301.

Media Literacy (2003). Center for Media Literacy. www.medialit.org/reading_room/article37.html

MSNBC (2006, May 24). *Countdown with Keith Olbermann*. www.msnbc.msn.com/id/12971702/

Potter, J.W. (2001/2008). *Media Literacy, second edition and fourth edition*. Thousand Oaks, CA: Sage.

Rodman, G. (2001). *Making Sense of Media*. Needham Heights, MA: Allyn and Bacon, 2001.

Shapiro, J.J., & Hughes, S.K. (1996, March/April). Information Literacy as a Liberal Art, Enlightenment Proposals for a New Curriculum, *Educom Review 31*, 1. www.educause.edu/pub/er/review/reviewArticles/31231.html (June 19, 2006).

Silverblatt, A. (1995). *Media Literacy, Keys to Interpreting Media Messages*, pp. 2–3, 128–131, 303. Westport, CT: Praeger.

Silverblatt, A., &, Zlobin, N. (2004). *International Communications: A Media Literacy Approach*. Armonk, NY: M.E. Sharpe.

Stern, M. (2014, January 22). "To Be Takei" Traces George Takei's Journey from Japanese Internment Camp to Cultural Icon. *The Daily Beast*. www.thedailybeast.com/articles/2014/01/22/to-be-takei-traces-george-takei-s-journey-from-japanese-internment-camps-to-cultural-icon.html

Stevenson, N. (1995) *Understanding Media Cultures*. London: Sage.

Tewksbury, D., & Rittenberg, J. (2012). *News on the Internet, Information and Citizenship in the 21st Century*. Oxford, UK: Oxford University Press.

University of Kansas, Board of Regents (2013). Suspensions, Terminations and Dismissals (6)(b) Other. www.kansasregents.org/policy_chapter_ii_c_suspensions

Vered, K.O. (2001). Intermediary Space and Media Competency: Children's Media Play in "Out of School Hours Care" Facilities in Australia. *Studies in Media & Information Literacy Education 1*, 1–4. www.utpjournals.com/simile

Widzinski, L. (2001). The Evolution of Media Librarianship: A Tangled History of Change and Constancy. *Studies in Media & Information Literacy Education 1*, 1–4. www.utpjournals.com/simile

Yates, B.L. (2004). Applying Diffusion Theory: Adoption of Media Literacy Programs in Schools. *Studies in Media & Information Literacy Education 4*, 1–4. www.utpress.utoronto.ca/journal/ejournals/simile

GLOSSARY

Advertising—paid and commercial messages purchased by an advertiser or agency representative to appear within mainstream traditional or hybrid digital media. Sponsored content or "native advertising" mimics the look and feel of editorial or news content, but it is sponsored as a single ad or part of a larger ad campaign buy.

Analytics—measurement of social media behavior through a variety of metrics. A stream of new tools has been developed to present real-time and near real-time data on social media dashboards, such as Google Analytics.

Apps—short for *applications*, an app is software, for use on a desktop, laptop, tablet or smartphone, that allows the user to apply the power of system software for a particular purpose.

Arab Spring—political uprisings across the Middle East beginning in 2009, and continuing, that generated large-scale public protests, political shifts toward removal of longtime rulers and dictators, and intense social media and network activity. Mainstream media coverage included following social media content.

Augmented reality (AR)—use of geographic data and mobile smartphone data and images to augment physical spaces with vast amounts of computer data.

Benchmark data—use of foundational data within a social media campaign. By benchmarking, a social media entity may set and track longer-term goals and objectives, as well as effectiveness of tactics.

Best practices—standard practices of an industry, developed gradually, that are the processes and social media content that have worked well over time.

Blog—these are online sites, often owned media, in which somewhat formal and regular posts (information and commentary) are published. Early blogs were characterized by authenticity, which is the idea that the author presents a more "real" and unfiltered identity.

Board—Pinterest uses the term "board' to reflect the online space where users "pin" content to a virtual message board.

Branding—the marketing technique of emphasizing a brand for a product, service, organization or individual. A logo, face or even a song may reinforce the brand for consumers.

Breaking news—real-time events and news that happen as developing news stories. Traditional media emphasize breaking news, and this content frequently is spread on social networks.

Business-to business (B2B)—business between two businesses rather than between a business and consumer.

Buzz—the aggregate social network activity from a word, term, phrase or other content. On Twitter, for example, we can track #BreakingNews buzz on a graph of time (X) and total number of tweets (Y).

C-suite—top-level corporate executives making key decisions that may include social media policies.

Citizen journalism—individuals use online platforms to distribute news created as non-professional citizen journalists. This content may be "hyperlocal," with a neighborhood focus that does not attract large enough audiences to interest mainstream media.

Click-through rates (CTR)—a measure of user clicks on sponsored results.

Community—a core CMC concept that describes how individuals create groups, including interest groups, by sharing information within social networks.

Computer-mediated communication (CMC)—a social and research construct that begins to explain the nature of social network and social media behavior and culture.

Convergence—an early description of the merging of previously separate media, such as print (newspapers and magazines), broadcasting (radio and television), advertising, public relations and marketing. So-called "convergence newsrooms" were developed to allow content producers to work across online media platforms.

Conversation monitoring—the process of monitoring online activity, emphasizing engagement through responding to comments, reactions and posts by others.

Conversion—marketers convert social media activity to sales.

Cost of Ignoring (COI)—a newer metric developed in response to criticism of the lack of social media ROI; it emphasizes the need for online engagement.

Cost Per Click (CPC)—a social media alternative advertising measure to the traditional cost per thousand mainstream method for pricing commercial messages. CPC charges advertisers for every audience user click.

Cost Per Thousand (CPM)—a traditional advertising price method estimating how much to charge for each 1,000 audience members who will see the ad. For example, one online national video service charges about $25 CPM. The Super Bowl, which has the largest national audience, has increased over the years from $5 to $27 CPM, while a popular primetime show may cost $35 CPM.

Credibility—is related to trust and believability. In media research, we talk about source and message credibility. The more content has both, the more likely audience members will be to trust it.

Crowdsourcing—social networks allow individuals to interact in real time. Crowdsourcing is defined as a method for gathering, filtering, generating and distributing information within a social network. On Twitter, for example, crowdsourcing is used during breaking news to separate facts from rumors.

Customer relationship management (CRM)—organizes engagement around customer satisfaction, loyalty and retention.

Digital Rights Management (DRM)—systems of control over content access to seek user payments.

Diffusion—the spread of new ideas, new practices, new processes and new products. Diffusion research identifies the earliest innovators (2.5%), early adopters (13.5%), early majority (34%), late majority (34%), and laggards (16%). The percentage of adopters (Y) is graphed using an S-shaped curve over time (X).

Direct Message (DM)—In Twitter, followers may send private messages that are not broadcast on the larger network.

Early adopters—in a diffusion cycle, the first to adopt new technologies and/or ideas.

Earned exposure—customer reviewer expressions of positive feelings about products or services.

Earned media—public relations professionals work to receive positive attention for their clients through content that is not paid advertising. Earned media may be the product of media relations, a campaign, real-time engagement or other activities.

eCommerce—online sales and business.

Electronic Frontier Foundation (EFF)—organization promoting free and open Internet.

Engagement—the term that describes strengthening social network interaction from passive to more active. It goes beyond passive viewing to clicking on a link, liking content, sharing content and responding to content in some way that can be seen by social media users.

Entrepreneurs—social media sites have been created and developed by the technology sector, which values an innovative culture. Personal computer hardware and software were first developed by young entrepreneurs, such as Bill Gates and Steve Jobs, and the current industry features inventors and their start-ups.

Fan—A Facebook user may like a page and become a fan. By doing this, the posts on this page appear on the user's news feed.

Gatekeepers—those who perform a traditional news editorial function of story selection.

Hardware—the physical computing equipment, such as a desktop, laptop, tablet or smartphone. We also speak of components—keyboard, mouse, monitor, router, modem, etc.—as hardware.

Hashjacking—hijacking a hashtag already in use on Twitter for an event.

Hashtag (#)—the number sign is used on Twitter and, more recently, Facebook as a filtering device. By searching for and using hashtags, subsets of the larger feed can be seen and used.

Human-computer-interaction (HCI)—early research into how humans engaged with computer hardware and software.

Hybrid media—new media that incorporate some older media rules, such as news editorial practices.

Hyperlinks—Web links to other content via an Internet URL address.

Idea starter—a type of user identified by Edelmen TweetLevel as someone who begins discussion or is an early participant. Specifically, these users on Twitter are rewarded with a high score for "originating detailed opinion and thought leadership."

Identity—what we present online through the use of words, photographs, sounds, videos, emoticons, avatar or other means. Each time we decide to communicate (and even when we do not) we suggest an identity to social network site users.

Impressions—awareness of information, such as from seeing it during a search.

Influence—users with a lot of fans, followers or connections tend to be considered influencers. These social media accounts may have high Klout, Tweetlevel or other measured scores.

Innovation—a business culture favoring change over stability.

Interaction—each engagement with another SNS account reflects a decision to interact. Interaction and engagement are a key foundation for social media use.

Internet Protocol (IP) an address number attached to a user computer or location.

Key Performance Indicators (KPI)—continuous monitoring of important business variables.

Keywords—words used within SEO to move page placement higher in a search by relating to common user language.

Live tweeting—during an event or breaking news, eyewitnesses and commentators may tweet in real time with updates on any new information.

Location-based services (LBS)—designed to allow users to check in at locations.

Marketing—promoting and selling products and services targeted at a specific market. Research is usually utilized to focus marketing, which may involve use of advertising and social media marketing.

Measurement error—all measurement has error, and researchers estimate amounts.

Media cloverleaf—Edelman PR divides the media environment into four overlapping parts: traditional media, owned media, hybrid media and social media.

Media literacy—is a way to describe the need for media audience members to possess skills that allow them to deconstruct and understand media content. For example, an information literacy approach would emphasize knowledge and learning. Media literacy scholars suggest that children need to be taught to realize when they are being sold products and services through sophisticated advertising and marketing campaigns.

Meme—social media content that features cultural imitation. Production typically uses easily identifiable characters, iterations and humor. For example, there is a persistent use of an image from the 1971 *Willy Wonka and the Chocolate Factory* movie because of an early meme generator site.

Metrics—the measurement of behavior within social media. A variety of social media "dash-boards," such as Google Analytics, Sprout, Chartbeat, Hootsuite, Cision, Tweetdeck, Argyle Social, Sprout Social and Radian6 are in use.

Microblog—short, or limited space, blogging began with Twitter and its 140 character limit. Micro-blogging became a genre to comment through without taking the time and energy to publish a more formal blog site. Even for those blogging, microblogs are used to push out links and drive traffic back to the site.

Mobile communication—smartphones and tablets connected through WiFi or cellphone data. Mobile Internet connections allow for the use of a wide variety of social media apps.

Narrative—use of storytelling techniques, such as a story arc.

Network visualization—social networks generate large amounts of data that may be viewed as a series of network maps of communication hubs and spokes. Visualization depicts through graphs the social space between SNS accounts.

Non-Governmental Organization (NGO)—entities operating in the non-profit sector rather than government or commercial for-profit businesses.

Objectivity—a norm within journalism placing value and emphasis on balance, fairness and telling at least two sides to every story. In the second half of the 20th century, journalists strived for objectivity. Recent scholars see it as an unachievable ideal. Social media users of social networks frequently emphasize subjectivity and opinion.

Opportunity costs—the cost of using money on one expense and not having it available for other possibilities.

Organic—is a way to describe naturally evolving social media content. Facebook contrasts content that organically circulates on the social network with paid content that is then boosted to the top of feeds, or given more prominent placement.

Owned media—typically company-owned media, such as a website.

Packet switching—the method of moving Internet data in packet chunks and re-assembling content upon arrival.

Paid search—search engines charge advertisers for top placement within search results.

Pandora—a streaming music service.

Paywall—a system requiring registration and payment by users.

Pins—Pinterest describes any posting on a user board as a pin, which is the online metaphor for placing a scrap of paper on a bulletin board.

Platforms—online sites that offer various social media services.

Posting—is the act of uploading media content to a social media site. Beyond organic content, the text, photographs or video distributed through a posting may receive wider distribution by paying for a promoted post or sponsored content on a site.

Promoted posts—social media sites charge advertisers to appear in prominent positions that are likely to be seen.

Privacy—a concept first suggested in the late 19th century that calls for legal protection of intimate details of life, especially when a person seeks to protect these from public view.

Propaganda—information designed to promote or advance a view, cause, person, product or idea. Before World War II, propaganda was simply considered persuasion. However, World War II propaganda caused people to associate the term with a pejorative meaning such that now it suggests the spread of false information.

Public relations (PR)—seeks through professional best practices to present, maintain and manage public images and reputations. Ongoing campaigns use media relations tactics to present perceived positives. Reputation management efforts may be in response to a crisis from perceived negative information.

Reach—a traditional mass media measure of distribution, social media are also interested in measuring the broad distribution of content.

Real-time social engagement—current PR best practices include nearly immediate response to conversation monitoring of social media. Within a relatively short time, sometimes a matter of minutes, a brand engages on a social network about a trending topic, issue or person.

Reliability—social scientific measures of consistency or reproducibility of results.

Return on Investment (ROI)—calculation of a financial gain minus the cost of an investment. ROI is expressed as a percentage or ratio and is sometimes considered a measure of efficiency.

Retweet—re-distributing a previous tweet with the letters RT in front of it, this allows Twitter users to easily share content to their social network. Twitter users also post MT for modified tweets and PRT, if an item is a partial retweet.

Roles—individuals adopt roles, much as an actor might. A social media professional, for example, may perceive and express the role of an innovator or entrepreneur.

Search Engine Optimization (SEO)—Google algorithms produce a system for pushing some Internet content to the top of any specific search.

Search Engine Result Placements (SERP)—using SEO techniques to drive high placement during keyword searches.

Sentiment analysis—computer and human coding for positive, neutral and negative comments.

Smartphones—mobile telephones connected on cellular networks that provide an Internet connection through devices that have personal computer capabilities.

Social graph—on Facebook, this is a user's complete social network.

Social media dashboard—measurement tools that organize data for efficient analysis.

Social networks—an array of online platforms used to connect with others.

Social Network Site (SNS)—any online platform that enables communication between site accounts.

Software—computer code that allows hardware to be used via an operating system, programs and applications.

Sponsored content—paid media content that may appear near editorial media content and free social media content.

Start-ups—new business ventures, sometimes with the funding help of "angel investors," launch social media sites and apps. An innovation culture, annual events such as "South By Southwest" (#SXSW) and the tech journalism community drive interest and activity in the diffusion of new ideas and products.

Storytelling—a fundamental concept in journalism and media communication. People have told stories since the development of language and oral tradition. Storytelling techniques, including the use of narrative, drive interest in content.

Tactics—strategic PR campaigns devise a set of tactics used to achieve communication goals. For example, if a campaign is designed to raise awareness about an issue, a tactic may be to create a YouTube video that can be shared by bloggers.

Tagging—On Facebook, a person can be tagged in a photograph. In doing so, a name is associated with a face and perhaps a place, and these data can be shared across the social network. More generally, geotagging is use of a computer software code that identifies location. A smartphone photograph may be geotagged with the location, and this data can be presented or used within the context of an application.

Thought leader—in each area of the social media communication industry, leaders emerge who can communicate as influencers of the field. These thought leaders may be very active in social media and are asked to speak at conferences and meetings. They frequently blog and publish articles and books.

Transparency—the social media approach of disclosing all relevant interests and not having a hidden agenda.

Trending—on Twitter, different words and hashtags trend at any given time. These are the most talked-about items. These can be organic or "promoted" as advertising.

Trust—is considered an important and fundamental characteristic for a lot of influential social media content. Trust is related to credibility and believability, which frequently is assessed by judging previous behavior, including communication.

Tweet—Twitter limits each individual message to no more than 140 characters, and calls it a tweet.

User-generated content (UGC)—created content by users, often not sponsored by traditional professional media organizations.

User profiles—online descriptions of user identities.

Uses and gratifications—a research perspective emphasizing active audience participation.

Validity—in social science, the determination that measurement is conceptually what it was planned to be.

Verification and verified accounts—authenticity of identity is an important online concern. Twitter created a blue checkmark to identify those accounts that have been verified through its internal process, and this also appears on some Facebook pages. Additionally, Facebook users may take advantage of a two-step verification for login that includes a text message code to a mobile phone for account security.

Viral—content that is shared quickly and widely because of high interest. Social media enables individuals to post viral videos on YouTube and rise to almost-instant fame.

Virtual communities—online spaces creating a community experience among users.

Vlog—video bloggers use video posts instead of text. Vlogs are regular commentary in a video medium.

Word clouds—a word visualization of frequently used social media language.

Word of mouth (WOM)—personal influence is spread through word of mouth communication. In the past, this was mostly done face-to-face. Now, CMC allows for mediated WOM through social media communication.

INDEX

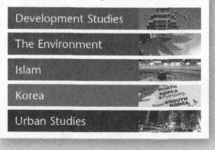